IT Essentials
Lab Manual,
Version 6

Cisco Networking Academy

Cisco Press
800 East 96th Street
Indianapolis, Indiana 46240 USA

IT Essentials Lab Manual
Version 6

Cisco Networking Academy

Copyright© 2016 Cisco Systems, Inc.

Published by:
Cisco Press
800 East 96th Street
Indianapolis, IN 46240 USA

Printed in the United States of America

First Printing April 2016

Library of Congress Control Number: 2016939206

ISBN-13: 978-1-58713-354-1
ISBN-10: 1-58713-354-7

Warning and Disclaimer

Trademark Acknowledgments

This book is part of the Cisco Networking Academy® series from Cisco Press. The products in this series support and complement the Cisco Networking Academy curriculum. If you are using this book outside the Networking Academy, then you are not preparing with a Cisco trained and authorized Networking Academy provider.

·ı|ı·ı|ı·
CISCO.

For more information on the Cisco Networking Academy or to locate a Networking Academy, please visit www.cisco.com/edu.

Feedback Information

At Cisco Press, our goal is to create in-depth technical books of the highest quality and value. Each book is crafted with care and precision, undergoing rigorous development that involves the unique expertise of members from the professional technical community.

Readers' feedback is a natural continuation of this process. If you have any comments regarding how we could improve the quality of this book, or otherwise alter it to better suit your needs, you can contact us through email at feedback@ciscopress.com. Please make sure to include the book title and ISBN in your message.

We greatly appreciate your assistance.

Editor in Chief	Mark Taub
Business Operation Manager, Cisco Press	Jan Cornelssen
Executive Editor	Mary Beth Ray
Managing Editor	Sandra Schroeder
Project Editor	Mandie Frank
Proofreader	Sarah Kearns
Editorial Assistant	Vanessa Evans
Cover Designer	Chuti Prasertsith

CISCO

Americas Headquarters
Cisco Systems, Inc.
170 West Tasman Drive
San Jose, CA 95134-1706
USA
www.cisco.com
Tel: 408 526-4000
800 553-NETS (6387)
Fax: 408 527-0883

Asia Pacific Headquarters
Cisco Systems, Inc.
168 Robinson Road
#28-01 Capital Tower
Singapore 068912
www.cisco.com
Tel: +65 6317 7777
Fax: +65 6317 7799

Europe Headquarters
Cisco Systems International BV
Haarlerbergpark
Haarlerbergweg 13-19
1101 CH Amsterdam
The Netherlands
www-europe.cisco.com
Tel: +31 0 800 020 0791
Fax: +31 0 20 357 1100

Cisco has more than 200 offices worldwide. Addresses, phone numbers, and fax numbers are listed on the Cisco Website at **www.cisco.com/go/offices.**

Contents

Chapter 0: Course Introduction 1

Lab 0.2.2.2 - Worksheet - Job Opportunities 1

Chapter 1: Introduction to the Personal Computer 3

Lab 1.1.1.4 - Ohm's Law 3

Lab 1.2.1.13 - Research Computer Components 4

Lab 1.3.1.7 - Build a Specialized Computer System 7

Chapter 2: Introduction to Lab Procedures and Tool Use 13

Lab 2.2.2.3 - Diagnostic Software 13

Lab 2.2.4.4 - Using a Multimeter and a Power Supply Tester 14

Lab 2.2.4.7 - Computer Disassembly 18

Chapter 3: Computer Assembly 23

Lab 3.1.1.3 - Install the Power Supply 23

Lab 3.1.2.6 - Install the Motherboard 24

Lab 3.1.3.3 - Install the Drives 26

Lab 3.1.4.4 - Install Adapter Cards 27

Lab 3.1.5.5 - Install Internal Cables 29

Lab 3.1.5.8 - Install Front Panel Cables 31

Lab 3.1.5.12 - Complete the Computer Assembly 32

Lab 3.2.2.8 - Boot the Computer 33

Lab 3.3.1.6 - BIOS File Search 36

Lab 3.3.3.2 - Upgrade Hardware 38

Chapter 4: Overview of Preventive Maintenance

Chapter 5: Windows Installation 41

Lab 5.1.2.3 - Search NOC Certifications and Jobs 41

Lab 5.1.4.4 - Data Migration in Windows 43

Lab 5.2.1.7 - Install Windows 7 or Vista 69

Lab 5.2.1.7 - Install Windows 8 94

Lab 5.2.1.10 - Check for Updates in Windows 7 and Vista 103

Lab 5.2.1.10 - Check for Updates in Windows 8 109

Lab 5.2.4.7 - Create a Partition in Windows 7 and Vista 114

Lab 5.2.4.7 - Create a Partition in Windows 8 126

Chapter 6: Windows Configuration and Management..**139**

Lab 6.1.1.5 - Task Manager in Windows 7 and Vista 139

Lab 6.1.1.5 - Task Manager in Windows 8 154

Lab 6.1.1.9 - Install Third-Party Software in Windows 7 and Vista 166

Lab 6.1.1.9 - Install Third-Party Software in Windows 8 175

Lab 6.1.2.3 - Create User Accounts in Windows 7 and Vista 184

Lab 6.1.2.3 - Create User Accounts in Windows 8 192

Lab 6.1.2.5 - Configure Browser Settings in Windows 7 and Vista 207

Lab 6.1.5.2 - Configure Browser Settings in Windows 8 217

Lab 6.1.2.12 - Manage Virtual Memory in Windows 7 and Vista 227

Lab 6.1.2.12 - Manage Virtual Memory in Windows 8 239

Lab 6.1.2.14 - Device Manager in Windows 7 and Vista 251

Lab 6.1.2.14 - Device Manager in Windows 8 256

Lab 6.1.2.16 - Region and Language Options in Windows 7 and Vista 261

Lab 6.1.2.16 - Region and Language Options in Windows 8 269

Lab 6.1.3.6 - Monitor and Manage System Resources in Windows 7 and Vista 275

Lab 6.1.3.6 - Monitor and Manage System Resources in Windows 8 305

Lab 6.1.4.2 - Hard Drive Maintenance in Windows 7 and Vista 325

Lab 6.1.4.2 - Hard Drive Maintenance in Windows 8 334

Lab 6.1.4.4 - Managing System Files in Windows 338

Lab 6.1.5.4 - Common Windows CLI Commands 345

Lab 6.1.5.6 - System Utilities in Windows 353

Lab 6.3.1.2 - Managing the Startup Folder in Windows 7 and Vista 363

Lab 6.3.1.2 - Managing the Startup Folder in Windows 8 368

Lab 6.3.1.5 - Task Scheduler in Windows 7 and Vista 378

Lab 6.3.1.5 - Task Scheduler in Windows 8 390

Lab 6.3.1.7 - System Restore in Windows 7 and Vista 402

Lab 6.3.1.7 - System Restore in Windows 8 412

Chapter 7: Networking Concepts **423**

Lab 7.3.2.6 - Build and Test Network Cables 423

Lab 7.4.1.11 - Configure a NIC to Use DHCP in Windows 428

Chapter 8: Applied Networking **435**

Lab 8.1.2.10 - Connect to a Router for the First Time 435

Lab 8.1.2.12 - Configure Wireless Router in Windows 442

Lab 8.1.2.14 - Test the Wireless NIC in Windows 454

Lab 8.1.3.9 - Share Resources in Windows 460

Lab 8.1.4.3 - Remote Assistance in Windows 484

Lab 8.1.4.4 - Remote Desktop in Windows 7 and Vista 498

Lab 8.1.4.4 - Remote Desktop in Windows 8 512

Chapter 9: Laptops and Mobile Devices **525**

Lab 9.1.1.6 - Research Docking Stations 525

Lab 9.3.1.5 - Research Laptop RAM 526

Lab 9.3.2.3 - Research Laptop Batteries 527

Lab 9.3.2.5 - Research Laptop Screens 528

Lab 9.3.2.7 - Research Laptop Hard Drives 529

Lab 9.3.2.14 - Research Building a Specialized Laptop 530

Lab 9.6.2.2 - Research Laptop Problems 533

Lab 9.6.2.3 - Gather Information from the Customer 534

Lab 9.6.2.4 - Investigate Support Websites and Repair Companies 535

Chapter 10: Mobile, Linux, and OS X Operating Systems **537**

Lab 10.1.2.3 - Working with Android 537

Lab 10.1.3.3 - Working with iOS 549

Lab 10.1.5.3 - Mobile Device Features 562

Lab 10.1.5.4 - Mobile Device Information 573

Lab 10.2.1.2 - Passcode Locks 575

Lab 10.3.1.2 - Mobile Wi-Fi 586

Lab 10.4.1.4 - Install Linux in a Virtual Machine and Explore the GUI 592

Lab 10.4.3.3 - Working with Linux Command Line 605

Lab 10.5.2.2 - Troubleshooting Mobile Devices 614

Chapter 11: Printers **617**

Lab 11.2.1.6 - Install a Printer in Windows 7 and Vista 617

Lab 11.2.1.6 - Install a Printer in Windows 8 619

Lab 11.3.2.5 - Share a Printer in Windows 7 and Vista 621

Lab 11.3.2.5 - Share a Printer in Windows 8 633

Chapter 12: Security **639**

Lab 12.2.1.8 - Configure Windows Local Security Policy 639

Lab 12.3.1.3 - Configure Data Backup and Recovery in Windows 7 and Vista 648

Lab 12.3.1.3 - Configure Data Backup and Recovery in Windows 8 669

Lab 12.3.1.5 - Configure the Firewall in Windows 7 and Vista 679

Lab 12.3.1.5 - Configure the Firewall in Windows 8 699

Lab 12.3.1.9 - Configure Users and Groups in Windows 710

Lab 12.4.2.2 - Document Customer Information in a Work Order 724

Chapter 13: The IT Professional **727**

Lab 13.1.1.3 - Technician Resources 727

Chapter 14: Advanced Troubleshooting **729**

Lab 14.1.1.2 - Troubleshooting Hardware Problems 729

Lab 14.1.1.3 - Remote Technician - Repair Boot Problem 731

Lab 14.2.1.2 - Troubleshoot Operating System Problems 733

Lab 14.2.1.3 - Remote Technician - Fix an Operating System Problem 745

Lab 14.3.1.2 - Troubleshooting Network Problems 747

Lab 14.3.1.3 - Remote Technician - Fix a Network Problem 749

Lab 14.4.1.2 - Troubleshoot Security Problems 751

Lab 14.4.1.3 - Remote Technician - Fix a Security Problem 755

About This Lab Manual

IT Essentials Lab Manual is a supplemental book prepared for students in the Cisco® Networking Academy IT Essentials v6 course. All the hands-on labs and worksheets from the course are printed within this book to provide practical, hands-on experience with the course content. IT Essentials covers fundamental computer and career skills for entry-level IT jobs.

Practicing and performing all these tasks will reinforce the concepts, skills, and procedures and help prepare the student to take the CompTIA® A+ 220-901 and 220-902 exams.

Chapter 0: Course Introduction

Lab 0.2.2.2 - Worksheet - Job Opportunities

Use the Internet, magazines, or a local newspaper to gather information for jobs in the computer service and repair field. Be prepared to discuss your research in class.

a. Research three computer-related jobs. For each job, write the company name and the job title in the column on the left. Write the job details that are most important to you, as well as the job qualifications in the column on the right. An example has been provided for you.

Company Name and Job Title	Details and Qualifications
Gentronics Flexible Solutions/ Field Service Representative	Company offers continuing education. Work with hardware and software. Work directly with customers. Local travel. • A+ certification preferred • 1 year installation or repair experience of computer hardware and software required • Requires a valid driver's license • Must have reliable personal transportation • Mileage reimbursement • Ability to lift and carry up to 50 lbs

b. Based on your research, which job would you prefer and why? Be prepared to discuss your answer in class.

_____

_____

Chapter 1: Introduction to the Personal Computer

Lab 1.1.1.4 - Ohm's Law

Answer the following questions based on electricity and Ohm's Law. Show all steps when solving problems.

a. What are the four basic units of electricity? Provide the variable name and symbol, and unit name and symbol.

    _____

    _____

b. Write the equation for Ohm's Law.

    _____

c. Re-arrange the Ohm's Law equation to solve the following:

    I = _____   R = _____

d. Power is equal to voltage multiplied by current. Add the missing information in each of the following power equations.

    P = V _____   P = R _____   P = V² _____

e. The yellow wire connected to a power supply carries 12V. If the power supply provides 60W of power to the yellow wire, how much current is passing through the yellow wire?

    _____

f. There are 3.3V passing through an orange power supply cable, and there are 0.025 ohms of resistance in the orange wire. How much power is supplied to the orange wire by the power supply?

    _____

g   A wire from the power supply is carrying 120W of power and 24A of current. Which color(s) of cable is the wire?

    _____

Lab 1.2.1.13 - Research Computer Components

Use the Internet, trade publications, or a local store to gather information about the components you will need to complete your customer's computer. Information is provided for the components that your customer already has. Use these specifications to make sure that the components you research are compatible with the components your customer already owns. Be prepared to discuss your selections.

Step 1:   Answer the following PC component questions.

a.   List three components that must have the same compatible form factor.

_____

b.   List three components that must conform to the same socket type.

_____

c.   List two components that must utilize the same front side bus speed.

_____

d.   List three considerations when you choose memory.

_____

e.   What component must be compatible with every other component of the computer?

_____

Step 2: Perform research for compatible components for your customer.

Your customer already owns the components described in the table below.

Component	Brand and Model Number	Features	Cost
Case	NZXT Source 210	ATX Mid Tower 2 x USB 2.0 Front Ports Bottom-Mounted PSU Wire Management Support Dual 120mm Front Intake Also fits 2 x 120/140mm fan	$39.99
Motherboard	ASUS H97-PRO Gamer	LGA 1150 Core i7 / i5 / i3 Intel H97 Chipset DDR3 1600/1333 MHz Non-ECC, Un-buffered 32GB Maximum Dual Channel Memory Supported 1 x PCIe 3.0/2.0 x16 1 x PCIe 2.0 x16 2 x PCI Express x1 4 x SATA 6Gb/s 4 x USB 3.0	$104.99
Hard Drive	Western Digital WD5000AAKX	SATA 6.0Gb/s 500GB 7200 RPM 16MB Cache	$52.99

Search the Internet, trade publications, or a local store to research the following components, make sure they are compatible with the components that your customer owns. Enter the specifications in the table below.

Component	Brand and Model Number	Features	Cost
Power Supply			
CPU			
Heatsink/Fan			
RAM			
Video Adaptor Card			

Lab 1.3.1.7 - Build a Specialized Computer System

Use the Internet, a newspaper, or a local store to gather information about building a specialized computer system that supports hardware and software that allows a user to perform tasks that an off-the-shelf system cannot perform. Be prepared to discuss your selections.

For this worksheet, assume the customer's system will be compatible with the parts you order.

a. The customer runs an audio and video editing workstation to record and mix music, create music CDs, CD labels, and create home movies. The customer wishes to upgrade the components listed in the table.

Brand and Model Number	Features	Cost
Audio card		
Video card		
Hard drive		
Dual monitors		

Provide reasons for the components purchased. How will they support the customer's needs?

_____

_____

_____

_____

b. The customer runs computer-aided design (CAD) or computer-aided manufacturing (CAM) software and wishes to upgrade the components listed in the table.

Brand and Model Number	Features	Cost
CPU		
Video card		
RAM		

Provide reasons for the components purchased. How will they support the customer's needs?

_____

_____

_____

_____

c. The customer uses virtualization technologies to run several different operating systems to test software compatibility. The customer wishes to upgrade the components listed in the table.

Brand and Model Number	Features	Cost
RAM		
CPU		

Provide reasons for the components purchased. How will they support the customer's needs?

_____

_____

_____

_____

d.   The customer wishes to upgrade an HTPC with the components listed in the table.

Brand and Model Number	Features	Cost
Case		
Power supply		
Surround sound audio		
TV tuner and cable cards		

Provide reasons for the components purchased. How will they support the customer's needs?

_____

_____

_____

_____

e. The customer wishes to upgrade a gaming computer with the components listed in the table.

Brand and Model Number	Features	Cost
CPU		
Video card		
Sound card		
Cooling system		
RAM		
Hard drive		

Provide reasons for the components purchased. How will they support the customer's needs?

_____

_____

_____

_____

Chapter 2: Introduction to Lab Procedures and Tool Use

Lab 2.2.2.3 - Diagnostic Software

Use the Internet, a newspaper, or a local store to gather information about a hard drive diagnostic program. Be prepared to discuss the diagnostic software you researched.

a. Based on your research, list at least two different hard drive manufacturers.

_____

_____

b. Based on your research, choose a hard drive manufacturer. Does this manufacturer offer hard drive diagnostic software to go with their products? If so, list the name and the features of the diagnostic software.

_____

_____

_____

_____

_____

c. Why do manufacturers offer hard drive diagnostic software? What are the potential benefits of doing so to the manufacturer and/or customer?

_____

_____

_____

_____

_____

Lab 2.2.4.4 - Using a Multimeter and a Power Supply Tester

Introduction

In this lab, you will learn how to use and handle a multimeter and a power supply tester.

Recommended Equipment

- A digital multimeter
- The multimeter manual
- A battery to test
- A power supply tester
- A manual for the tester
- A power supply

Note: The multimeter is a sensitive piece of electronic test equipment. Do not drop it or handle it carelessly. Be careful not to accidentally nick or cut the red or black wires or leads, called probes. Because it is possible to check high voltages, take extra care to avoid electrical shock.

Part 1:   Multimeter

Step 1:   Set up the multimeter.

a.   Insert the red and black leads into the jacks on the meter. The black probe should go in the COM jack and the red probe should go in the + (plus) jack.

b.   Turn on the multimeter (consult the manual if there is no ON/OFF switch).

What is the model of the multimeter?

_____

What action must be taken to turn on the meter?

_____

Step 2:   Explore the different multimeter measurements.

a.   Switch or turn to different measurements. For example, the multimeter can be adjusted to measure Ohms.

How many different switch positions does the multimeter have?

_____

What are they?

_____

b.   Switch or turn the multimeter to the DC voltage measurement.

What symbol is shown for this?

_____

Step 3:   Measure the voltage of a battery.

a.   Place the battery on the table. Touch the tip of the red (positive) probe to the positive (+) side of a battery. Touch the tip of the black (negative) probe to the other end of the battery.

What is shown on the display?

_____

_____

If the multimeter does not display a number close to the battery voltage, check the multimeter setting to ensure it is set to measure voltage, or replace the battery with a known good battery. If the number is negative, reverse the probes.

b.   Name one thing you should not do when using a multimeter.

_____

_____

c.   Name one important function of a multimeter.

_____

_____

d. Disconnect the multimeter from the battery. Switch the multimeter to OFF. Part 1 of the lab is complete. Have your instructor verify your work.

Why is a digital multimeter an important piece of equipment for a technician? Explain your answer.

_____

_____

_____

Part 2:   Power Supply Tester

Complete only the steps for the connectors supported by the power supply tester that you are using.

Step 1:   Check the testing ports for the power supply tester.

Many power supply testers have connector ports to test the following power supply connectors:

- 20-pin/24-pin motherboard connector
- 4-pin Molex connector
- 6-pin PCI-E connector
- P4 +12V connector
- P8 +12V EPS connector
- 4-pin Berg connector
- 15-pin SATA connector

Which connectors does the power supply tester you are using have?

_____

Step 2:   Test the power supply motherboard connector.

Complete the following steps for the connectors supported by the power supply tester that you are using:

a. Set the power supply switch (if available) to the OFF (or 0) position.

b. Plug the 20-pin or 24-pin motherboard connector into the tester.

c. Plug the power supply into an AC outlet.

d. Set the power supply switch (if available) to the ON (or 1) position.

If the power supply is working, LEDs will illuminate and you might hear a beep. If the LED lights do not illuminate, it is possible the power supply could be damaged or the motherboard connector has failed. In this instance, you must check all connections, ensure the power supply switch (if available) is set to ON (or 1) and try again. If the LEDs still do not illuminate, consult your instructor.

Possible LED lights include +5 V, -5 V, +12 V, +5 VSB, PG, -12 V, and +3.3 V.

Which LED lights are illuminated?

_____

Step 3:   Test the power supply Molex connector.

Plug the 4-pin Molex connector into the tester. The LED illuminates on +12 V and +5 V. (If the power output fails, the LEDs will not illuminate.)

Which LED lights are illuminated?

_____

Step 4:   Test the 6-pin PCI-E connector.

Plug the 6-pin PCI-E connector into the tester. The LED will illuminate on +12 V. (If the power output fails, the LED will not illuminate.)

Does the LED light illuminate?

_____

Step 5:   Test the 5-pin SATA connector.

Plug the 5-pin SATA connector into the tester. The LED will illuminate on +12 V, +5 V, and +3.3 V. (If the power output fails, the LEDs will not illuminate.)

Which LED lights are illuminated?

_____

Step 6:   Test the 4-pin Berg connector.

Plug the 4-pin Berg connector into the tester. The LED will illuminate on +12 V and +5 V. (If the power output fails, the LEDs will not illuminate.)

Which LED lights are illuminated?

_____

Step 7:   Test the P4/P8 connectors.

a.   Plug the P4 +12 V connector into the tester. The LED will illuminate on +12 V. (If the power output fails, the LEDs will not illuminate.)

b.   Plug the P8 +12 V connector into the tester. The LED will illuminate on +12 V. (If the power output fails, the LEDs will not illuminate.)

Which LED lights are illuminated?

_____

c.   Switch the power supply to OFF (or 0) if available. Disconnect the power supply from the AC outlet. Disconnect the power supply from the power supply tester. The lab is complete. Have your instructor verify your work.

Why is a power supply tester an important piece of equipment for a technician? Explain your answer.

_____

_____

_____

Lab 2.2.4.7 - Computer Disassembly

In this lab, you will disassemble a computer using safe lab procedures and the proper tools. Use extreme care and follow all safety procedures. Familiarize yourself with the tools you will be using in this lab.

Note: If you cannot locate or remove the correct component, ask your instructor for help.

Recommended Tools

Safety glasses	Part retriever
Antistatic wrist strap	Thermal compound
Antistatic mat	Can of compressed air
Flat head screwdrivers	Cable ties
Phillips head screwdrivers	Parts organizer
Torx screwdrivers	Containers for storing computer parts
Hex driver	Antistatic bags for electronic parts

Step 1:   Power Off the Computer.

Turn off the power to the computer and disconnect the power cable from the wall and the power supply.

Step 2:   Open the Computer Case.

Locate all of the screws that secure the side panels to the back of the computer. Use the proper size and type of screwdriver to remove the side panel screws. Do not remove the screws that secure the power supply to the case. Put all of these screws in one place, such as a compartment in the parts organizer or small cup. Label the compartment or cup with a piece of masking tape on which you have written "side panel screws". Remove the side panels from the case.

If you have a camera or smartphone, take a picture of the inside of the computer case to be used as a reference when reassembling the computer.

Note: Some manufacturers do not use screws to fasten components inside of the computer case. Some may use plastic or metal clips that fasten components to the computer chassis. Be careful to remove only screws that are holding components in place, and not the screws that hold components together.

What type of screwdriver did you use to remove the screws?

_____

How many screws secured the side panels?

_____

Step 3:   Antistatic Wrist Strap.

Put on an antistatic wrist strap. Connect one end of the conductor to the wrist strap. Clip the other end of the conductor to an unpainted, metal part of the case.

If you have an antistatic mat, place it on the work surface and put the computer case on top of it. Ground the antistatic mat to an unpainted, metal part of the case.

Step 4:   Remove the Hard Drive.

a.   Locate the hard drive. Carefully disconnect the power and data cables from the back of the hard drive.

Which type of data cable did you disconnect?

_____

b.   Locate all of the screws that hold the hard drive in place. Use the proper size and type of screwdriver to remove the hard drive screws. Put all of these screws in one place and label them.

What type of screws secured the hard drive to the case?

_____

How many screws secured the hard drive to the case?

_____

Is the hard drive connected to a mounting bracket? If so, what type of screws secure the hard drive to the mounting bracket?

_____

Caution: Do NOT remove the screws that hold the hard drive together.

c.   Gently remove the hard drive from the case. Look for a jumper reference chart on the hard drive. If there is a jumper installed on the hard drive, use the jumper reference chart to see if the hard drive is set for a Master, Slave, or Cable Select (CS) drive. Place the hard drive in an antistatic bag.

What is the jumper setting of the hard drive?

_____

Step 5:   Remove Optical Drive.

a.   Locate the optical drive (Blu-ray, DVD, etc.). Carefully disconnect the power and data cables from the optical drive. Remove the audio cable from the optical drive if there is one connected.

What kind of data cable did you disconnect?

_____

Is there a jumper on the optical drive? What is the jumper setting?

_____

b.   Locate and remove all of the screws that secure the optical drive to the case. Put all of these screws in one place and label them. Place the optical drive in an antistatic bag.

How many screws secured the optical drive to the case?

_____

Step 6:   Remove the Power Supply.

a.   Locate the power supply. Find the power connection(s) to the motherboard.

b.   Gently remove the power connection(s) from the motherboard. How many pins are there in the motherboard connector?

_____

c.   Disconnect the power cables from any case fans.

d.   Disconnect the power cable from the video card if it requires one.

e.   Disconnect any other power supply cables from where they were connected.

If there were additional cables disconnected, to what were they connected?

_____

f.   Locate and remove all of the screws that secure the power supply to the case. Put all of these screws in one place and label them.

How many screws secure the power supply to the case?

_____

g.   Carefully remove the power supply from the case. Place the power supply with the other computer components.

Step 7:   Remove Adapter Cards.

a.   Locate any adapter cards that are installed in the computer, such as a video, NIC, or sound card.

b.   Locate and remove the screw that secures the adapter card to the case. Put the adapter card screws in one place and label them.

c.   Carefully remove the adapter card from the slot. Be sure to hold the adapter card by the mounting bracket or by the edges. Place the adapter card in an antistatic bag. Repeat this process for all of the adapter cards.

Note: Be very careful when removing video adapters. There is often a locking tab on the slot that must be released before the card can be removed.

d.   List the adapter cards and the slot types below.

Adapter Card	Slot Type

Step 8:   Remove Memory Modules.

a.   Locate the memory modules on the motherboard.

What type of memory modules are installed on the motherboard?

_____

How many memory modules are installed on the motherboard?

_____

b.   Remove the memory modules from the motherboard. Be sure to release any locking tabs that may be securing the memory module. Hold the memory module by the edges and gently lift out of the slot. Put the memory modules in an antistatic bag.

Step 9:   Remove Data Cables.

a.   Remove all data cables from the motherboard. Make sure to note the connection location of any cable you disconnect.

What types of cables were disconnected?

_____

_____

b.   You have completed this lab. The computer case should contain the motherboard, the CPU, and any cooling devices. Do not remove any additional components.

Chapter 3: Computer Assembly

Lab 3.1.1.3 - Install the Power Supply

Introduction

In this lab, you will install a power supply in a computer case.

Recommended Equipment

- Power supply with a compatible form factor to the computer case
- Computer case
- Tool kit
- Power supply screws

Step 1:   Open the Computer Case.

a.   Remove the screws from the side panels.

b.   Remove the side panels from the computer case.

Step 2:   Install the Power Supply.

a.   Align the screw holes in the power supply with the screw holes in the case.

b.   Secure the power supply to the case with the power supply screws.

c.   If the power supply has a voltage selection switch, set this switch to match the voltage in your area.

What is the voltage in your area?

_____

How many screws secure the power supply in the case?

_____

What is the total wattage of the power supply?

_____

d.   This lab is complete. Please ask the instructor to verify your work.

Lab 3.1.2.6 - Install the Motherboard

Introduction

In this lab, you will install a CPU, a heat sink/fan assembly, and RAM module(s) on the motherboard. You will then install the motherboard in the computer case.

Recommended Equipment

- Computer case with power supply installed
- Motherboard
- CPU
- Heat sink/fan assembly
- Thermal compound
- RAM module(s)
- Motherboard standoffs and screws
- Antistatic wrist strap and antistatic mat
- Tool kit
- Motherboard manual

Step 1:   Install the CPU.

a. Place the motherboard, the CPU, the heat sink/fan assembly, and the RAM module on the antistatic mat.

b. Put on your antistatic wrist strap and attach the grounding cable to the antistatic mat.

c. Locate Pin 1 on the CPU. Locate Pin 1 on the socket.

   Note: The CPU may be damaged if it is installed incorrectly.

d. Align Pin 1 on the CPU with Pin 1 on the socket.

e. Place the CPU into the CPU socket.

f. Close the CPU load plate and secure it in place by closing the load lever and moving it under the load lever retention tab.

g. Apply a small amount of thermal compound to the CPU.

   Note: Thermal compound is only necessary when it is not included on the heat sink. Follow all instructions provided by the manufacturer for specific application details.

h. Align the heat sink/fan assembly retainers with the holes in the motherboard around the CPU socket.

i. Place the heat sink/fan assembly onto the CPU and the retainers through the holes in the motherboard.

j. Tighten the heat sink/fan assembly retainers to secure it.

k. Plug the fan connector into the motherboard. Refer to the motherboard manual to determine which set of fan header pins to use.

Step 2:   Install the RAM.

a.   Locate the RAM slots on the motherboard.

In what type of slot(s) will the RAM module(s) be installed?

_____

_____

How many notches are found on the bottom edge of the RAM module?

_____

_____

b.   Align the notch(es) on the bottom edge of the RAM module to the notches in the slot.

c.   Press down until the side tabs secure the RAM module.

d.   Ensure that none of the RAM module contacts are visible. Reset the RAM module if necessary.

e.   Check the latches to verify that the RAM module is secure.

f.   Install any additional RAM modules using the same procedure.

Step 3:   Install the Motherboard.

a.   Install the motherboard standoffs.

b.   Install the I/O connector plate in the back of the computer case.

c.   Align the connectors on the back of the motherboard with the openings in the back of the computer case.

d.   Place the motherboard into the case and align the holes for the screws with the stand-offs. You may need to adjust the motherboard to line up the holes for the screws.

e.   Attach the motherboard to the case using the appropriate screws.

This lab is complete. Please have the instructor verify your work.

Lab 3.1.3.3 - Install the Drives

Introduction

In this lab, you will install the hard disk and optical drives.

Recommended Equipment

- Computer case with power supply and motherboard installed
- Antistatic wrist strap and antistatic mat
- Tool kit
- Hard disk drive
- Hard disk drive screws
- Optical drive
- Optical drive screws
- Motherboard manual

Step 1:   Install the Hard Disk Drive.

a.   Align the hard disk drive with the 3.5-inch drive bay.

b.   Slide the hard disk drive into the bay from the inside of the case until the screw holes line up with the holes in the 3.5-inch drive bay.

c.   Secure the hard disk drive to the case using the proper screws.

Step 2:   Install the Optical Drive.

Note: Remove the 5.25-inch cover from one of the 5.25-inch external drive bays if necessary.

a.   Align the optical drive with the 5.25-inch drive bay.

b.   Insert the optical drive into the drive bay from the front of the case until the screw holes line up with the holes in the 5.25-inch drive bay and the front of the optical drive is flush with the front of the case.

c.   Secure the optical drive to the case using the proper screws.

This lab is complete. Please have the instructor verify your work.

Lab 3.1.4.4 - Install Adapter Cards

Introduction

In this lab, you will install a NIC, a wireless NIC, and a video adapter card.

Recommended Equipment

- Computer with power supply, motherboard, and drives installed
- NIC
- Wireless NIC
- Video adapter card
- Adapter card screws
- Antistatic wrist strap and antistatic mat
- Tool kit
- Motherboard manual

Step 1:   Install the wired NIC.

a.   What type of expansion slot is compatible with the NIC?

_____

b.   Locate a compatible expansion slot for the NIC on the motherboard.

c.   Remove the slot cover from the back of the case, if necessary.

d.   Align the NIC to the expansion slot.

e.   Press down gently on the NIC until the card is fully seated.

f.   Secure the NIC by attaching the PC mounting bracket to the case with a screw.

Step 2:   Install the wireless NIC.

a.   What type of expansion slot is compatible with the wireless NIC?

_____

b.   Locate a compatible expansion slot for the wireless NIC on the motherboard.

c.   Remove the slot cover from the back of the case, if necessary.

d.   Align the wireless NIC to the expansion slot.

e.   Press down gently on the wireless NIC until the card is fully seated.

f.   Secure the wireless NIC by attaching the PC mounting bracket to the case with a screw.

Step 3:   Install the video adapter card.

a.   What type of expansion slot is compatible with the video adapter card?

_____

b.   Locate a compatible expansion slot for the video adapter card on the motherboard.

c.   Remove the slot cover(s) from the back of the case, if necessary.

d.   Align the video adapter card to the expansion slot.

e. Press down gently on the video adapter card until the card is fully seated.

f. Secure the video adapter card by attaching the PC mounting bracket(s) to the case with a screw.

This lab is complete. Please have the instructor verify your work.

Lab 3.1.5.5 - Install Internal Cables

Introduction

In this lab, install the internal power and data cables in the computer.

Recommended Equipment

- Computer with power supply, motherboard, drives, and adapter cards installed
- Hard disk drive data cable
- Optical drive data cable
- Antistatic wrist strap and antistatic mat
- Tool kit
- Motherboard manual

Step 1:   Connect the motherboard power supply connector.

a.   Align the motherboard power supply connector to the socket on the motherboard.

b.   Gently press down on the connector until the clip clicks into place.

Step 2:   Connect the auxiliary power connector.

a.   Align the auxiliary power connector to the auxiliary power socket on the motherboard.

b.   Gently press down on the connector until the clip clicks into place.

Note: This step is necessary only if your computer has an auxiliary power connector.

Step 3:   Connect the internal disk drive power connectors.

Plug a power connector into the hard disk drive and the optical drive.

Step 4:   Connect the video adapter card power cable.

Plug the PCIe power connector to the video adapter card.

Note: This step is necessary only if your video adapter card has a PCIe power connector.

Step 5:   Connect the fan power connector.

Connect the fan power connector into the appropriate fan header on the motherboard.

Note: This step is necessary only if your computer has a fan power connector.

Step 6:   Connect the hard disk data cable.

a.   Align and plug the hard disk drive data cable into the motherboard connector.

b.   Align and plug the other end of the hard disk drive data cable into the hard disk drive connector.

Note: SATA cables are keyed to ensure correct orientation with the connector.

Step 7:   Connect the optical drive data cable.

a.   Align and plug the optical drive data cable into the motherboard connector.

b.   Align and plug the other end of the optical drive data cable into the optical drive connector.

Step 8:   Verify the connections.

This lab is complete. Please have the instructor verify your work.

Lab 3.1.5.8 - Install Front Panel Cables

Introduction

In this lab, install the front panel cables in the computer.

Recommended Equipment

- Computer with power supply, motherboard, drives, and adapter cards installed
- Antistatic wrist strap and antistatic mat
- Tool kit
- Motherboard manual

Step 1:   Connect the reset switch connector.

Gently press down on the reset switch connector until the pins are fully inserted.

Step 2:   Connect the power switch connector.

Gently press down on the power switch connector until the pins are fully inserted.

Step 3:   Connect the power LED connector.

Gently press down on the power LED connector until the pins are fully inserted.

Step 4:   Connect the HDD LED connector.

Gently press down on the HDD LED connector until the pins are fully inserted.

Step 5:   Connect the speaker connector.

Gently press down on the speaker connector until the pins are fully inserted.

Step 6:   Connect the USB and front audio jacks.

If your case also has front USB and front audio jacks, gently press down on the connector until the clip clicks into place or the pins are fully inserted.

Step 7:   Verify the connections.

Note: If any LED or switch does not work when the computer is first started, remove the connector for that item, turn it around, and reconnect it.

Lab 3.1.5.12 - Complete the Computer Assembly

Introduction

In this lab, you will install the side panels and the external cables on the computer.

Recommended Equipment

- Computer with power supply, motherboard, drives, and adapter cards installed, and internal cables connected
- Monitor cable (HDMI, DVI, or VGA)
- Keyboard
- Mouse
- Network cable
- Wireless antenna
- Power cable
- Tool kit
- Motherboard manual

Step 1:   Attach the side panels.

a.   Attach the side panels to the computer case.

b.   Secure the side panels to the computer using the panel screws.

Step 2:   Attach the monitor cable.

a.   Attach the monitor cable to the video port.

b.   Secure the cable by tightening the screws on the connector.

Step 3:   Attach the keyboard cable.

Plug the keyboard cable into the USB or PS/2 keyboard port.

Step 4:   Attach the mouse cable.

Plug the mouse cable into the USB or PS/2 mouse port.

Step 5:   Attach the Ethernet cable.

Plug the Ethernet cable into the Ethernet port.

Step 6:   Attach the wireless antenna.

Connect the wireless antenna to the antenna connector.

Step 7:   Attach the power cable.

Plug the power cable into the power socket of the power supply.

Step 8:   Verify connections.

This lab is complete. Please have the instructor verify your work.

Lab 3.2.2.8 - Boot the Computer

Introduction

In this lab, you will boot the computer for the first time, explore the firmware setup utility program, and change the boot order sequence.

Recommended Equipment

- Assembled computer with no operating system installed
- Motherboard manual

Step 1: Power on the computer.

a. Plug the power supply cable into an AC wall outlet.

b. If there is a power switch on the power supply, set the switch to "1" or "on".

c. Turn on the computer with the power button on the front panel.

Note: If the computer beeps more than once, or if the power does not come on, notify your instructor.

Step 2: Enter the firmware setup program.

During POST, press the firmware setup key or key combination. The firmware setup utility program screen will appear.

What is the key or combination of keys used to enter the firmware setup utility program?

_____

Who manufactures the BIOS for your computer?

_____

What is the BIOS version?

_____

Step 3: List the main menu options.

List the main menu options and describe what is monitored in each menu?

_____

_____

_____

Step 4: Find the security settings.

Navigate through each screen to find the security settings.

What security settings and features are available?

_____

_____

Step 5: Find the CPU settings.

Navigate through each screen to find the CPU settings.

What is the CPU speed?

_____

What other information is listed for the CPU?

_____

Step 6:   Find the RAM settings.

Navigate through each screen to find the RAM settings.

What is the RAM speed?

_____

What other information is listed for the RAM?

_____

Step 7:   Find the hard drive settings.

Navigate through each screen to find the hard drive settings.

What information is listed for the hard drive?

_____

_____

Step 8:   Find the boot order sequence.

Navigate through each screen to find the boot order sequence.

What is the first boot device in the boot order sequence?

_____

How many additional devices can be assigned in the boot order sequence?

_____

Step 9:   Set the device boot order settings.

a.   Ensure that the first boot order device is the optical drive.

b.   Ensure that the second boot order device is the hard disk drive.

Why would you change the first boot device to the optical drive?

_____

What happens when the computer boots and the optical drive does not contain bootable media?

_____

Step 10: Find the power management setup or ACPI screen.

Navigate through each screen to find the power management setup screen, or ACPI screen.

What power management settings are available?

_____

_____

Step 11: Find the PnP settings.

Navigate through each screen to find the PnP settings.

What PnP settings are available?

_____

_____

Step 12: Find the splash screen settings.

Navigate through each screen to find the splash screen settings.

What splash screen settings are available?

_____

_____

Step 13: Save and exit the setup utility program.

Save the new BIOS/UEFI settings and exit the setup utility program. The computer should restart automatically.

Note: An error message stating that an OS cannot be found (or a similar error) will appear on the screen after the computer boots. An operating system must now be installed to prevent this error. It is safe to turn off the computer at this time.

This lab is complete. Please have the instructor verify your work.

Lab 3.3.1.6 - BIOS File Search

Introduction

In this lab, you will identify the current BIOS version, and then search for BIOS update files.

Recommended Equipment

- Classroom computer with an operating system installed
- Internet access

Step 1:   Boot your computer.

During POST, BIOS information is displayed on the screen for a short period of time.

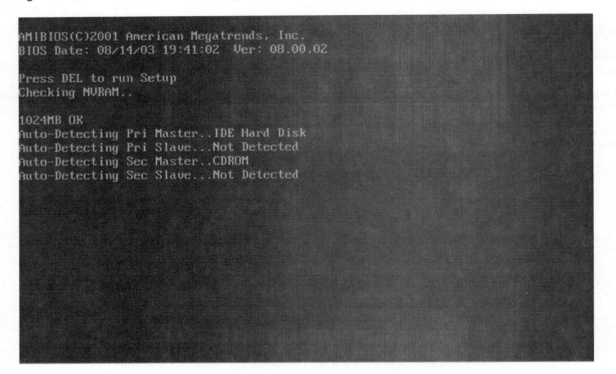

```
AMIBIOS(C)2001 American Megatrends, Inc.
BIOS Date: 08/14/03 19:41:02  Ver: 08.00.02

Press DEL to run Setup
Checking NVRAM..

1024MB OK
Auto-Detecting Pri Master..IDE Hard Disk
Auto-Detecting Pri Slave...Not Detected
Auto-Detecting Sec Master..CDROM
Auto-Detecting Sec Slave...Not Detected
```

Do not log on to Windows.

What key or combination of keys is used to run Setup on your computer?

_____

Step 2:   Restart your computer and enter Setup.

The BIOS Setup Utility or UEFI screen appears.

Who is the manufacturer of the BIOS?

_____

Which BIOS version is installed in your computer?

_____

Step 3:   Search the Internet to find the most current version of BIOS for the motherboard.

Use the information from the previous step to search the Internet to find the most current version of the BIOS for the motherboard in your computer. The following screen is an example of the type of information you would look for to answer the questions below.

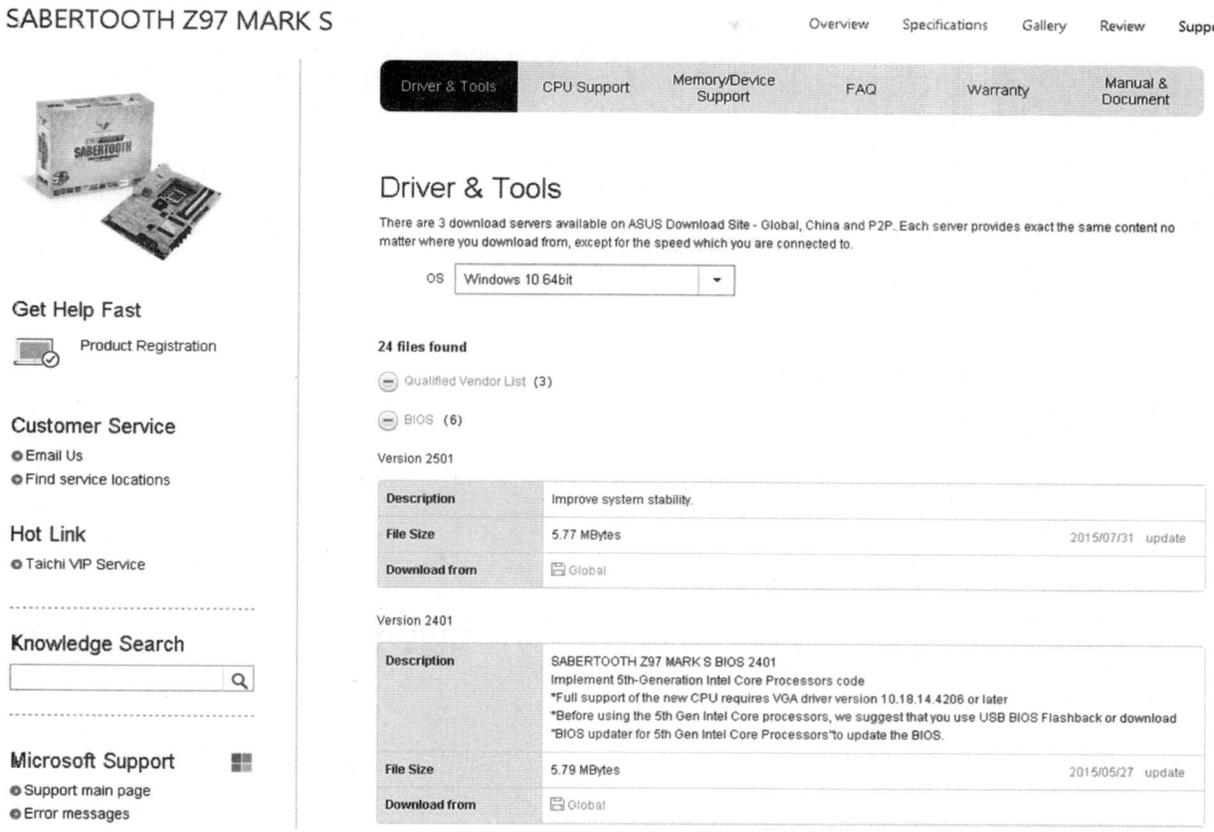

SABERTOOTH Z97 MARK S

Overview   Specifications   Gallery   Review   Support

| Driver & Tools | CPU Support | Memory/Device Support | FAQ | Warranty | Manual & Document |

Driver & Tools

There are 3 download servers available on ASUS Download Site - Global, China and P2P. Each server provides exact the same content no matter where you download from, except for the speed which you are connected to.

OS   Windows 10 64bit

Get Help Fast

Product Registration

Customer Service
- Email Us
- Find service locations

Hot Link
- Taichi VIP Service

Knowledge Search

Microsoft Support
- Support main page
- Error messages

24 files found

Qualified Vendor List (3)

BIOS (6)

Version 2501

Description	Improve system stability.	
File Size	5.77 MBytes	2015/07/31 update
Download from	Global	

Version 2401

Description	SABERTOOTH Z97 MARK S BIOS 2401 Implement 5th-Generation Intel Core Processors code *Full support of the new CPU requires VGA driver version 10.18.14.4206 or later *Before using the 5th Gen Intel Core processors, we suggest that you use USB BIOS Flashback or download "BIOS updater for 5th Gen Intel Core Processors"to update the BIOS.	
File Size	5.79 MBytes	2015/05/27 update
Download from	Global	

Caution: Do not update your BIOS at this time.

What is the current BIOS version available for the motherboard?

What features, if any, have been added to the new BIOS version?

What changes, if any, have been made to the new BIOS version to fix problems?

What are the instructions to update the new BIOS version?

Lab 3.3.3.2 - Upgrade Hardware

Introduction

Use the Internet, a newspaper, or a local store to gather information about hardware components. Your customer's computer currently has one module of 2 GB of RAM, a 500 GB hard disk drive, and a PCIe video adapter card with 256 MB of RAM. Your customer wants to be able to play advanced video games.

Step 1:   Research memory options.

Shop around, and in the table below, list the brand, model number, features, and cost for two different 4 GB modules of DDR3-1600 (PC3-12800).

Brand and Model Number	Features	Cost

Based on your research, which RAM would you select? Be prepared to discuss your decisions regarding the RAM you select.

_____

_____

Step 2:   Research hard disk drive options.

Shop around, and in the table below, list the brand, model number, features, and cost for two different 2 TB 7200 rpm SATA 3 hard disk drives.

Brand and Model Number	Features	Cost

Based on your research, which hard disk drive would you select? Be prepared to discuss your decisions regarding the hard disk drive you select.

_____

_____

Step 3:   Research video adapter card options.

Shop around, and in the table below, list the brand, model number, features, and cost for two different PCIe video adapter cards with 1 GB RAM.

Brand and Model Number	Features	Cost

Based on your research, which video adapter card would you select? Be prepared to discuss your decisions regarding the video adapter card you select.

_____

_____

Chapter 5: Windows Installation

Lab 5.1.2.3 - Search NOC Certifications and Jobs

In this lab, you will use the Internet, a newspaper, or magazines to gather information about network operating system certifications and jobs that require these certifications.

Web sites such as Monster.com, Indeed.com, Simplyhired.com, or Linkedin.com can be used.

a. Use the Internet to research three different network operating system certifications. Based on your research, complete the table below.

Company	Network Operating System(s) Covered	Certification(s) Title	Courses/Training Required for Certification

b. Use the Internet, a newspaper, or a magazine to find at least two network jobs available in your area. Describe the network jobs and the required certifications needed for the position.

_____

_____

_____

_____

_____

_____

_____

c.   Which job would you prefer? List reasons for your selection.

_____

_____

_____

_____

Lab 5.1.4.4 - Data Migration in Windows

Introduction

When a new computer is purchased or a new operating system is installed, it is often desirable to migrate a user's data to the new computer or OS. Windows has a built-in tool called **Windows Easy Transfer** that allows you to select files and folders to migrate. These files and folders are written to a file which is used to restore them to the same locations on the new computer or OS.

The Windows Easy Transfer tool cannot be used to migrate from Windows 8.1 to another installation of Windows 8.1, so instructions are not included in this lab. Also, Windows 8.0 has the same steps and screens that are used by Windows 7, but the windows look slightly different, so Windows 8.0 instructions are not included in this lab.

Recommended Equipment

The following equipment is required:

- A computer with Windows 7 installed
- A USB flash drive

Part 1:   Windows 7

Step 1:   Prepare for data migration.

a.   Log on to the computer.

b.   Right-click the desktop and choose **New > Folder**.

c.   Type **For Transferring** and press **Enter** to name the folder.

d.   Click **Start > All Programs > Accessories > Notepad** to open Notepad.

e.   Type **From older PC** in Notepad.

f.   Click **File > Save As**.

g.   Navigate to **Desktop > For Transferring**.

h.   Type **Data** in the File Name box and press **Enter**.

i.   Click **File > Exit**.

j. You should now have a file named **Data** in a folder called **For Transferring**.

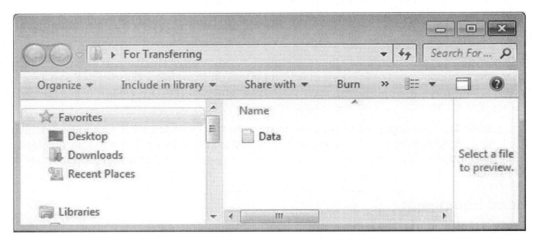

Step 2: Prepare the flash drive.

a. Open the **For Transferring** folder.

b. Connect the USB flash drive to the computer.

c. Navigate to **Computer** and open the USB flash drive.

d. Create a folder on the USB flash drive and name it **Transfer data files**.

Step 3: Create the Easy Transfer file.

a. Click **Start > All Programs > Accessories > System Tools > Windows Easy Transfer**. The **Windows Easy Transfer** window opens.

![Windows Easy Transfer welcome window]
Welcome to Windows Easy Transfer

Windows Easy Transfer lets you copy files and settings from one computer to another. No information is deleted from your old computer.

You can transfer:

- User accounts
- Documents
- Music
- Pictures

- E-mail
- Internet favorites
- Videos
- And more

When the transfer is done, you'll see a list of what was transferred, programs you might want to install on your new computer, and links to other programs that you might want to download.

Tip: If you're upgrading this computer to Windows 7, think of "old computer" as referring to your "old version of Windows" and "new computer" as referring to your "new version of Windows."

Next

b.   Click **Next**. The **What do you want to use to transfer items to your new computer?** window opens.

c.   Click **An external hard disk or USB flash drive**. The **Which computer are you using now?** window opens.

d.   Click **This is my old computer**. The **Checking what can be transferred...** window opens.

The **Choose what to transfer from this computer** window opens.

e.   Uncheck the box next to each account.

f. Click **Customize** for the account to which you are logged in.

g. When the customize window opens, click **Advanced**.

h. Navigate to the **For Transferring** folder that is on the desktop. This will be the location where files are transferred from.

    i.   Select the **Data** file and click **Save**. The **Choose what to transfer from this computer** window opens.

What is the size of the file being transferred?

_____

    j.   Click **Next**. The **Save your files and settings for transfer** window opens.

Because you are transferring the files back to the same computer, a password is not required.

k. Click **Save**.

l. Locate the folder called **Transfer data files** on the USB flash drive and click **Save**. The **These files and settings have been saved for your transfer** window opens.

m. Click **Next**. The **Your transfer file is complete** window opens.

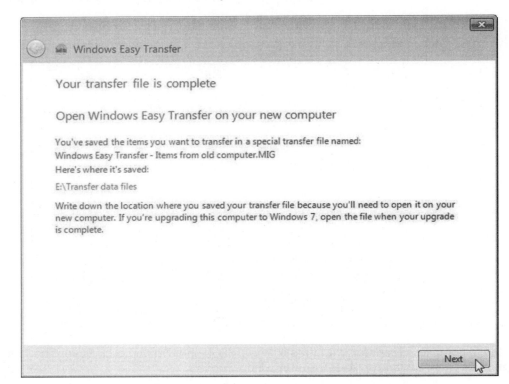

n. Click **Next**. The **Windows Easy Transfer is complete on this computer** window opens.

o. Click **Close**.

Step 4:   Delete the original data.

    a.   Locate and delete the **Data** file in the **For Transferring** folder that is located on the desktop.

    b.   Right-click the **Recycle Bin > Empty Recycle Bin**.

Step 5:   Receive the transfer file.

    a.   Click **Start > All Programs > Accessories > System Tools > Windows Easy Transfer**. The **Welcome to Windows Easy Transfer** window opens.

    b.   Click **Next**. The **What do you want to use to transfer items to your new computer?** window opens.

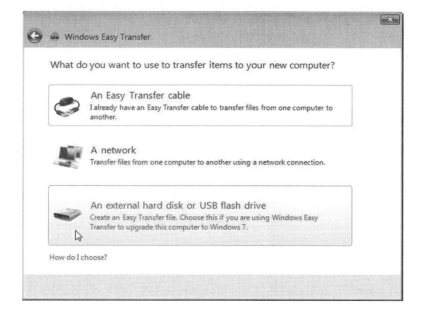

c. Select **An external hard disk or USB flash drive**. The **Which computer are you using now?** window opens.

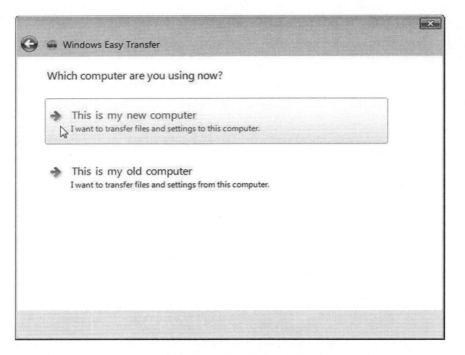

d. Select **This is my new computer**. The **Has Windows Easy Transfer already saved your files from your old computer to an external hard disk or USB flash drive?** window opens.

e. Click **Yes**.

f.   Locate and open the **Transfer data files** folder on the USB flash drive.

g.   Select the **Windows Easy Transfer** file, and then click **Open**. The **Choose what to transfer to this computer** window opens.

h.   Click **Transfer**. The **Transfer items to this computer** window opens.

The **Your transfer is complete** window opens.

i.   Click **See what was transferred**.

j.   Click **Details** below **1 document**.

The **Documents successfully transferred** window opens.

What do you notice about the location of the Data file?

_____

k. Close the **Detail View** window.

l. Close the **Windows Easy Transfer Reports** window.

m. When the **Window Easy Transfer** window opens, click **Close**.

Step 6: Verify the transfer.

a. Navigate to and open the **For Transferring** folder located on the desktop. Notice the **Data** file has been transferred.

b. If advised by the instructor, delete all folders and files created on the desktop and USB flash drive during this lab.

Part 2: Windows Vista

Step 1: Prepare for data migration.

  a.   Log on to the computer.

  b.   Right-click the desktop and choose **New > Folder**.

  c.   Type **For Transferring** and press **Enter** to name the folder.

  d.   Click **Start > All Programs > Accessories > Notepad** to open Notepad.

  e.   Type **From older PC** in Notepad.

  f.   Click **File > Save As**.

  g.   Navigate to **Desktop > For Transferring**.

  h.   Type **Data** in the File Name box and press **Enter**.

  i.   Click **File > Exit**.

  j.   You should now have a file named **Data** in a folder called **For Transferring**.

Step 2: Prepare the flash drive.

  a.   Connect the USB flash drive to the computer.

  b.   Open the **For Transferring** folder.

  c.   Navigate to **Computer** and open the USB flash drive.

  d.   Create a folder on the USB flash drive and name it **Transfer data files**.

Step 3: Create the Easy Transfer file.

a.   Click **Start > All Programs > Accessories > System Tools > Windows Easy Transfer**. The **Windows Easy Transfer** window opens.

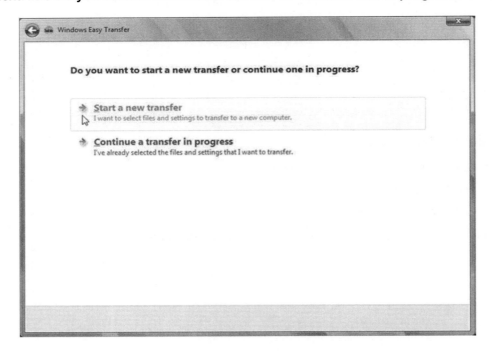

b.   Click **Next**. The **Do you want to start a new transfer or continue one in progress?** window opens.

c.   Click **Start a new transfer**. The **Which computer are you using now?** window opens.

d.   Click **My old computer**. The **Choose how to transfer files and settings to your new computer** window opens.

e. Click **Use a CD, DVD, or other removable media**. The **Choose how to transfer files and program settings** window opens.

f. Click **USB flash drive**. The **Plug in an empty USB flash drive** window opens. Because you are transferring the files back to the same computer, a password is not required.

g. Click **Next**. The **What do you want to transfer to your new computer?** window opens.

h. Click **Advanced options**. The **Select user accounts, files, and settings to transfer** window opens.

i.   Remove the check mark from each box in the window.

j. Click **Add files**.

k. Navigate to the **For Transferring** folder that is on the desktop. This will be the location where files are transferred from.

l. Select the **Data** file and click **Open**. The **Select user accounts, files, and settings to transfer** window opens.

m. Click **Next**. The **You're ready to transfer files and settings to your new computer** window opens.

n. Click **Close**.

Step 4: Delete the original data.

a. Locate and delete the **Data** file in the **For Transferring** folder that is located on the desktop.

b. Right-click the **Recycle Bin > Empty Recycle Bin**.

Step 5:   Receive the transfer file.

a.   Click **Start > All Programs > Accessories > System Tools > Windows Easy Transfer**. The **Welcome to Windows Easy Transfer** window opens.

b.   Click **Next**. The **Do you want to start a new transfer or continue one in progress?** window opens.

c. Click **Continue a transfer in progress**. The **Are your computers connected to a network?** window opens.

d. Click **No, I've copied files and settings to a CD, DVD, or other removable media**. The **Where did you save the files and settings you want to transfer?** window opens.

e. Click **On a USB flash drive**. The **Plug in the flash drive** window opens.

f. Click **Next**. The **Review selected files and settings** window opens.

g. Click **Transfer**. The **The transfer is complete** window opens.

h. Click **Show me everything that was transferred**. The **Windows Easy Transfer Report** window opens.

What do you notice about the location of the new Data file?

_____

i. Click **OK**.

j. Close the **Detail View** window.

k.   When the **Window Easy Transfer** window opens, click **Close**.

Step 6: Verify the transfer.

a.   Navigate to and open the **For Transferring** folder located on the desktop. Notice the **Data** file has been restored.

b.   If advised by the instructor, delete all folders and files created on the computer desktop and USB flash drive during this lab.

Lab 5.2.1.7 - Install Windows 7 or Vista

Introduction

In this lab, you will install the Windows 7 or Vista operating system.

Recommended Equipment

- A computer with a blank hard disk drive
- Windows 7 or Vista installation DVD or USB flash drive

Part 1: Windows 7 Installation

Step 1: Starting the installation media.

a. Insert the Windows 7 installation DVD into the DVD-ROM drive or plug the USB flash drive into a USB port.

b. When the computer starts up, watch for the message **Press any key to boot from CD or DVD**. If the message appears, press any key on the keyboard to boot the computer from the DVD. If the **press any key message** does not appear, the computer automatically starts loading files from the DVD.

c. The computer starts loading files from the DVD or USB flash drive.

d.   The Windows 7 boot screen appears.

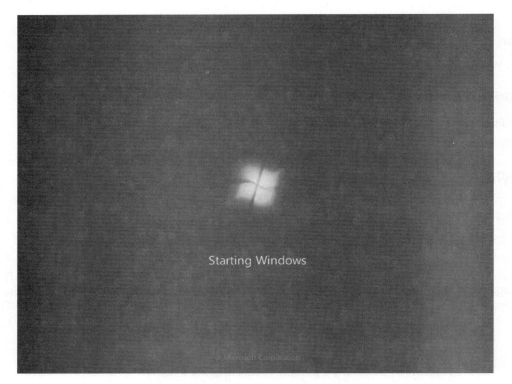

Step 2:   Configuring Initial Settings.

a.   The **Install Windows** window opens. Press **Next** unless you need to change the default settings.

b.   Press **Install now** to continue.

Step 3:   Collecting information.

a.   The **Setup is starting...** screen appears.

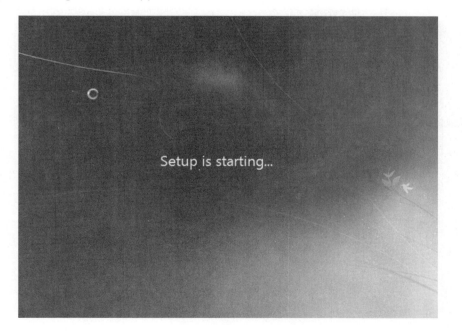

b.   The **Please read the license terms** window opens. Read and confirm that you accept the license by selecting **I accept the license terms**. Click **Next**.

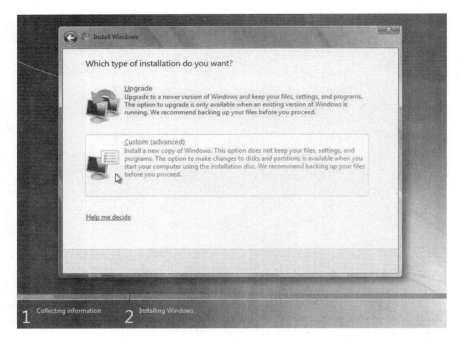

c.   When the **Which type of installation do you want?** window opens, click **Custom (advanced)** to continue.

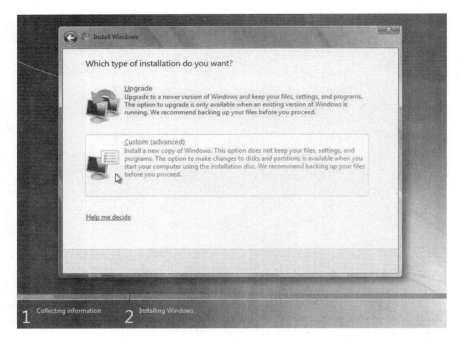

d. The **Where do you want to install Windows?** window opens. Select the hard drive or partition on which Windows 7 will be installed. Click **Next** to select **Disk 0 Unallocated Space**, which is the default setting.

Step 4:   Installing Windows.

a. The **Installing Windows...** window opens. Windows 7 Setup may take up to 50 minutes to configure your computer.

b.   The **Windows needs to restart to continue** window opens. Your computer will automatically restart or you can click **Restart now**.

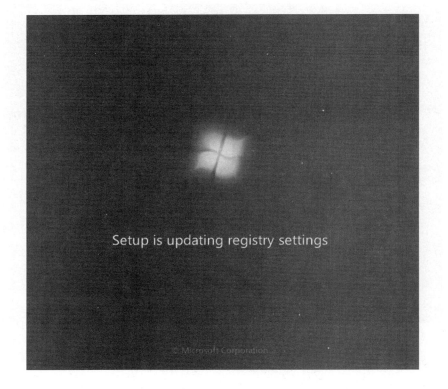

c.   If you get the message **Press any key to boot from CD or DVD…**, do not press any key and Windows will boot from the hard disk to continue the installation.

Press any key to boot from CD or DVD...

d.   The **Setup is updating registry settings** screen appears.

Setup is updating registry settings

© Microsoft Corporation

e.   The **Setup is starting services** screen appears.

f.   The **Installing Windows…** window opens. Windows may reboot a few more times. This may take several minutes.

Step 5:   Setting up Windows.

a.   Type the user name and computer name provided by your instructor. Click **Next**.

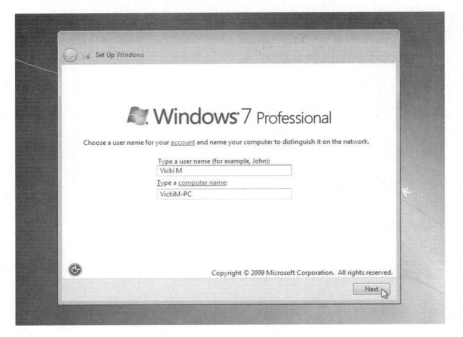

b.   The **Set a password for your account** window opens. Type the password provided by your instructor. Retype the password and enter the password hint. Click **Next**.

c.   The **Type your Windows product key** window opens. On this page, type your product key. Click **Next**.

Note: You can find the product key on the case or sleeve in which the Windows DVD was packaged, or you can get it from your instructor.

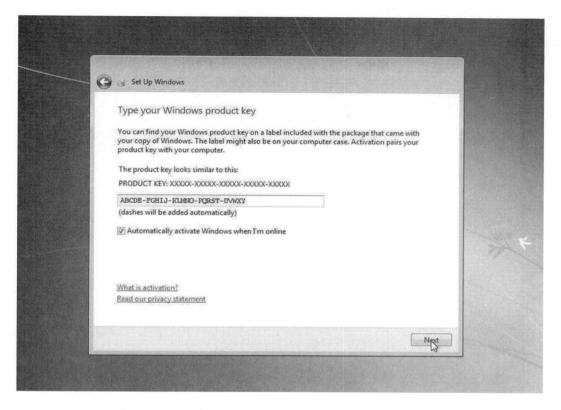

Note: If you entered your product key, Setup will not ask you the following:

Do you want to enter your product key now? If you were instructed not to enter a product key, click **No**.

d. In the **Help protect your computer and improve Windows automatically** window, click **Use recommended settings**.

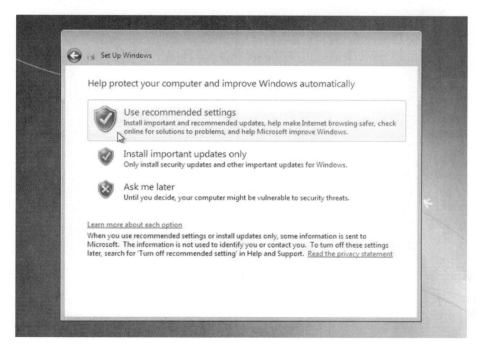

e. In the **Review your time and date settings** window, configure the computer clock to match your local date, time, and time zone. Click **Next**.

f. The **Select your computer's current location** window opens. Select the option provided by your instructor.

Note: This window will not show up if the installation did not correctly install drivers for the network card.

g.   The **Windows is finalizing your settings** window opens.

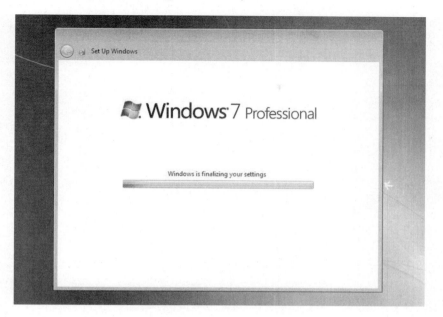

Step 6:   Logging into Windows.

a.   The **Welcome** screen appears.

b.   The **Preparing your desktop...** screen appears.

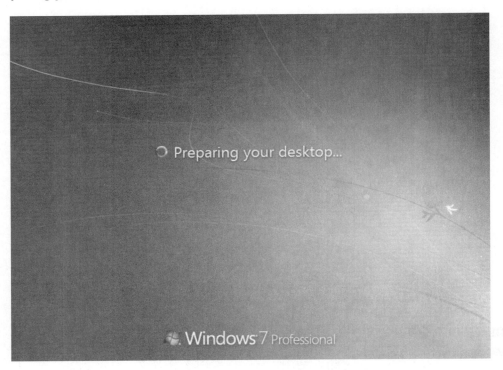

c.   You are logged on to Windows 7 for the first time.

Part 2:   Windows Vista Installation

Step 1:   Starting the installation media.

a.   Insert the Windows Vista installation DVD into the DVD-ROM drive or plug the USB flash drive into a USB port.

b.   When the computer starts up, watch for the message **Press any key to boot from CD or DVD**. Press any key to continue.

If the **press any key** message does not appear, the computer automatically starts loading files from the DVD.

c.   The computer starts loading files from the DVD or USB flash drive.

d. The Windows Vista boot screen appears.

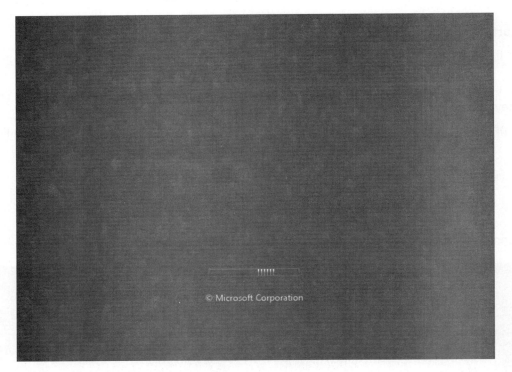

Step 2:   Configuring the initial settings.

a. The **Install Windows** window opens. Press **Next** unless you need to change the default settings.

b.   Click **Install now** to continue.

Step 3:   Collecting information.

a.   The **Type your product key for activation** screen appears. On this page, type your product key. Click **Next**.

Note: You can find the product key on the case or sleeve in which the Windows DVD was packaged, or you can get it from your instructor.

Note: If you entered your product key, Setup will determine the Vista product edition to install and will not display the next two screens. Skip to step d.

b.   Because you have left the product key field blank, the **Do you want to enter your product key now?** window opens. If you were instructed not to enter a product key, click **No**.

c.   Setup now prompts you to select the Vista version you purchased. In general, you should choose the version you purchased, but note that you can install any Vista version listed and experiment with it for a limited time before product activation requires you to activate the version you purchased.

Note: Your product key will only activate the version of Vista you purchased.

d.   Select the Windows Vista version that will be installed, check the item title **I have selected the edition of Windows that I purchased**, and then click **Next**.

e.   The **Please read the license terms** window opens. Read and confirm that you accept the license by
     selecting the box **I accept the license terms**. Click **Next** to continue.

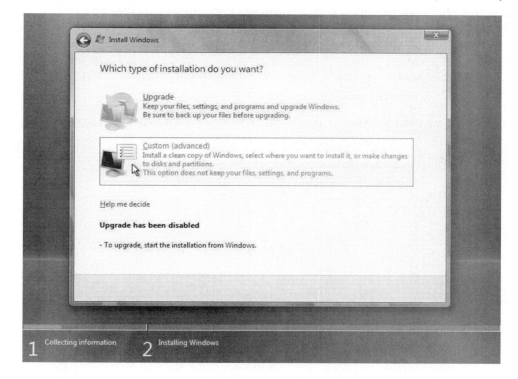

f.   The **Which type of installation do you want?** window opens. Click **Custom (advanced)**.

g.   The **Where do you want to install Windows?** window opens. Select the hard drive or partition on which Windows Vista will be installed. Click **Next** to select **Disk 0 Unallocated Space**, which is the default setting.

Step 4:   Installing Windows Vista.

a.   The **Installing Windows…** window opens. Windows Vista Setup may take up to 50 minutes to configure your computer.

b. The **Windows needs to restart to continue** window opens. Your computer will automatically restart or you can click **Restart now**.

c. If you get the message **Press any key to boot from CD or DVD**, do not press any key and Windows will boot from the hard disk to continue the installation.

d. The **Please wait while Windows continues setting up your computer...** screen appears.

e. The **Installing Windows…** window opens. Windows may reboot a few more times. This may take several minutes.

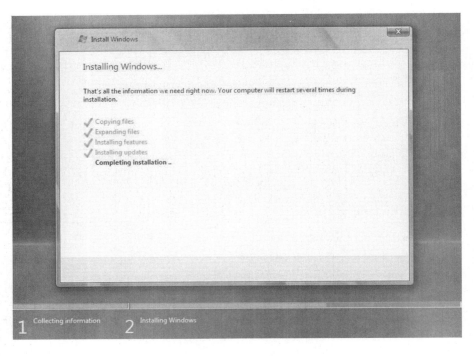

Step 5:   Setting up Windows.

a. The **Choose a user name and picture** window opens. Type the name provided by your instructor. Type the Administrator password provided by your instructor. When you type in a password, two new fields will appear. Retype the password and the password hint. Click **Next**.

b. The **Type a computer name and choose a desktop background** window opens. Type the computer name provided by your instructor. Click **Next**.

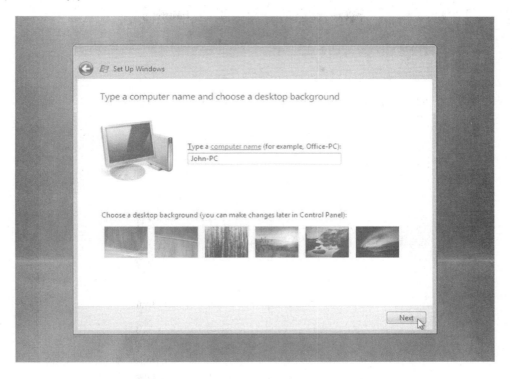

c. In the **Help protect Windows automatically** window, click **Use recommended settings**.

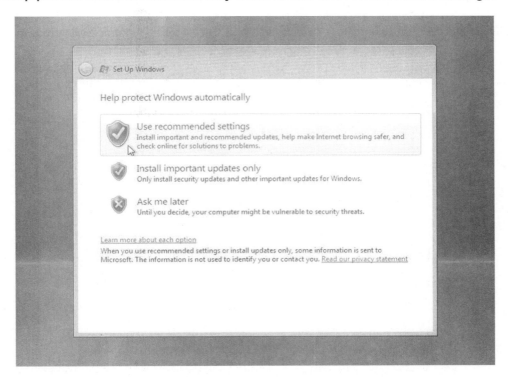

d. In the **Review your time and date settings** window, configure the computer clock to match your local date, time, and time zone. Click **Next**.

e. The **Select your computer's current location** window opens. Select the option provided by your instructor.

Note: This screen will not show up if the installation did not correctly install drivers for the network card.

f.   In the **Thank you** window, click **Start**.

g.   The **Set Up Windows** section is completed.

h.   The **Please wait while Windows checks your computer's performance** screen appears.

i.   Windows Vista boots for the first time.

j.   The login screen appears. Enter the password that you used during the install process and click the **blue arrow** to login.

k.   The **Preparing your desktop…** screen appears. Your account profile is created and configured.

l.   The **Welcome** screen appears. Windows Vista is now installed.

Lab 5.2.1.7 - Install Windows 8

Introduction

In this lab, you will install Windows 8.1 and 8.0.

Recommended Equipment

- A computer with a blank hard disk drive
- Windows 8.1 and 8.0 installation DVD or USB flash drive

Step 1: Starting the installation media.

a. Insert the Windows 8 installation DVD into the DVD-ROM drive or plug the USB flash drive into a USB port.

b. When the computer starts up, watch for the message **Press any key to boot from CD or DVD.**

   If the message appears, press any key on the keyboard to boot the computer from the DVD. If the **press any key message** does not appear, the computer automatically starts loading files from the DVD.

c. The computer starts loading files from the DVD or USB flash drive.

Step 2: Configuring initial settings.

a. The **Windows Setup** window opens. Click **Next** to continue unless you need to change the default settings.

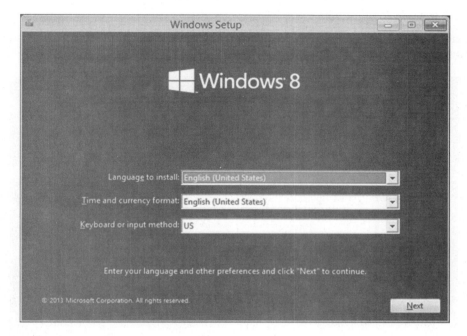

b. Click **Install now** to continue the installation.

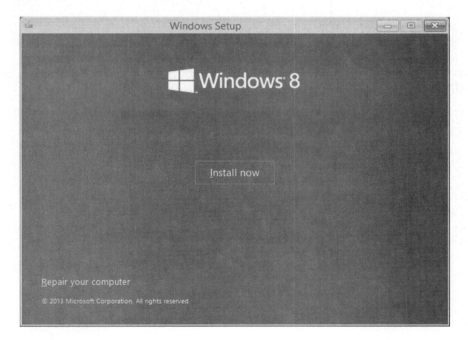

Step 3: Collecting information.

a. In the **Enter the product key to activate Windows** window, enter the product key.

    Note: You can find the product key on the case or sleeve in which the Windows DVD was packaged, or you can get it from your instructor.

b. The **License terms** window opens. Read and confirm that you accept the license by selecting the box **I accept the license terms**. Click **Next**.

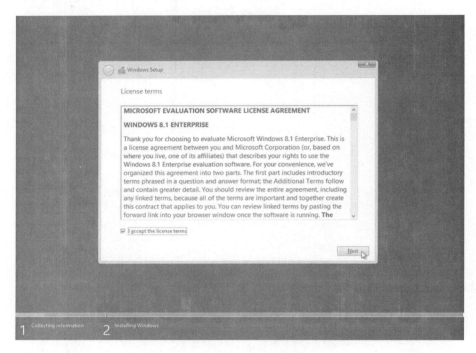

c. The **Which type of installation do you want?** window opens. Click **Custom: Install Windows only (advanced)**.

d. The **Where do you want to install Windows?** window opens. Select the hard drive or partition on which Windows 7 will be installed. In this example, click to select **Disk 0 Unallocated Space**. Click **Next** to continue. Setup has finished collecting information for the installation.

Step 4: Installing Windows.

a. The **Installing Windows** window opens. Windows 8 will take some time to copy the files and install the OS on your computer. During the setup, the computer will restart several times.

b. When the **Windows needs to restart to continue** window opens, your computer will automatically restart or you can click **Restart now**.

c. If you get the message **Press any key to boot from CD or DVD...**, do not press any key and Windows will boot from the hard disk to continue the installation.

Step 5: Personalize your Windows installation.

a. After the device's setup is complete and Windows is ready for more customization, the **Personalize** screen displays. Enter the name of this PC in the **PC name** field. Click **Next** to continue.

b. The **Settings** screen displays. At this screen, you can click **Customize** to configure the settings, such as Windows Update, according to your preference. In this lab, click **Use express settings** to continue.

Step 6: Account setup.

In this step, you will set up a local account to access the computer. You will not be creating a Microsoft account for this exercise. If you already have an account or choose to do so, you may use your Microsoft account for this step.

a. When the **Sign in to your Microsoft account** screen displays for Window 8.1 installation, click **Create a new account** to continue. If you already have a Microsoft account and choose to use it, enter the required information and click **Next** to continue.

   For **Window 8.0 installation**, click **Sign in without a Microsoft account**. Click **Local account** to continue and skip to step c.

b. On the **Create a Microsoft account** screen, do not fill in the information. Click **Sign in without a Microsoft account** to continue.

c. On the **Your account** screen, enter a username. Enter a password and a password hint provided by your instructor. It is highly recommended to create a password to protect your user account and data. Click **Finish** to continue.

Step 7: Finishing the installation.

a. When you are finished with the installation, Windows continues to finalize your settings and install your apps.

b. After the installation is completed, the Desktop displays and you are logged into Windows for the first time.

    For Windows 8.0, the **Start** screen displays when you are logged in for the first time.

Lab 5.2.1.10 - Check for Updates in Windows 7 and Vista

Introduction

In this lab, you will configure the operating system so you can select which updates are installed and then change the settings so updates are downloaded and installed automatically.

Recommended Equipment

The following equipment is required for this exercise:

- A computer with a new installation of Windows 7 or Vista

Step 1:   Check for updates on your computer.

a. Boot the computer. Navigate to the **Change Settings** window by clicking **Control Panel > Windows Update > Change settings**.

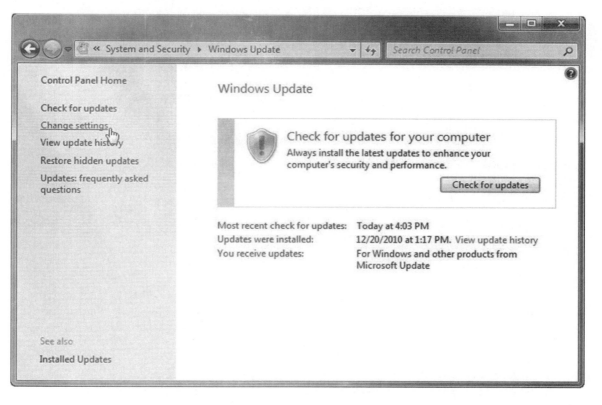

b. In the **Important updates** drop-down menu, select **Check for updates but let me choose whether to download and install them**.

c. Click **OK**.

Step 2: Select updates to apply, and install the updates.

a. From the **Windows Update** window, click the link that shows how many updates have been downloaded. Example: **16 important updates are available**.

Note: If no important updates are shown, click **Check for updates**.

b. The **Select update to install** window opens. Place a check mark next to the important and optional updates to be installed, and click **OK**.

Note: Before selecting which updates to be installed, ask the instructor for permission to install the updates.

c.   In the **Windows Update** window, click **Install updates**.

d.   The **Windows Update** window will display the status of the update process. Once all of the selected updates have been installed, you may receive a message stating that a reboot is required. If you receive that message, reboot the computer.

Step 3:   Open the Windows Update utility program. (Optional)

If you rebooted your computer, re-open the **Windows Update** window by clicking **Control Panel > Windows Update > Change settings**.

Step 4:   Change the Windows Updates to install updates automatically.

a.   From the **Windows Update** window, click **Change settings**.

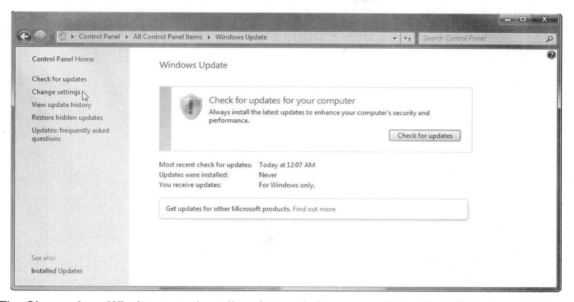

b.   The **Choose how Windows can install updates** window opens. Select **Install updates automatically (recommended)** from the drop-down menu.

c.   Click **OK** to accept the change.

d.   Close all open windows.

Reflection

Why is it recommended to set important updates to install automatically?

_____

_____

_____

_____

Lab 5.2.1.10 - Check for Updates in Windows 8

Introduction

In this lab, you will configure the operating system so you can select which updates are installed and then change the settings so updates are downloaded and installed automatically.

Recommended Equipment

The following equipment is required for this exercise:

- A computer with a new installation of Windows 8

Step 1:   Check for updates on your computer.

a.   Boot the computer. Navigate to the **Change Settings** window by clicking **Control Panel > Windows Update > Change settings**.

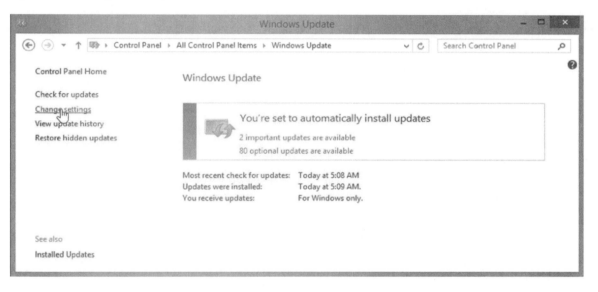

b. In the **Important updates** drop-down menu, select **Check for updates but let me choose whether to download and install them**.

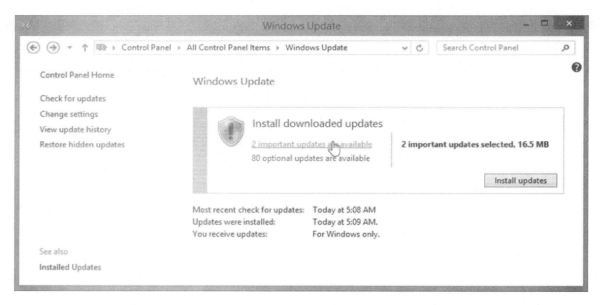

c. Click **OK**.

Step 2:   Select updates to apply, and install the updates.

a. In the **Windows Update** window, click the link that shows how many updates have been downloaded. Example: **2 important updates are available**.

Note: If no important updates are shown, click **Check for updates**.

b. The **Select updates to install** window opens. Place a check mark next to the important and optional updates to be installed, and then click **Install**.

Note: Before selecting which updates to be installed, ask the instructor for permission to install the updates.

c. The Windows Update window reappears and provides the progress status of the update operation.

d.   The Windows update window will notify you when all updates have been downloaded and installed.

Note: A **Restart now** button may appear to the right of the **updates were installed** message. If you see this message, it is necessary to reboot the computer in order to apply some operating system updates. If you see this button, click **Restart now**.

Step 3:   Open the Windows Update utility program. (Optional)

If you rebooted your computer, re-open the **Windows Update** window by clicking **Control Panel > Windows update**.

Step 4:   Change the Windows Updates to install updates automatically.

a.   In the **Windows Update** window, click **Change settings**.

b.   In the **Change settings** window, select **Install updates automatically (recommended)** from the **Important updates** drop-down menu.

c.   Click **OK** to accept the change.

d.   Close all open windows.

Reflection

Why does Microsoft recommend selecting the setting to install updates automatically?

_____

_____

_____

_____

Lab 5.2.4.7 - Create a Partition in Windows 7 and Vista

Introduction

In this lab, you will create a FAT32 formatted partition on a disk. You will convert the partition to NTFS. You will then identify the differences between the FAT32 format and the NTFS format.

Recommended Equipment

- Computer running Windows 7 or Vista
- Un-partitioned space of at least 1 GB on the hard disk drive

Step 1:   Start the Computer Management Utility.

Note: You must have administrative rights to work with the Computer Management Utility.

a. Click **Start**.

b. Click **Control Panel > Administrative Tools > Computer Management**.

c. In the **Computer Management** window, click **Disk Management**.

Step 2:   Create a new disk volume in the free space.

a.   Right-click on the block of **Free Space** or **Unallocated** space, and then click **New Simple Volume**.

b.   The **New Simple Volume Wizard** window opens. Click **Next**.

c.   The **Specify Volume Size** window opens. Type **2000** in the **Simple volume size in MB** field, and then click **Next**.

New Simple Volume Wizard

Specify Volume Size
Choose a volume size that is between the maximum and minimum sizes.

Maximum disk space in MB: 8191

Minimum disk space in MB: 8

Simple volume size in MB: 2000

< Back   Next >   Cancel

d.   Click the **Assign the following drive letter:** radio button. Select **I** from the drop-down menu, and then click **Next**.

New Simple Volume Wizard

Assign Drive Letter or Path
For easier access, you can assign a drive letter or drive path to your partition.

◉ Assign the following drive letter: E ▼
○ Mount in the following empty NTFS folder:
                                          Br
○ Do not assign a drive letter or drive path

B
E
F
G
H
I
J
K
L
M
N
O
P
Q
R
S
T
U

< Back   Next >   Cancel

Note: You may need to substitute different drive letters for the letters shown in this lab.

e. Click the **Format this volume with the following settings:** radio button. Select **FAT32** from the File system drop-down menu, and then click **Next**.

f. The **Completing the New Simple Volume Wizard** window opens. Click **Finish**.

g. The **Computer Management** window displays the status of the **NEW VOLUME**. Close the **Computer Management** window.

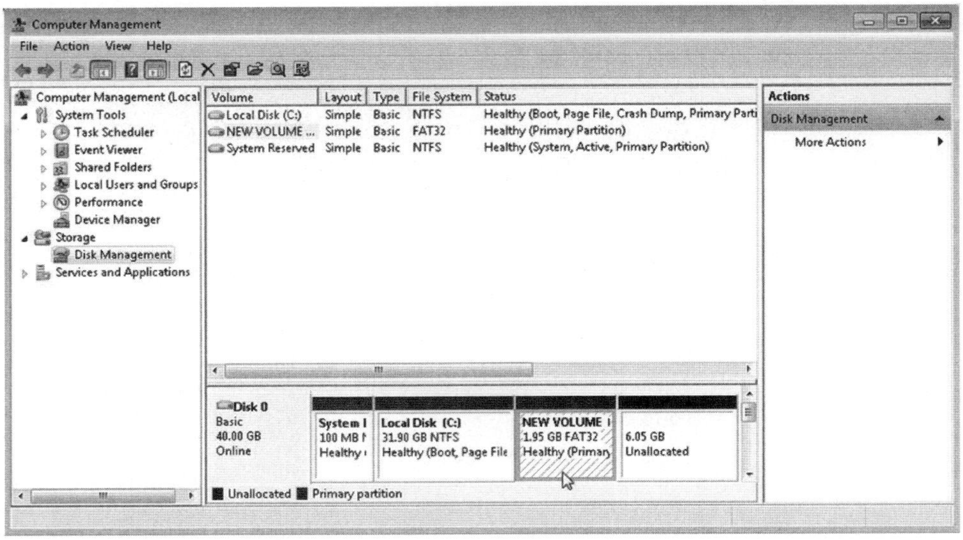

Step 3: **Open the Computer window to review information about the new disk partition.**

a. Click **Start > Computer** to open the **Computer** window.

b. Click to highlight the **NEW VOLUME (I:)** drive and basic information about the drive will appear at the bottom of the **Computer** window.

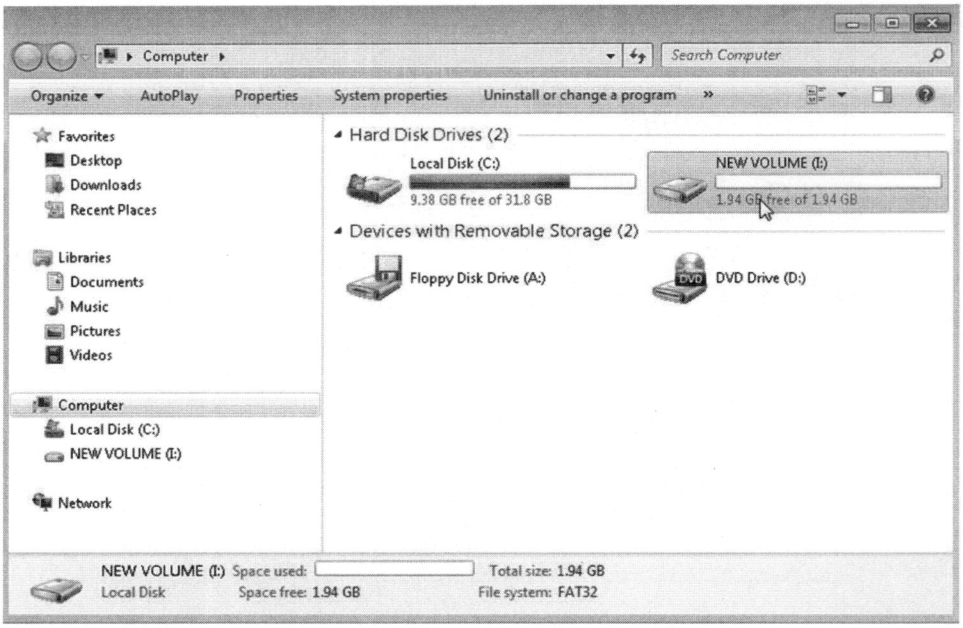

What type file system is used on the NEW VOLUME (I:)?

_____

How much Free Space is shown?

_____

c. Right-click the **NEW VOLUME (I:)** drive, then select **Properties**.

d. The **NEW VOLUME (I:) Properties** window opens.

List the tabs found in the **NEW VOLUME (I:) Properties** window.

_____

e. On the **General** Tab, rename the volume from **NEW VOLUME** to **ITE**, and then click **OK**.

Step 4:   Create a text document and save it to the ITE drive.

    a.   Click **ITE (I:)** in the left panel of the **Computer** window, then right-click anywhere in the white space of the right panel.

    b.   Click **New > Text Document**.

    c.   Rename the **New Text Document** to **ITE Test Document** and press **Enter**.

d. Right-click on the **ITE Test Document** and choose **Properties**. This opens the **ITE Test Document Properties** window.

What tabs are listed in the ITE Test Document Properties window?

_____

e. Click **OK** to close the **ITE Test Document Properties** window. Close the **Computer** window.

Step 5:   Convert the ITE volume from FAT32 to NTFS without losing data.

a.   Click **Start**, then type **cmd** in the search field just above the start button. Right-click on the **command** program that appears, and click **Run as administrator**.

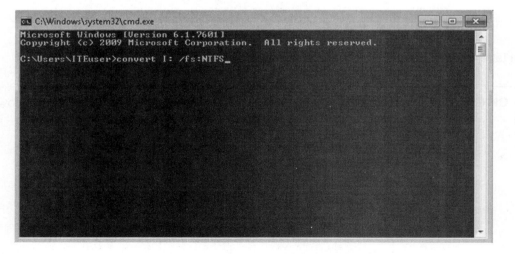

b.   The **Administrator: C:\Windows\System32\cmd.exe** window opens. At the command prompt, type **convert I: /fs:NTFS** and then press **Enter**.

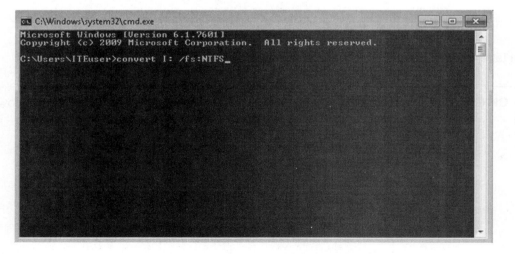

c. You will be prompted to enter the current volume label for drive **I:**. Type **ITE** and press the **Enter** key.

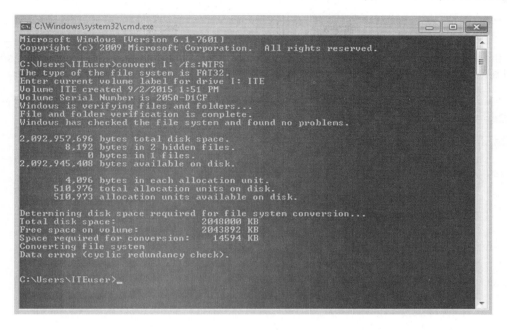

d. Review the information displayed by the convert command. To close the **Administrator: C:\Windows\System32\cmd.exe** window, type **exit** at the command prompt and then press **Enter**.

Step 6:   Open the Computer window to work with the ITE volume.

a. Click **Start > Computer** to open the **Computer** window.

b. Right-click on the **ITE (I:)** volume, and select **Properties** from the drop-down menu.

What type of File System is used for the ITE (I:) drive?

_____

What are the tabs in the ITE (I:) Properties window?

_____

_____

When the volume was FAT32, there were seven tabs. What are the names of the new tabs that were added after the volume was converted to NTFS?

_____

c.   Click **Cancel** to close the **ITE (I:) Properties** window.

Step 7:   Display the properties of the ITE Test Document.

a.   In the left pane of the **Computer** window, click **ITE (I:)**.

b.   Right-click on the **ITE Test Document**, then select **Properties** from the drop-down menu.

What are the tabs in the **ITE Test Document Properties** window?

_____

_____

When the volume was FAT32, there were three tabs. What is the name of the new tab that was added after the volume was converted to NTFS?

_____

c. Close all open windows.

Reflection

Why is there an additional Security tab in the properties windows for documents stored on an NTFS volume?

_____

_____

_____

_____

Lab 5.2.4.7 - Create a Partition in Windows 8

Introduction

In this lab, you will create a FAT32 formatted partition on a disk. You will convert the partition to NTFS. You will then identify the differences between the FAT32 format and the NTFS format.

Recommended Equipment

- Computer running Windows 8
- Un-partitioned space of at least 1 GB on the hard disk drive

Step 1:   Start the Computer Management Utility program.

Note: You must have administrative rights to work with the Computer Management Utility program.

a.   Click **Control Panel > Administrative Tools > Computer Management**.

Note: To open the Disk Management window in Windows 8.0, click **Search** and then type **diskmgmt.msc** and press **Enter**.

b.   In the **Computer Management** window, click **Disk Management**.

Step 2:   Create a new disk volume in the free space.

    a.   Right-click on the block of **Free Space** or **Unallocated** space. Click **New Simple Volume**.

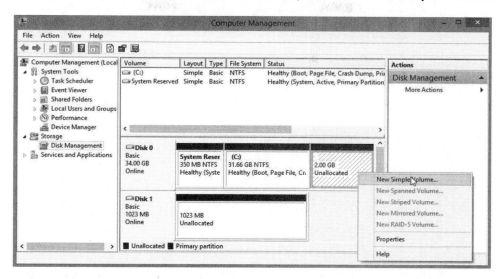

    b.   The **New Simple Volume Wizard** window opens. Click **Next**.

c.   Type **2000** in the **Simple volume size in MB** field, and then click **Next**.

d.   Click the **Assign the following drive letter:** radio button. Select **I** from the drop-down menu, then click **Next**.

Note: You may need to substitute different drive letters for the letters shown in this lab.

e. Click the **Format this volume with the following settings:** radio button. Select **FAT32** from the **File system** drop-down menu, and then click **Next**.

f. Click **Finish** to complete the **New Simple Volume Wizard**.

g. The **Computer Management** window will display the status of the **NEW VOLUME**. Close the **Computer Management** window.

   Note: In Windows 8.0, close the Disk Management window.

Step 3:   Open the This PC window to review information about the new disk partition.

a. Click **Start,** type **this pc**, and press **Enter** to open the **This PC** window.

Note: In Windows 8.0, click **Search**, type **compute**r, and then press **Enter** to open the **Computer** window. This window will allow you to do the same operations that the **This PC** windows does in Windows 8.1.

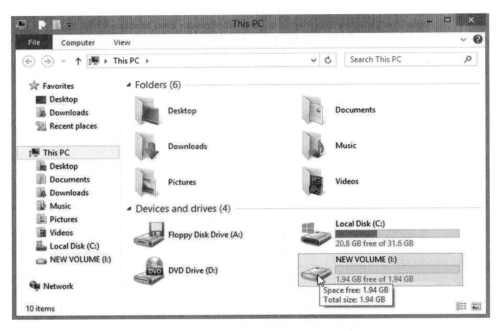

b. Right-click on the **NEW VOLUME (I:)** drive and then select **Properties** from the drop-down menu.

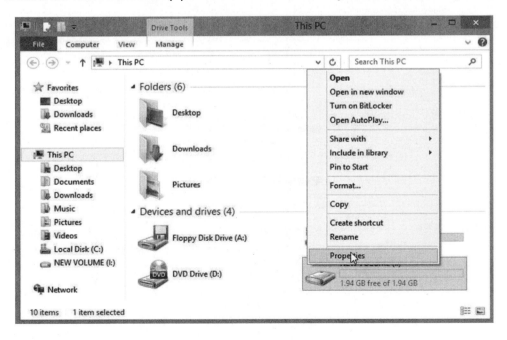

What type of File System is used on the NEW VOLUME (I:)?

_____

How much Free Space is shown?

_____

List the tabs found in the **NEW VOLUME (I:) Properties** window.

_____

c.   On the **General** tab, rename the volume from **NEW VOLUME** to **ITE**, and then click **OK**.

d.   If an **Access Denied** window opens, click **Continue** to complete the operation.

Step 4:   Create a text document and save it to the ITE drive.

a.   Double-click on the **ITE (I:)** disk icon to view the contents of the drive. You should see a message in the middle of the screen stating that this folder is empty. Right-click anywhere in the white space below that message to bring up a drop-down menu. Click **New > Text Document**.

b.   Rename the **New Text Document** to **ITE Test Document** and press **Enter**.

c. Right-click on the **ITE Test Document** and choose **Properties**. This opens the **ITE Test Document Properties** window.

What tabs are listed in the ITE Test Document Properties window?

_____

d. Click **OK** to close the **ITE Test Document Properties** window. Close the **ITE (I:)** window.

Step 5:   Convert the ITE volume from FAT32 to NTFS without losing data.

a.   Click **Start**, then type **cmd** (the search field will pop up as soon as you start typing). Right-click on the **Command Prompt** program that appears, and then click **Run as administrator**.

Note: In Windows 8.0, right-clicking on the **Command Prompt** will display options at the bottom of the screen. Click **Run as administrator**.

b.   The **User Account Control** window opens asking if you want to allow the following program to make changes to this computer. Click **Yes**.

c.   The **Administrator: Command Prompt** window opens. At the command prompt, type **convert I: /fs:NTFS** and then press **Enter**.

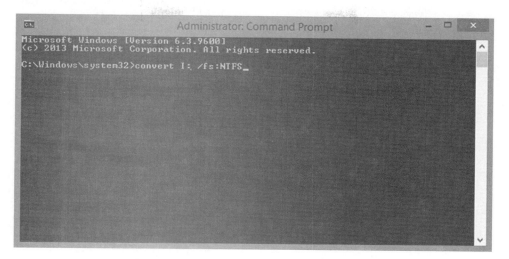

d.   You will be prompted to enter the current volume label for drive **I:**. Type **ITE** and press **Enter**.

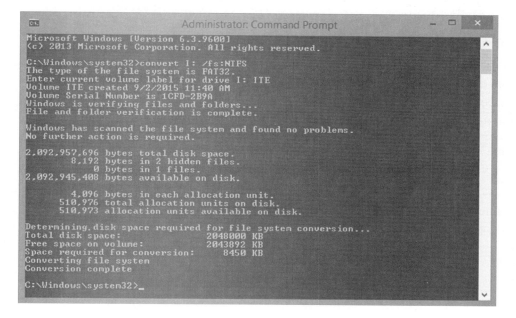

e.   Review the information displayed by the convert command. To close the **Administrator: Command Prompt** window, type **exit** at the command prompt and then press **Enter**.

Step 6:   Open the This PC window to work with the ITE volume.

a.   Click **Start,** then type **Computer** to open the **This PC** window.

b.   Right-click on the **ITE (I:)** volume, and select **Properties** from the drop-down menu.

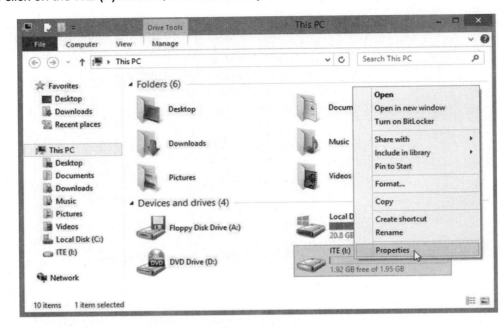

What type of File System is used for the ITE (I:) drive?

_____

What are the tabs in the ITE (I:) Properties window?

_____

_____

When the volume was FAT32, there were six tabs. What are the names of the new tabs that were added after the volume was converted to NTFS?

_____

c.   Click **Cancel** to close the **ITE (I:) Properties** window.

Step 7:   Display the properties of the ITE Test Document.

a.   In the **This PC** window, double-click on the **ITE (I:)** disk icon.

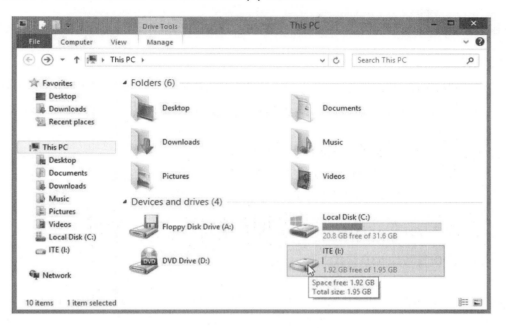

b.   Right-click on the **ITE Test Document**, then select **Properties** from the drop-down menu.

What are the tabs in the **ITE Test Document Properties** window?

_____

When the volume was FAT32, there were three tabs. What is the name of the new tab that was added after the volume was converted to NTFS?

_____

c.   Close all open windows.

Reflection:

Why is there an additional Security tab in the properties window of documents stored on an NTFS volume?

_____

_____

_____

_____

Chapter 6: Windows Configuration and Management

Lab 6.1.1.5 - Task Manager in Windows 7 and Vista

Introduction

In this lab, you will explore Task Manager and manage processes from within Task Manager.

Recommended Equipment

The following equipment is required for this exercise:

- A computer running Windows 7 or Vista

Step 1:   Work in the Applications tab of Windows Task Manager.

a.   Log on to Windows as an administrator.

b.   Open a browser and a folder.

c.   Click the **desktop** and press **Ctrl-Alt-Delete > Start Task Manager > Applications** tab.

d.   Select the open browser and then click **Switch To**.

What happened to the browser?

_____

e. Bring **Windows Task Manager** to the front of the desktop. Click **New Task** to open the **Create New Task** window.

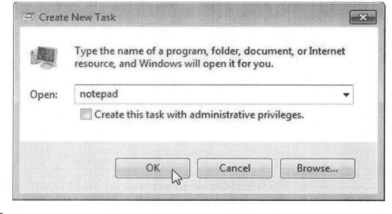

f. In the **Open** field, type **Notepad** and click **OK**.

What happens?

_____

g. Navigate back to the **Windows Task Manager**, select **Notepad**, and click **End Task**.

What happens?

_____

Step 2:   Work in the Services tab of Windows Task Manager.

    a.   Click the **Services** tab. Use the scroll bar on the right of the **Services** window to view all the services listed.

What are the statuses listed?

_____

Step 3: Work in the Performance tab of Windows Task Manager.

a. Click the **Performance** tab.

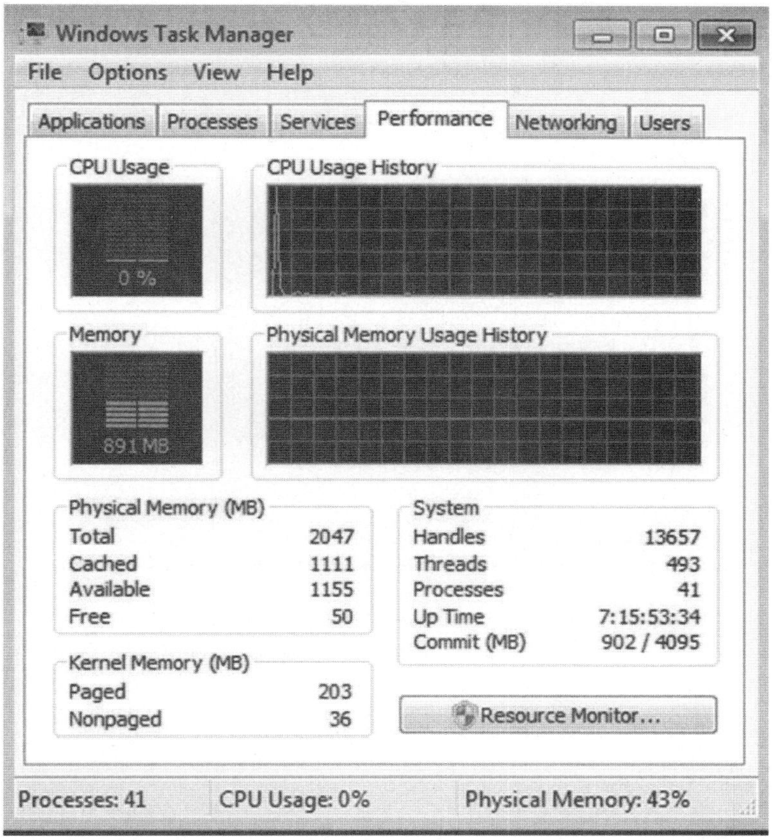

How many threads are running?

_____

How many processes are running?

_____

What is the total physical memory (MB)?

_____

What is the available physical memory (MB)?

_____

How much physical memory (MB) is being used by the system?

_____

Step 4:   Work in the Networking tab of Windows Task Manager.

a.   Click the **Networking** tab.

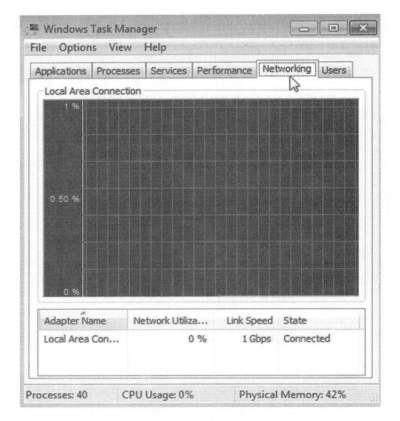

What is the link speed?

_____

Step 5:   Work in the Users tab of Windows Task Manager.

a.   Click the **Users** tab.

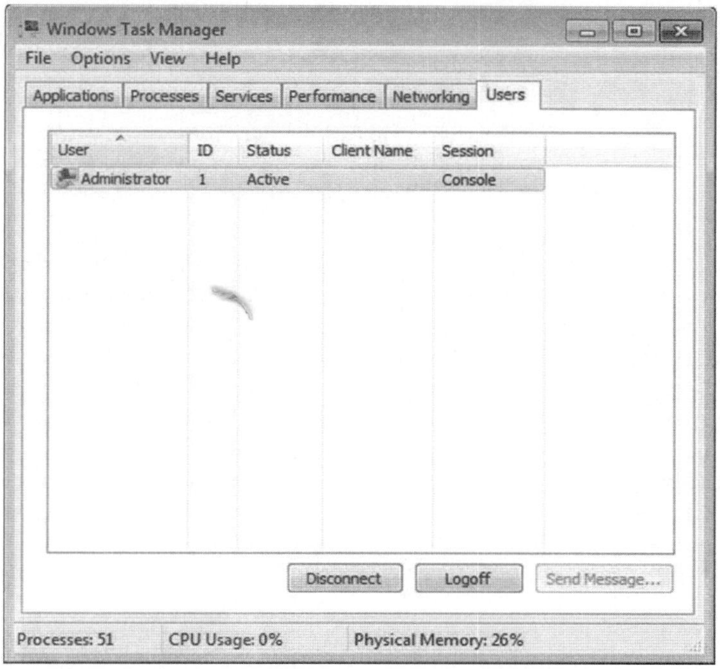

List all users and their status.

_____

What actions can you perform on the user from this window?

_____

Step 6:   Work in the Processes tab of Windows Task Manager.

   a.   Click the **Processes** tab.

b. Check the checkbox **Show processes from all users**.

c. Double-click the white border around the Processes tab. This changes the view of Windows Task Manager to compact mode.

Note: The **User Account Control** window may open in Vista asking for permission to continue. Click **Continue**.

d. Click the heading **Image Name**. Click **Image Name** again.

Image Name	User Name	CPU	Memory (Private Working Set)	Description
audiodg.exe	LOCAL ...	00	7,872 K	Windows Audio Device Graph...
csrss.exe	SYSTEM	00	1,388 K	Client Server Runtime Process
csrss.exe	SYSTEM	00	4,856 K	Client Server Runtime Process
csrss.exe	SYSTEM	00	1,312 K	Client Server Runtime Process
dwm.exe	ITEuser	00	1,056 K	Desktop Window Manager
explorer.exe	ITEuser	00	22,692 K	Windows Explorer
GWX.exe	ITEuser	00	952 K	GWX
jusched.exe *32	ITEuser	00	964 K	Java Update Scheduler
LogonUI.exe	SYSTEM	00	9,516 K	Windows Logon User Interfa...
lsass.exe	SYSTEM	00	4,828 K	Local Security Authority Proc...
lsm.exe	SYSTEM	00	2,172 K	Local Session Manager Service
msdtc.exe	NETWO...	00	2,764 K	Microsoft Distributed Transac...
mstsc.exe	ITEuser	02	13,548 K	Remote Desktop Connection
rdpclip.exe	ITEuser	00	1,440 K	RDP Clip Monitor
SearchIndexe...	SYSTEM	00	11,068 K	Microsoft Windows Search In...
services.exe	SYSTEM	00	3,780 K	Services and Controller app
smss.exe	SYSTEM	00	316 K	Windows Session Manager
spoolsv.exe	SYSTEM	00	5,768 K	Spooler SubSystem App
svchost.exe	NETWO...	00	27,532 K	Host Process for Windows Se...
svchost.exe	SYSTEM	00	2,992 K	Host Process for Windows Se...
svchost.exe	NETWO...	00	3,608 K	Host Process for Windows Se...

☑ Show processes from all users   End Process

What effect does this have on the columns?

_____

e. Click **Memory (Private Working Set)**.

Image Name	User Name	CPU	Memory (Private Working Set)	Description
System Idle P...	SYSTEM	98	24 K	Percentage of time the proce...
System	SYSTEM	00	72 K	NT Kernel & System
smss.exe	SYSTEM	00	316 K	Windows Session Manager
GWX.exe	ITEuser	00	952 K	GWX
jusched.exe *32	ITEuser	00	964 K	Java Update Scheduler
wininit.exe	SYSTEM	00	968 K	Windows Start-Up Application
dwm.exe	ITEuser	00	1,056 K	Desktop Window Manager
csrss.exe	SYSTEM	00	1,312 K	Client Server Runtime Process
csrss.exe	SYSTEM	00	1,388 K	Client Server Runtime Process
rdpclip.exe	ITEuser	00	1,424 K	RDP Clip Monitor
winlogon.exe	SYSTEM	00	1,780 K	Windows Logon Application
vmware-usba...	SYSTEM	00	1,800 K	VMware USB Arbitration Service
taskmgr.exe	ITEuser	00	1,884 K	Windows Task Manager

☑ Show processes from all users   End Process

What affect does this have on the columns?

_____

f.   Double-click the outside border again to return to tabs mode.

g.   Open a browser.

Note: Firefox is used in this lab. However, any browser will work. Just substitute your browser name whenever you see the word **Firefox**.

h.   Return to the **Windows Task Manager**. Click **Image Name** so the list is in alphabetical order, then locate and select **firefox.exe**.

i.   Right-click **firefox.exe > Set Priority**.

What is the default priority for the browser?

_____

j. Set the priority to **Above Normal**. Then click **Change priority** in the Windows Task Manager warning message.

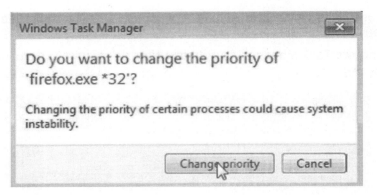

Step 7: Change the fields that are displayed in the Windows Task Manager.

a. Click **View > Select Columns**.

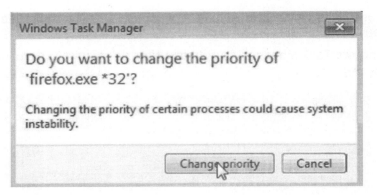

b. The **Select Process Page Columns** window opens. Check **Base Priority and** click **OK**.

c.   Expand the width of the **Windows Task Manager** so the **Base Priority** column is visible.

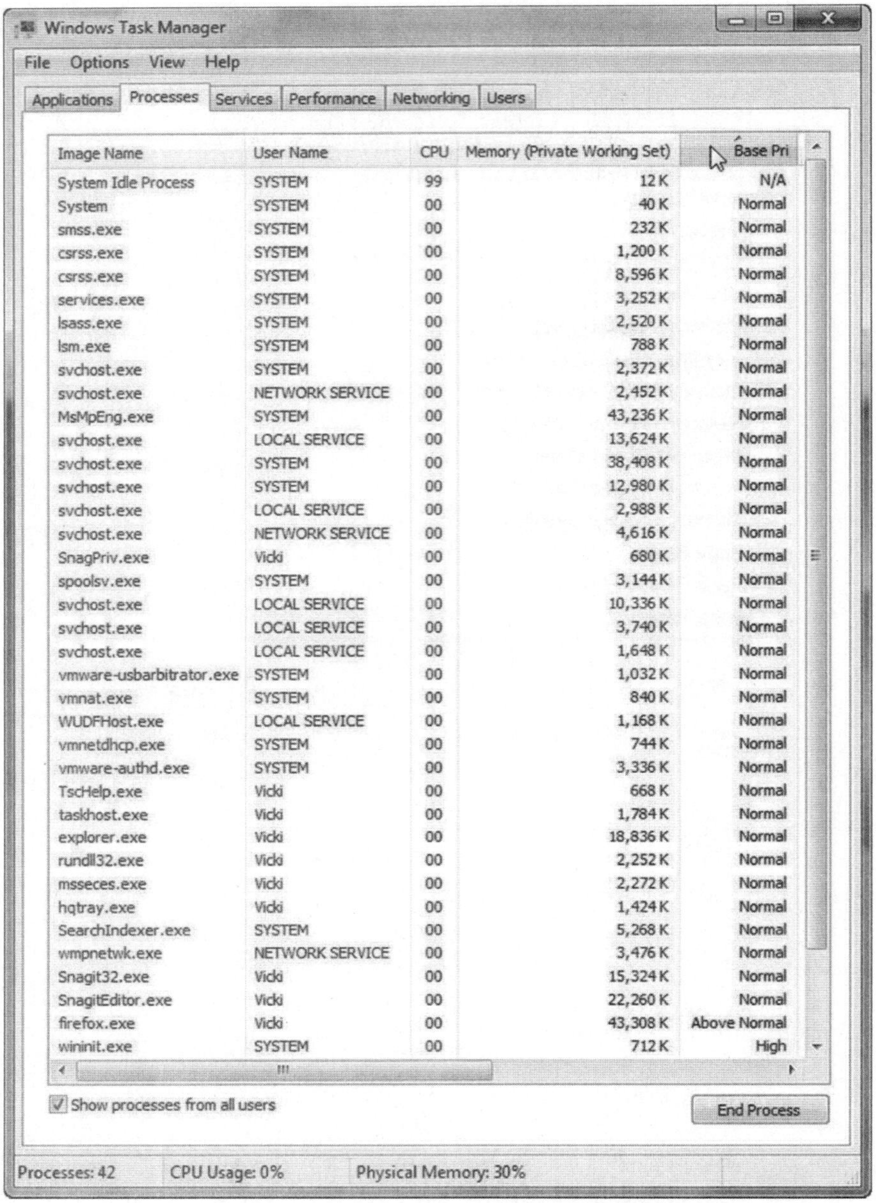

List the name of the image that has a base priority of Above Normal?

_____

Which image name has a base priority of N/A?

_____

d.   Reset Firefox.exe base priority to normal. To do this, right-click **firefox.exe > Set Priority > Normal > Change priority**.

e. Click **View > Select Columns**. Uncheck **Base Priority** and click **OK**.

f. Close **Firefox**.

Is Firefox listed as a process?

_____

g. Close all open windows.

Reflection

Why is it important for an administrator to understand how to work within the Windows Task Manager?

_____

_____

_____

_____

Lab 6.1.1.5 - Task Manager in Windows 8

Introduction

In this lab, you will explore Task Manager and manage processes from within Task Manager.

Recommended Equipment

The following equipment is required for this exercise:

- A computer running Windows 8

Step 1:   Work in the Applications tab of Task Manager.

a.   Log on to Windows as an administrator.

b.   Open a browser and a folder.

c.   Click **Start**, and type **task manager**. Press **Enter** to bring up the Task Manager utility.

Note: For Windows 8.0, bring up the charms menu and then click on the search icon. Type **task manager** and press **Enter** to open the Task Manager utility.

d.   Click **Fewer details** to view the list of open applications.

e.   Double-click the **open browser listing** in Task Manager.

What action took place on the desktop?

_____

f.   Bring up **Task Manager** again by clicking on its icon in the task bar. Highlight the browser, and click **End task**.

What happened?

_____

Step 2:   Work in the Services tab of Task Manager.

a.   Click **More Details** at the bottom-left corner of Task Manager.

b.   Click the **Services** tab. Use the scroll bar on the right side of the **Services** window to view all the services listed.

What statuses are listed?

_____

Step 3:   Work in the Performance tab of Task Manager.

a.   Click the **Performance** tab.

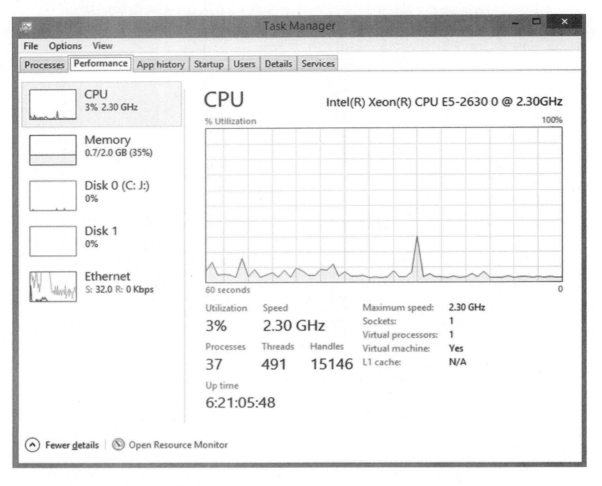

How many threads are running?

_____

How many processes are running?

_____

b. Click on the **Memory Chart** in the left panel of the **Performances** tab.

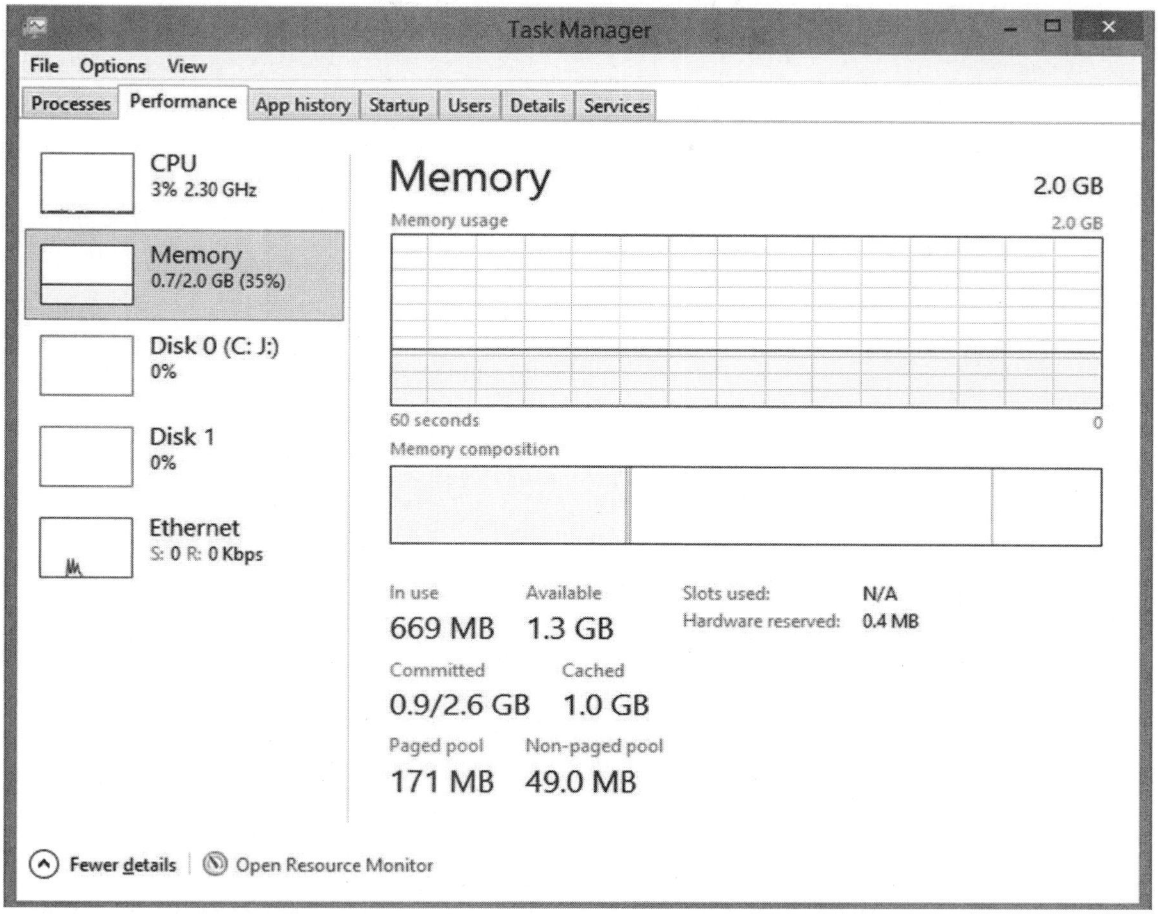

What is the total physical memory (MB)?

_____

What is the available physical memory (MB)?

_____

How much physical memory (MB) is being used by the computer?

_____

c.   Click the **Ethernet Chart** in the left panel of the **Performances** tab.

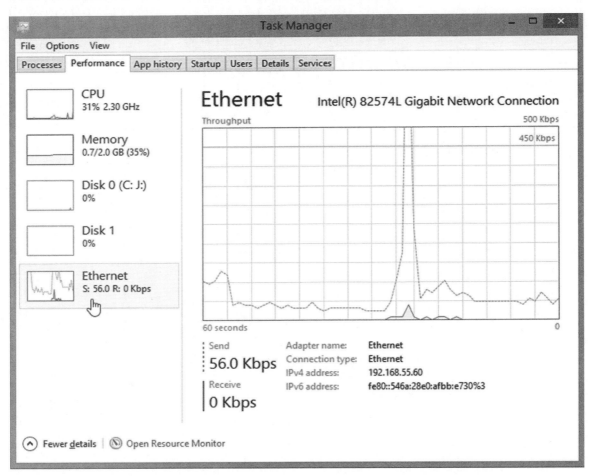

What is the link speed?

_____

What is the IPv4 address of the PC?

_____

Note: You can click **Open Resource Monitor** to bring up the Resource Monitor utility from the Performance tab in Task Manager.

Step 4:   Work in the Processes tab of Task Manager.

a. Click the **Processes** tab.

b.   Click the **Memory** heading. Click the **Memory** heading a second time.

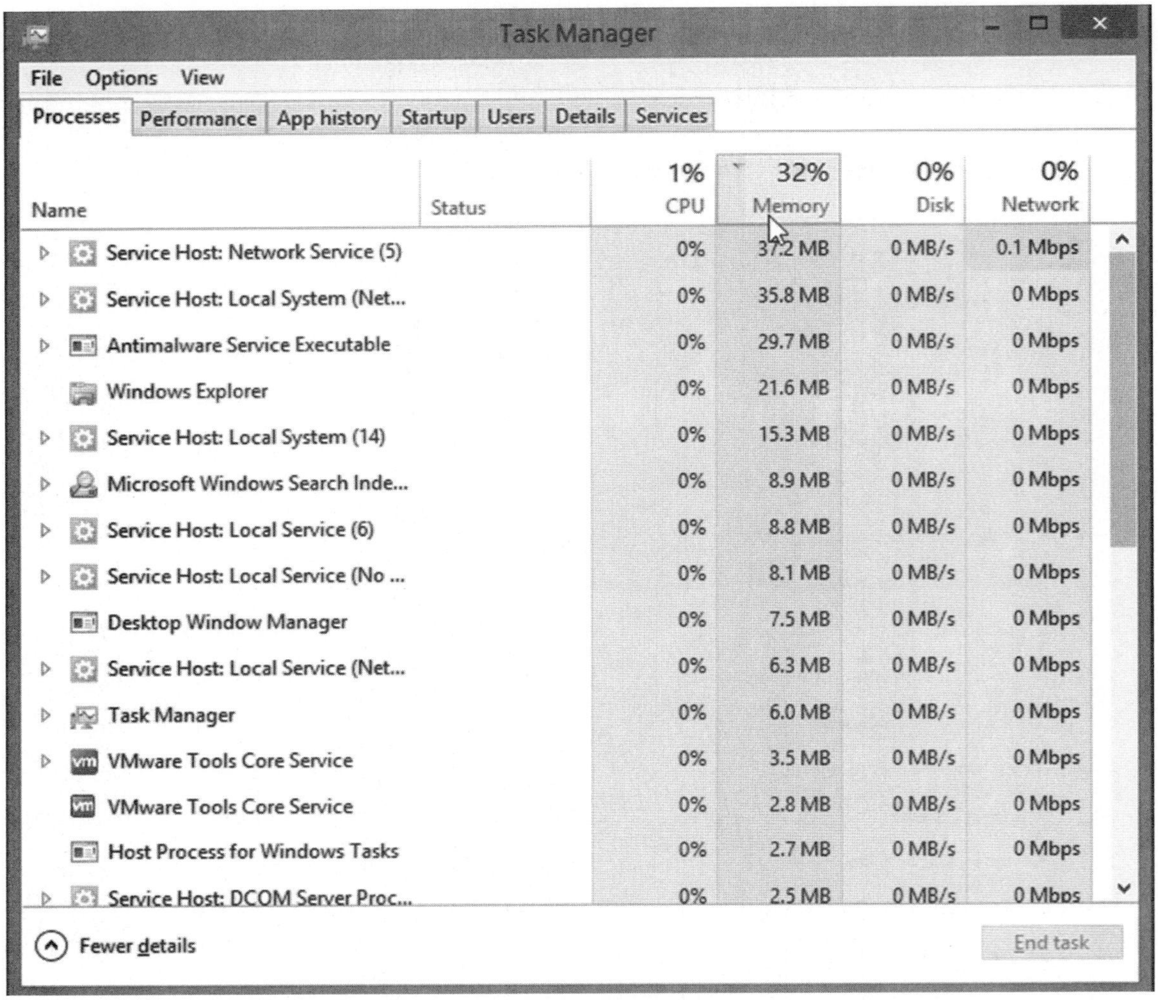

What effect does this have on the columns?

_____

_____

_____

c. Right-click on the **Memory** heading, and then select **Resource values > Memory > Percents**.

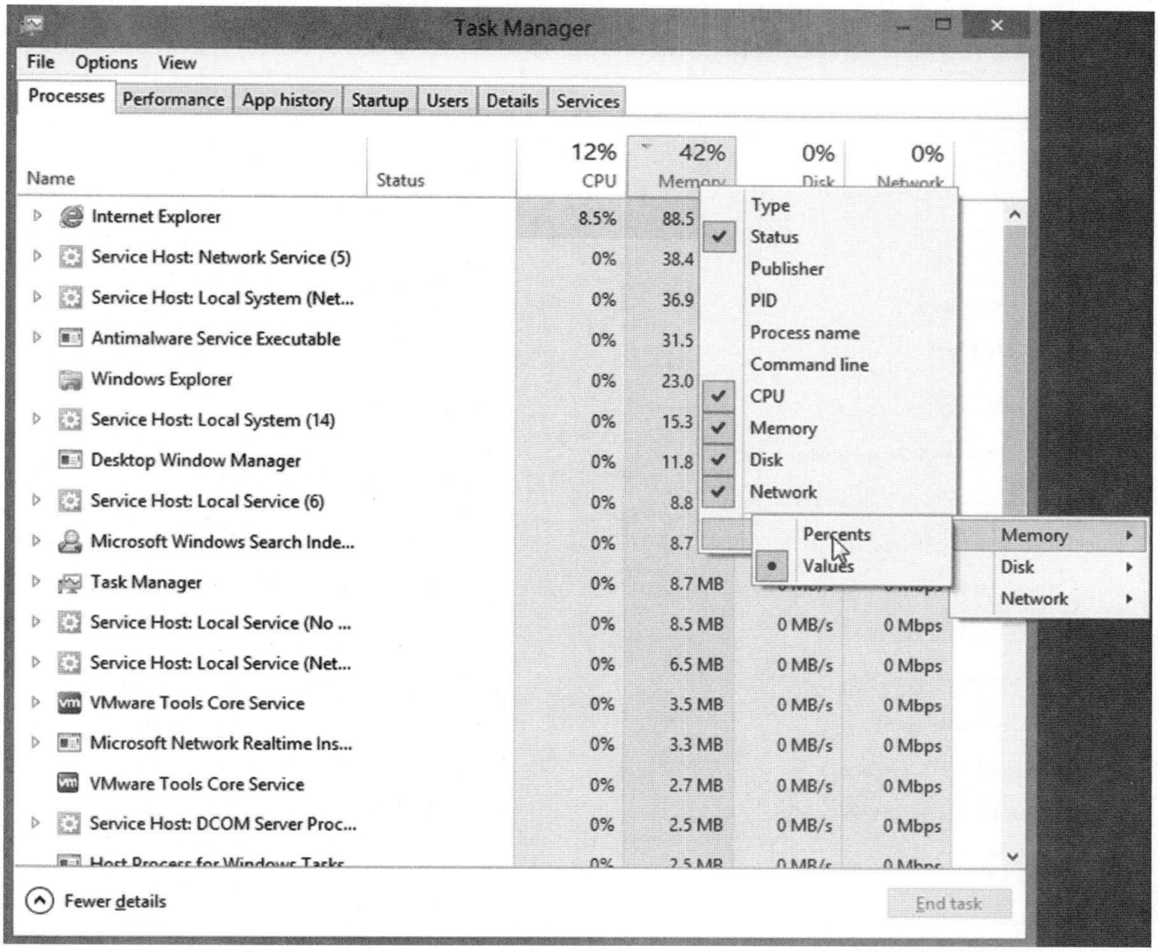

What affect does this have on the Memory column?

_____

How could this be useful?

_____

_____

_____

d. Open a browser.

Note: Internet Explorer is used in this lab. However, any browser will work. Just substitute your browser name whenever you see the **Internet Explorer**.

e.   Return to the **Task Manager**. Click the **Name** heading.

The listed processes are divided by categories. What categories are listed?

_____

f.   Select **Internet Explorer**, and click **End Task**.

Task Manager						
File Options View						
Processes	Performance	App history	Startup	Users	Details	Services
Name	Status	5% CPU	41% Memory	0% Disk	0% Network	

Name	Status	CPU	Memory	Disk	Network
Apps (2)					
▷ Internet Explorer		0%	11.5%	0 MB/s	0 Mbps
▷ Task Manager		0%	1.4%	0 MB/s	0 Mbps
Background processes (9)					
Adobe® Flash® Player Utility		0%	0.3%	0 MB/s	0 Mbps
Host Process for Windows Tasks		0%	0.3%	0 MB/s	0 Mbps
▷ Microsoft Distributed Transacti...		0%	0.1%	0 MB/s	0 Mbps
▷ Microsoft Windows Search Inde...		0%	1.1%	0 MB/s	0 Mbps
RDP Clipboard Monitor		0%	0.1%	0 MB/s	0 Mbps
▷ Spooler SubSystem App		0%	0.3%	0 MB/s	0 Mbps
VMware Tools Core Service		0%	0.4%	0 MB/s	0 Mbps
▷ VMware Tools Core Service		0%	0.5%	0 MB/s	0 Mbps
▷ Windows License Monitoring Se...		0%	0.1%	0 MB/s	0 Mbps
Windows processes (22)					
▷ Antimalware Service Executable		0%	3.8%	0 MB/s	0 Mbps
Client Server Puntime Proce...		0%	0.1%	0 MB/s	0 Mbps

⌃ Fewer details   End task

g.   Close all open windows.

Reflection

Why is it important for an administrator to understand how to work within the Task Manager?

_____

_____

_____

_____

Lab 6.1.1.9 - Install Third-Party Software in Windows 7 and Vista

Introduction

In this lab, you will install and remove a third-party software application supplied by your instructor. You will install the Packet Tracer Windows application.

Recommended Equipment

The following equipment is required for this exercise:

- A computer that is using Windows 7
- A flash drive or CD with the latest Packet Tracer Windows install package

Step 1:   Locating the installer.

a. Log on to the computer with the Administrator account and use Windows Explorer to navigate to the folder where the Packet Tracer installer is located. This folder could be on the local hard drive, on an external flash drive, or on a CD.

b. Locate the PacketTracer###_setup.exe (where ### is the version number) application. Click the **PacketTracer6.2_setup.exe** icon to start the installation process of the Packet Tracer application. You may need to double-click the icon to start the installation.

Note: The version shown in the file name depends on the version of Packet Tracer you are installing and may vary.

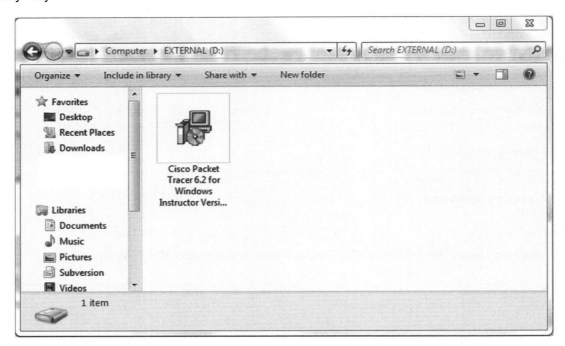

Note: If the **Open File – Security Warning** opens, click **Run** or **Continue**.

Step 2:   Running the Packet Tracer installer.

a. The **Setup – Cisco Packet Tracer 6.2 Instructor** window opens. Click **Next**.

   Note: The window name may not contain the word **Instructor**. It will depend on the version of Packet Tracer being installed.

b. The **License Agreement** window opens. Select **I accept the agreement** and click **Next**.

c.   The **Select Destination Location** window opens. Keep the default settings and click **Next**.

What is the default location for Packet Tracer?

_____

d.   The **Select Start Menu Folder** window opens. Keep the default settings and click **Next**.

e.   The **Select Additional Tasks** window opens. Keep the default settings. Click **Next**.

f.   The **Ready to Install** window opens. Click **Install**.

g.   The **Installing** progress window opens.

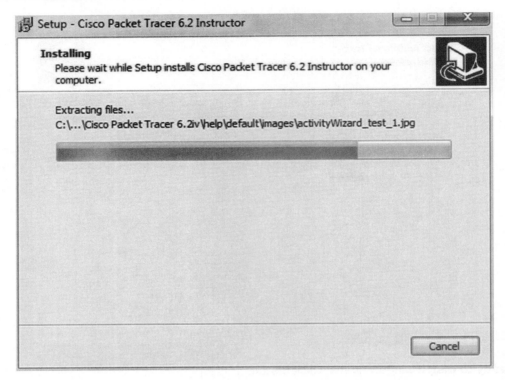

h.   If an information window opens, click **OK**.

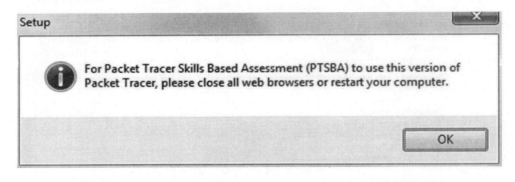

i. The **Completing the Cisco Packet Tracer 6.2 Setup Wizard** window opens. Click **Finish**.

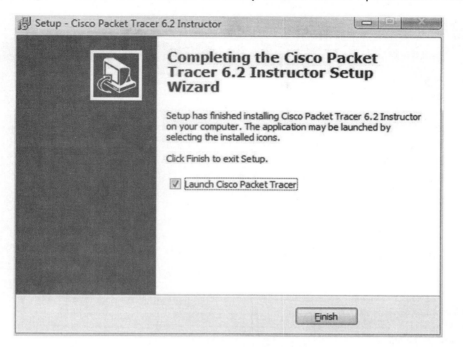

j. If the **You are running Packet Tracer for the first time** window opens, click **OK**.

k. If **Windows Security Alert** appears, click **Unblock**.

l.   Packet Tracer opens. Close Packet Tracer and all other open windows.

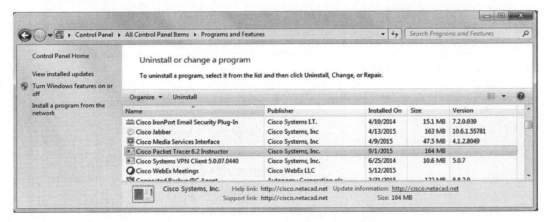

Step 3:   Uninstalling Packet Tracer.

a.   To uninstall a program, click **Control Panel > Programs and Features**. Click **Cisco Packet Tracer** in the list and click **Uninstall**.

b. The **Cisco Packet Tracer Uninstall** window opens. Click **Yes**.

c. When the successfully removed message appears, click **OK**.

d. Verify the application was removed from the list in the **Programs and Features** window. After the application removal process, the **Programs and Features** window no longer shows Cisco Packet Tracer in the list. Close all open windows.

e. Future activities in this course will require the use of Packet Tracer. Reinstall Packet Tracer.

Reflection

Why does Microsoft recommend using uninstall or change a program to remove an installed application?

_____

_____

_____

Lab 6.1.1.9 - Install Third-Party Software in Windows 8

Introduction

In this lab, you will install and remove a third-party software application supplied by your instructor. You will install the Packet Tracer Windows application.

Recommended Equipment

The following equipment is required for this exercise:

- A computer with Windows 8 installed
- A flash drive or CD with the latest Packet Tracer Windows install package

Step 1:   Locating the installer.

a. Log on to the computer with the Administrator account and use Windows Explorer to navigate to the folder where the Packet Tracer installer is located. This folder could be on the local hard drive, on an external flash drive, or on a CD.

b. Locate the PacketTracer###_setup.exe (where ### is the version number) application. Click the **PacketTracer6.2_setup.exe** icon to start the installation process of the Packet Tracer application. You may need to double-click the icon to start the installation.

Note: The version shown in the file name depends on the version of Packet Tracer you are installing and may vary.

Step 2:   Running the installer and installing Packet Tracer.

a. The **Setup – Cisco Packet Tracer 6.2** window opens. Click **Next**.

Note: The window name may not contain the word "Instructor". It will depend on the version of Packet Tracer being installed.

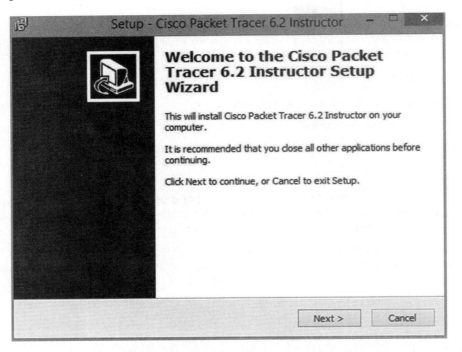

b.   The **License Agreement** window opens. Select **I accept the agreement,** and then click **Next**.

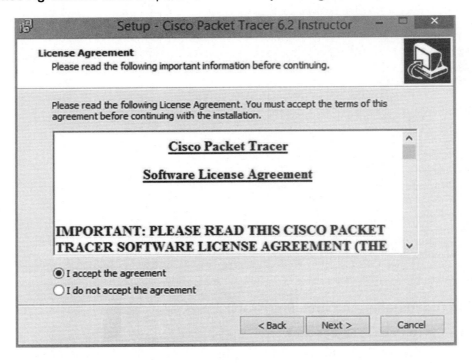

c.   The **Select Destination Location** window opens. Keep the default settings and click **Next**.

What is the default installation location for Packet Tracer?

d.   The **Select Start Menu Folder** window opens. Keep the default settings. Click **Next**.

e.   The **Select Additional Tasks** window opens. Keep the default settings. Click **Next**.

f.   The **Ready to Install** window opens. Click **Install**.

g. The **Installing** progress window opens.

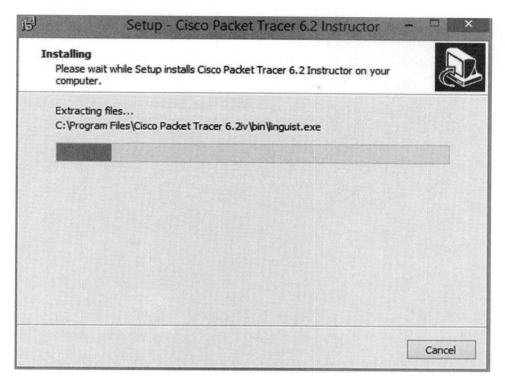

h. If an information window opens, click **OK**.

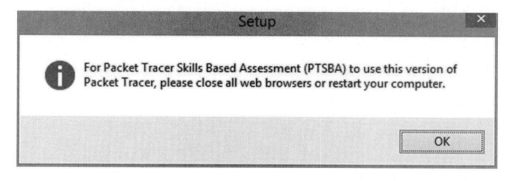

i.   The **Completing the Cisco Packet Tracer 6.2 Setup Wizard** window opens. Click **Finish**.

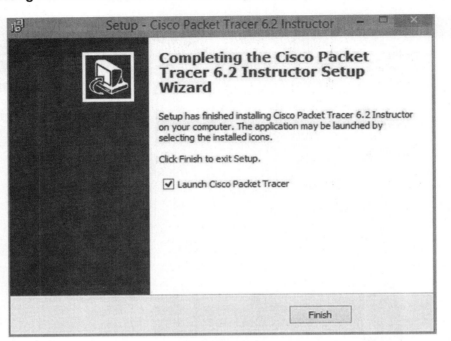

j.   If the **You are running Packet Tracer for the first time** window appears, click **OK**.

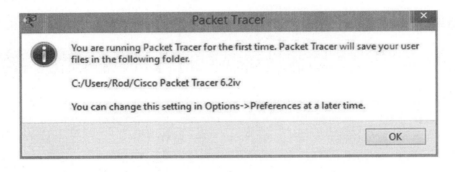

k. If the **Windows Security Alert** window opens, click **Allow access**.

l. Packet Tracer starts. Close Packet Tracer and all other open windows.

Step 3:   Uninstalling Packet Tracer.

    a.   To uninstall a program, click **Control Panel > Programs and Features**. Choose **Cisco Packet Tracer** in the list and click **Uninstall**.

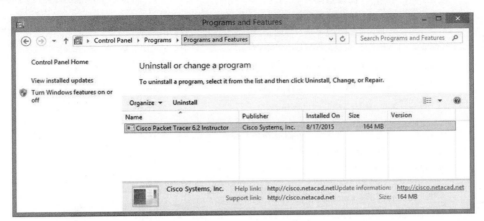

    b.   The **Cisco Packet Tracer 6.2 Uninstall** window opens. Click **Yes** to confirm the removal.

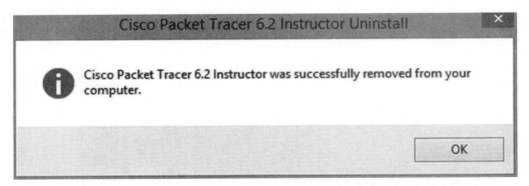

    c.   When the **successfully removed from your computer** message opens, click **OK**.

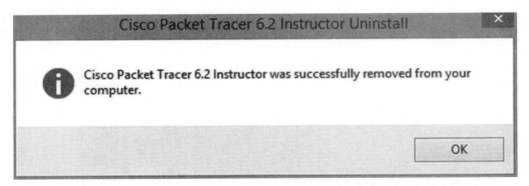

d. Verify the application was removed. After the application removal process, the **Programs and Features** window no longer shows Cisco Packet Tracer in the list. Close all open windows.

e. Future activities in this course will require the use of Packet Tracer. Reinstall Packet Tracer.

Reflection

Why does Microsoft recommend using Uninstall or change a program to remove an installed application?

_____

_____

_____

Lab 6.1.2.3 - Create User Accounts in Windows 7 and Vista

Introduction

In this lab, you will create user accounts in Windows 7 and Vista.

Recommended Equipment

The following equipment is required for this exercise:

- A computer with a new installation of Windows 7 or Vista

Step 1:   Open the User Account tool.

a.   Log on to the computer with an Administrator account.

b.   Click **Control Panel > User Accounts**.

Step 2: Create an account.

a. The User Accounts window opens. Click **Manage another account**.

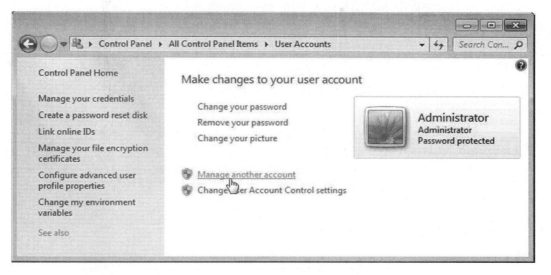

b. The **Manage Accounts** window opens. Click **Create a new account**.

c. The **Create New Account** window opens. Type the name provided by your instructor in the **Name the account and choose an account type** field and select **Standard user** as the account type.

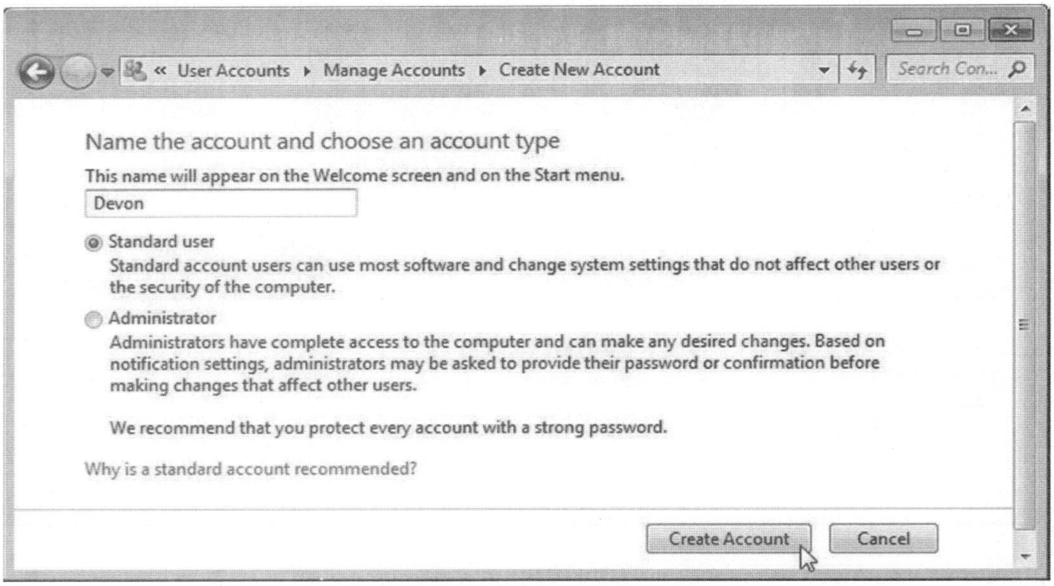

What can a user do with a limited account?

_____

What limitations does this type of an account have?

_____

d. Click **Create Account**.

Step 3:   Password protect the account.

a. Click the user account you just created.

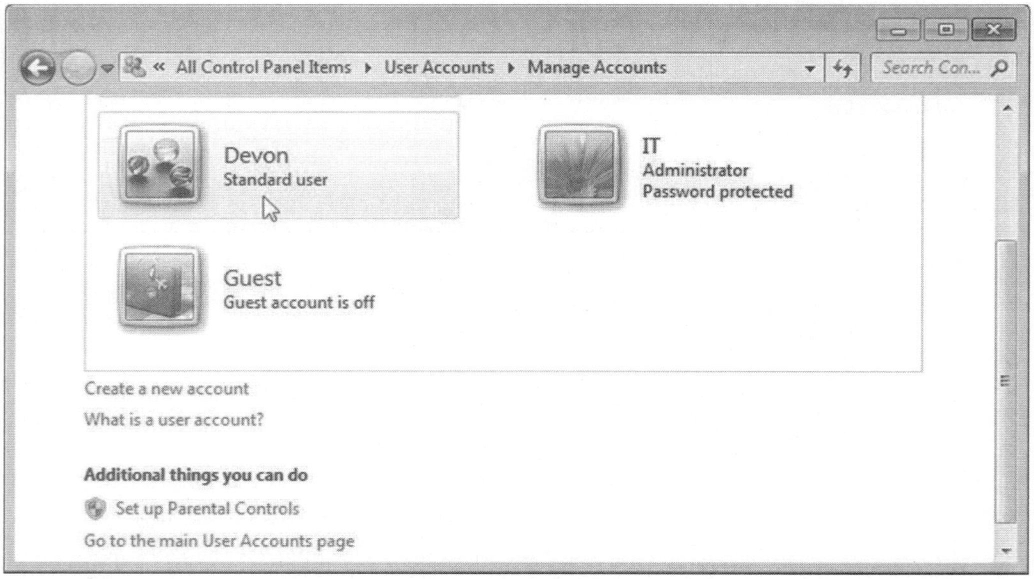

b.   The **Make changes to Devon's account?** window opens. Click **Create a password**.

What information is listed for the new account?

_____

c.   Type in the password provided by the instructor and then click **Create password**.

Step 4:   Change the account type.

a.   The **Make changes to Devon's account** window opens. Click **Change the account type**.

What information is listed for the new account?

_____

b.   The **Change Account Type** window opens. Select **Administrator** as the account type, and then click **Change Account Type**.

What can a user do with an administrator account?

_____

Step 5:   Delete the account.

a.   The **Make changes to Devon's account** window opens. Click **Delete the account**.

b.   The **Do you want to keep Devon's files?** window opens. Click **Delete Files**.

c.   The **Are you sure you want to delete Devon's account?** window opens. Click **Delete Account**.

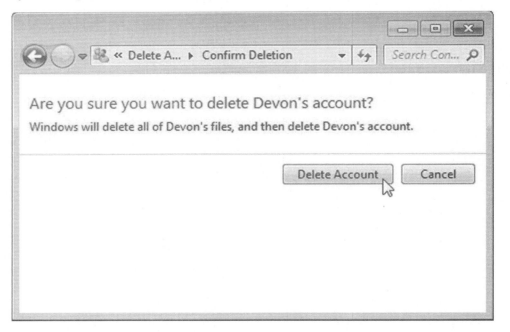

d.   Notice the account is no longer listed. Close all open windows.

Reflection

1.   Why is it important to protect all accounts with strong passwords?

_____

_____

_____

2. Why would you create a user with standard privileges?

    _____

    _____

    _____

Lab 6.1.2.3 - Create User Accounts in Windows 8

Introduction

In this lab, you will create user accounts in Windows 8.

Recommended Equipment

The following equipment is required for this exercise:

- A computer with a new installation of Windows 8

Part 1:   Windows 8.1

Step 1:   Open the User Account tool.

a.   Log on to the computer with an Administrator account.

b.   Click **Control Panel > User Accounts**.

Step 2:   Create an account.

a.   The **User Accounts** window opens. Click **Manage another account**.

b.   The **Manage Accounts** window opens. Click **Add a new user in PC settings**.

c.   The **Manage other accounts** window opens. Click **Add an account**.

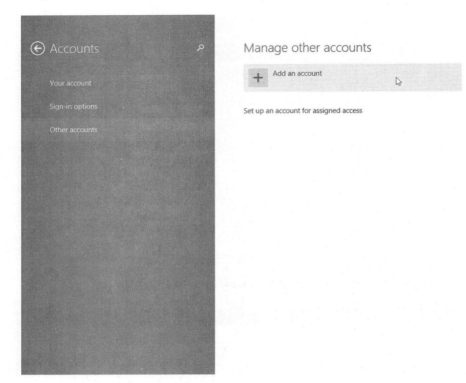

d.   The **How will this person sign in?** window opens. Click **Sign in without a Microsoft account (not recommended)**.

e. The **Add a user** window opens. Click **Local account**.

f. The second **Add a user** window opens. Type the name provided by your instructor in the **User name** field.

g. Type in the password provided by the instructor in the **Password** field.

h. Reenter the password in the **Reenter password** field.

i. Type a hint to help you remember the password in the **Password hint** field.

j. Click **Next**.

k. The final **Add a user** window opens. Click **Finish**.

Step 3: Change the account type.

a. The **Manage other accounts** window opens. Click on the user you just created, and then click **Edit**.

What information is listed for the new account?

_____

b. The **Edit Account** window opens. Select **Administrator** as the account type. Click **OK**.

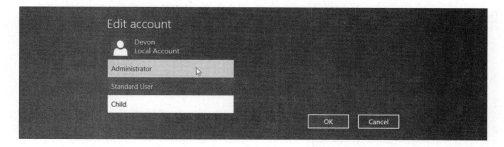

Step 4:   Delete the account.

a. The **Manage other accounts** window opens. Click **Remove**.

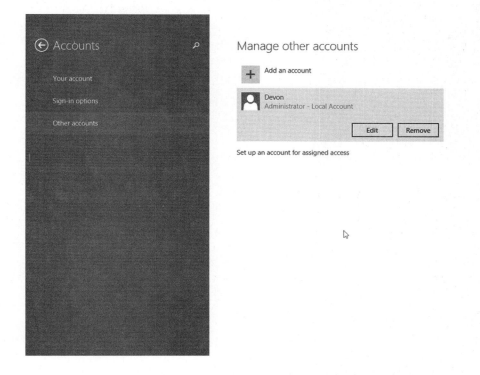

b. The **Delete account and data?** window opens. Click **Delete account and data**.

c.   Notice the account is no longer listed. Close all open windows.

Part 2:   Windows 8.0

Step 1:   Open the User Account tool.

a.   Log on to the computer with an Administrator account.

b.   Click **Control Panel > User Accounts**.

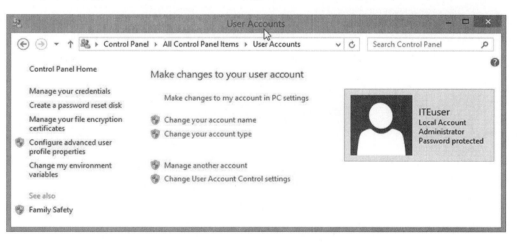

Step 2:   Create an account.

a.   The **User Accounts** window opens. Click **Manage another account**.

b.   The **Manage Accounts** window opens. Click **Add a new user in PC settings**.

c.   The **Manage other accounts** window opens. Click **Add a user**.

d. The **Add a user** window opens. Click **Sign in without a Microsoft account**.

e. The next **Add a user** window opens. Click **Local account**.

f.   The third **Add a user** window opens. Type the name provided by your instructor in the **User name** field.

g.   Type in the password provided by the instructor in the **Password** field.

h.   Reenter the password in the **Reenter password** field.

i.   Type a hint to help you remember the password in the **Password hint** field.

j.   Click **Next**.

k.   The final **Add a user** window opens. Click **Finish**.

l.   The **Your account** window opens. Close all open windows.

Step 3:   Change the account type.

a.   Click **Control Panel > User accounts > Manage another account**.

b.   The **Manage Accounts** window opens. Click the new account.

c.   The **Change an Account** window opens. Click **Change the account type**.

d.   Select **Administrator** as the account type. Click **Change Account Type**.

What can a user do with an administrator account?

_____

Step 4:   Delete the account.

a.   The **Change an Account** window opens. Click **Delete the Account**.

b. The **Delete Account** window opens. Click **Delete Files**.

c. The **Confirm Deletion** window opens. Click **Delete Account**.

d.   Notice the account is no longer listed. Close all opened windows.

Reflection

1.   Why is it important to protect all accounts with strong passwords?

_____

_____

2.   Why would you create a user with standard privileges?

_____

_____

_____

Lab 6.1.2.5 - Configure Browser Settings in Windows 7 and Vista

Introduction

In this lab, you will configure browser settings in Microsoft Internet Explorer.

Recommended Equipment

- A computer with Windows 7 and Vista installed
- An Internet connection

Step 1:   Setting Intenet Explorer as the default browser.

a.   Choose **Start > Search Programs and files** in Windows 7 or choose **Start > Start Search** in Windows Vista. Type **www.cisco.com**, and click the link **http://www.cisco.com**.

Which browser was used to open the web page?

_____

If your answer is not Internet Explorer, use the following steps to set Internet Explorer as your default browser. Otherwise, go to step b.

1) Choose **Start > All Programs > Internet Explorer**.

2) Choose **Tools > Internet options**, and then click the **Programs** tab.

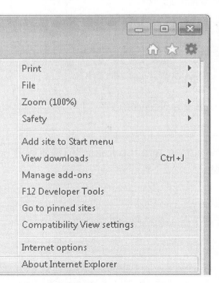

3) Select **Tell me if Internet Explorer is not the default web browser** and then click **OK**. Close the browser.

4) Choose **Start > All Programs > Internet Explorer**.

5) Click **Yes** to make Internet Explorer the default browser.

b. Click **Tools** (⚙) at the top-right corner of the window **> About Internet Explorer**.

If desired, right-click the title bar and select **Menu bar** to add the menu to Internet Explorer. Click **Help > About Internet Explorer**.

Which version of Internet Explorer is installed on your computer?

_____

Step 2:   Clear temporary Internet files.

a.   Choose **Tools > Internet options**. Click the **Settings** in the Browsing history section in the **General** tab.

b. In the **Website Data Settings** window, click **View files** in the Temporary Internet Files tab to list the temporary Internet files.

   Note: In Windows Vista, the window is called **Temporary Internet Files and History Settings**.

How many temporary Internet files were listed?

_____

c. Close the Temporary Internet Files window.

   In the **Temporary Internet Files** tab or section, which setting is configured for **Check for newer versions of stored pages**?

_____

   In the **History** tab or section, how many days is **History** set to store the list of visited websites?

_____

d. Close the **Website Data Settings** or **Temporary Internet Files and History Settings** window.

e.   In the **Internet Options** window, click **Delete…** in the **General** tab to remove Internet browsing history.

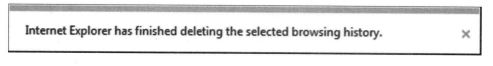

Which options are available in the **Delete Browsing History** for deleting browsing history?

_____

_____

f.   Uncheck all selected options except for **Temporary Internet files**. Click **Delete** to remove the temporary files. When completed, Internet Explorer displays the following message:

> Internet Explorer has finished deleting the selected browsing history.   ✕

g.   Close all opened windows except for Internet Explorer.

Step 3:   Clear Internet browsing history.

a.   Open Internet Explorer, if closed, and visit a few web sites using the same tab.

b. Click the **down** arrow at the right end of the **URL Address** field to view previously visited sites.

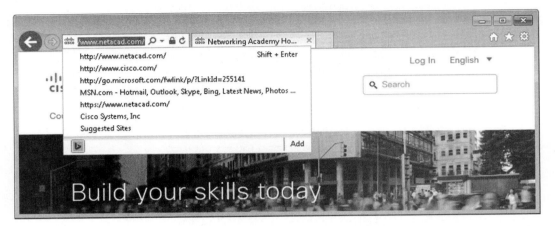

How many sites are listed in the drop-down box? _____

c. To clear the browser history, choose **Tools > Internet options > Delete**. Uncheck all selected options except for **History**. Click **Delete**.

d. Close all open windows except for Internet Explorer.

e. When completed, click the **down** arrow at the right end of the **address** field to view previously visited sites.

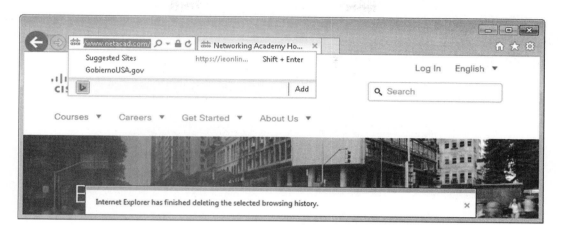

How many sites are now found in the drop-down box for browsing history? _____

Step 4: Configure the Security settings.

a. Open Internet Explorer as necessary.

b. Choose **Tools > Internet Options**, and then click the **Security** tab.

c.   Click each of the four zones and describe their security settings.

Internet: _____

Local intranet: _____

Trusted sites: _____

Restricted sites: _____

d.   Click **Custom level…**. In this window, you can select the options in the list that you wish to change for a zone. Click **Cancel** to close this window.

Step 5:   Configure Privacy settings.

a.   Open Internet Explorer if necessary. Click **Tools > Internet options** and select the **Privacy** tab. Click **Advanced** to open the **Advanced Privacy Settings** window.

b.   In the **Advanced Privacy Settings** window, click **Override automatic cookie handling** and change the setting for Third-party Cookies to **Prompt**.

c.   Click **OK** and close all open windows.

Reflection

Why would you want to clear temporary Internet files or Internet browsing history?

_____

_____

_____

Lab 6.1.5.2 - Configure Browser Settings in Windows 8

Introduction

In this lab, you will configure browser settings in Microsoft Internet Explorer.

Recommended Equipment

- A computer with Windows 8
- An Internet connection

Step 1: Set Internet Explorer as the default browser.

a. On the **Start** screen, type **www.cisco.com**, and click the link http://www.cisco.com.

Note: If **Quick Tasks** opens, click the **wrench icon** ( ) and click **View on the desktop**.

Which browser was used to open the web page?

_____

If your answer is not Internet Explorer, use the following steps to set Internet Explorer as your default browser. Otherwise, go to step b.

1) Navigate to the **Start** screen and type **Internet Explorer**. Select **Internet Explorer**.

2) Click **Set default browser** in the Internet Explorer window. Click **Tools** (⚙) icon **> Internet options** if the option is not available.

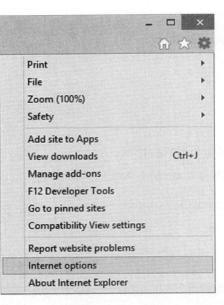

If desired, right-click the title bar and select **Menu bar** to add the menu to Internet Explorer. Click **Help** menu **> About Internet Explorer**.

3) In the **Internet Options** window, select the **Programs** tab, and click **Make Internet Explorer the default browser**.

4) In the **Set Default Programs** window, click **Internet Explorer** on the left panel. Click **Set this program as default**. Click **OK** in the **Set Default Programs** window to close it.

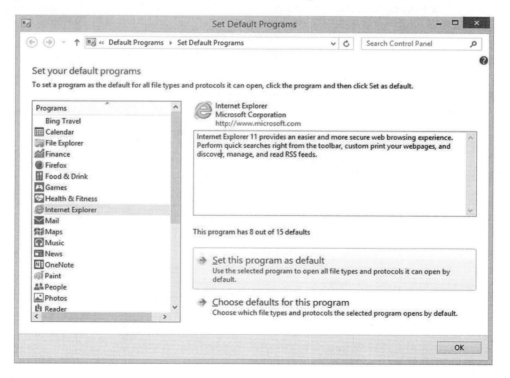

5) Click **OK** in the **Internet Options** window to continue.

b. Click **Tools** (⚙) icon > **About Internet Explorer** or click **Help** menu > **About Internet Explorer**.

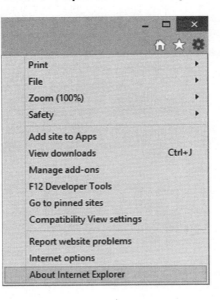

Which version of Internet Explorer is installed on your computer?

_____

c. Click **Close** to continue.

Step 2:   Clear temporary Internet files.

a. Select **Tools > Internet options**. Click **Settings** in the Browsing history section in the **General** tab.

b. In the **Temporary Internet Files** tab of the **Website Data Settings** window, click **View files** to list the temporary Internet files.

How many temporary Internet files were listed?

_____

c. Close the **INetCache** or **Temporary Internet Files** window.

In the **Temporary Internet Files** tab of the **Website Data Settings** window, which setting is configured for **Check for newer versions of stored pages**?

_____

In the **History** tab, how many days is **History** set to store list of visited websites?

_____

d. Click **OK** to close the **Website Data Settings**.

e. In the **General** tab of the **Internet Options** window, click **Delete…**.

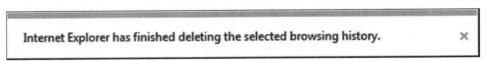

Which options are available in the **Delete Browsing History** for deleting browsing history?

_____

_____

f. Uncheck all selected options except for **Temporary Internet files**. Click **Delete** to remove the temporary files. When completed, Internet Explorer displays the following message:

Internet Explorer has finished deleting the selected browsing history.   ×

g. Close all open windows except for Internet Explorer.

Step 3: Clear Internet browsing history.

a. Open Internet Explorer if closed and visit a few web sites using the same tab.

b.   Click the **down** arrow, at the right end of the **URL Address** field, to view previously visited sites.

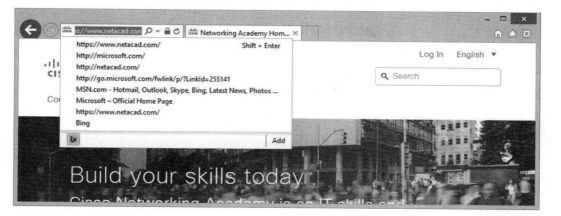

How many sites are listed in the drop-down box? _____

c.   To clear the browser history, select **Tools > Internet options > Delete**. Uncheck all selected options except for **History**. Click **Delete**.

d.   Close all open windows except for Internet Explorer.

e. When completed, click the **down** arrow at the right end of the **address** field to view previously visited sites.

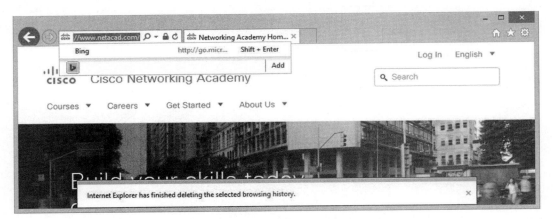

How many sites are now found in the drop-down box for browsing history? _____

Step 4: Configure the Security settings.

a. Open Internet Explorer as necessary.

b. Select **Tools > Internet options**, and then click the **Security** tab.

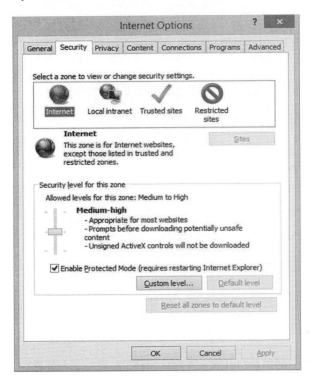

c.   Click each of the four zones and describe their security settings.

   Internet: _____

   Local intranet: _____

   Trusted sites: _____

   Restricted sites: _____

d.   Click the **Custom level... button**. In this window, you can select the options in the list that you wish to
   change for a zone. Click **Cancel** to close this window.

Step 5:   Configure Privacy settings.

a.   Open Internet Explorer if necessary. Click **Tools >Internet options > Privacy** tab. Click **Advanced.**

b.   In the **Advanced Privacy Settings** window, click **Override automatic cookie handling** and change the setting for Third-party Cookies to **Prompt**.

c.   Click **OK** and close all open windows.

Reflection

Why would you want to clear temporary Internet files or Internet browsing history?

_____

_____

_____

Lab 6.1.2.12 - Manage Virtual Memory in Windows 7 and Vista

Introduction

In this lab, you will customize virtual memory settings.

Recommended Equipment

- A computer with Windows 7 or Vista installed
- The hard drive must have two or more partitions

Note: At least 2 GB of free space is recommended on the second partition.

Step 1:   Open System Properties.

a.   Click **Start** > right-click **Computer** > **Properties** > **Advanced system settings**.

b.   The **System Properties** window opens. Select the **Advanced** tab and click **Settings** in the Performance area.

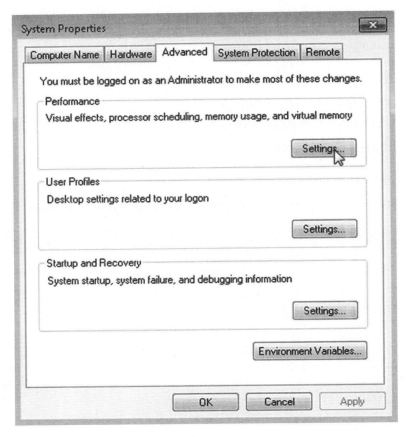

c.   The **Performance Options** window opens. Click the **Advanced** tab.

What is the current size of the virtual memory (paging file)?

_____

Step 2:   Make virtual memory changes.

a.   Click **Change** in the Virtual memory area to open the **Virtual Memory** window.

b.   Remove the check mark from **Automatically manage paging file size for all drives**.

What Drive [Volume Label] contains the paging file?

_____

c.   Choose the **I:** drive. Select the **Custom size:** radio button.

Virtual Memory

☐ Automatically manage paging file size for all drives

Paging file size for each drive

Drive [Volume Label]	Paging File Size (MB)
C: [Local Disk]	System managed
I: [ITE]	None

Selected drive: I: [ITE]
Space available: 4565 MB

◉ Custom size:
Initial size (MB):   [   ]

Maximum size (MB): [   ]

◯ System managed size
◯ No paging file   [Set]

Total paging file size for all drives

Minimum allowed: 16 MB
Recommended: 3070 MB
Currently allocated: 2047 MB

[OK]   [Cancel]

Note: Your drive letter and volume may be different than the example. Replace I: with the drive letter for your second partition on your PC.

What is the recommended paging file size for all drives?

_____

d. Enter a number smaller than the recommended file size in the **Initial size (MB):** field. Enter a number that is larger than the Initial size but smaller than the recommended file size in the **Maximum size (MB):** field. Click **Set**.

e. Select the **C:** drive. Select the **No paging file** radio button, and click **Set**.

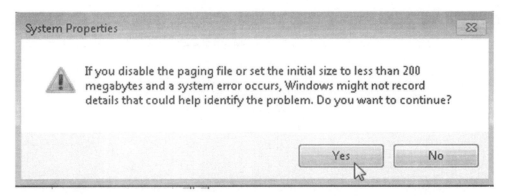

f. The System Properties warning message displays. Click **Yes**.

g. Click **OK** on the **Virtual Memory** window to accept the new virtual memory settings.

h. Click **OK** on the **Performance Options** window to close it.

i. Click **OK** on the **System Properties** window to close it.

Step 3:   Navigate back to the Virtual Memory window to verify changes.

a.   The **System Properties** window opens. Select the **Advanced** tab and click **Settings** in the Performance area.

b.   The **Performance Options** window opens. Select the **Advanced** tab, and click **Change**.

c.   The **Virtual Memory** window opens displaying the new paging file information. Verify that your changes have been made.

What Drive [Volume Label] contains the paging file?

_____

Step 4: Reset the virtual memory back to the original settings.

a. Select drive **C: [Local Disk] > System managed size > Set**.

b. Select **I: > No paging file > Set**.

c.   Check **Automatically manage paging file size for all drives**, and click **OK**.

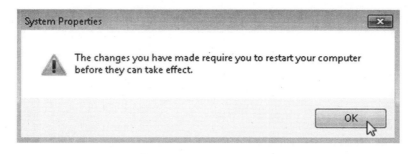

d.   The **System Properties** window opens, informing you that a restart is required before changes will take effect. Click **OK**.

e.   Click **OK** to close the **Performance Options** window. Click **OK** to close the **System Properties** window.

f.   The warning message displays: **You must restart your computer to apply these changes**.
     Click **Restart Now**.

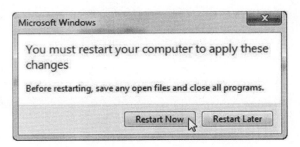

Reflection

Why would you ever change the default virtual memory page file settings in Windows?

_____

_____

_____

_____

_____

_____

Lab 6.1.2.12 - Manage Virtual Memory in Windows 8

Introduction

In this lab, you will customize virtual memory settings.

Recommended Equipment

- A computer with Windows 8 installed
- The hard drive must have two or more partitions

  Note: At least 2 GB of free space is recommended on the second partition.

Step 1:   Open System Properties.

a.   Right-click **Start** and select **System**.

Note: In Windows 8.0, bring up the charms menu, click **Search**, type **computer**, and press **Enter**. Right-click on **Computer** in the left pane of the **Computer** window and select **Properties**.

b.   In the **System** window, click **Advanced system settings**.

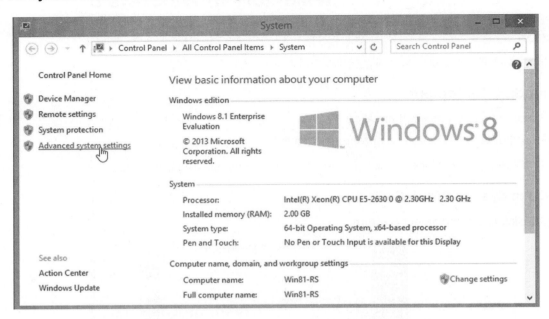

c.   The **System Properties** window opens. Select the **Advanced** tab and click **Settings** in the Performance area.

d.   The **Performance Options** window opens. Click the **Advanced** tab.

What is the current size of the virtual memory (paging file)?

Step 2:   Make virtual memory changes.

    a.   Click **Change** in the Virtual memory area to open the **Virtual Memory** window.

b.   Remove the check mark from **Automatically manage paging file size for all drives**.

What Drive [Volume Label] contains the paging file?

_____

c.   Choose the **I:** drive. Select the **Custom size:** radio button.

Note: Your drive letter and volume may be different than the example. Replace **I:** with the drive letter for your second partition on your PC.

What is the recommended paging file size for all drives?

_____

d. Enter a number smaller than the recommended file size in the **Initial size (MB):** field. Enter a number that
is larger than the Initial size but smaller than the recommended file size in the **Maximum size (MB):** field.
Click **Set**.

e.   Select the **C:** drive. Select the **No paging file** radio button, and click **Set**.

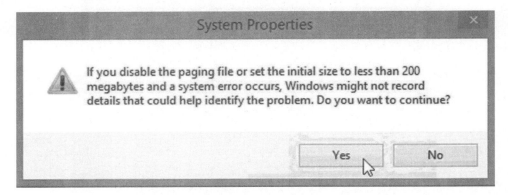

f.   The System Properties warning message displays. Click **Yes**.

g.   Click **OK** on the **Virtual Memory** window to accept the new virtual memory settings.

h.   Click **OK** on the **Performance Options** window to close it.

i.   Click **OK** on the **System Properties** window to close it.

Step 3:   Navigate back to the Virtual Memory window to verify changes.

a.   The **System Properties** window opens. Select the **Advanced** tab and click **Settings** in the Performance area.

b.   The **Performance Options** window opens. Select the **Advanced** tab and click **Change**.

c.   The **Virtual Memory** window opens, displaying the new paging file information. Verify that your changes have been made.

What Drive [Volume Label] contains the paging file?

_____

Step 4:   Reset the virtual memory back to the original settings.

a.   Select drive **C: [Local Disk] > System managed size > Set**.

b.   Select **I: > No paging file > Set**.

c.   Check **Automatically manage paging file size for all drives**, and then click **OK**.

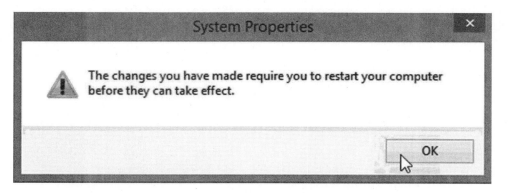

d.   The **System Properties** window opens, informing you that a restart is required before changes will take effect. Click **OK**.

e.   Click **OK** to close the **Performance Options** window. Click **OK** to close the System Properties window.

f.   The warning message displays: You must restart your computer to apply these changes. Click **Restart Now**.

Reflection

Why would you ever change the default virtual memory page file settings in Windows?

_____

_____

_____

_____

_____

_____

Lab 6.1.2.14 - Device Manager in Windows 7 and Vista

Introduction

In this lab, you will open Device Manager to display devices listed on your computer. You will also display the monitor settings.

Recommended Equipment

The following equipment is required for this exercise:

- A computer running Windows 7 or Vista

Step 1: Open Device Manager.

a. Log on to the computer as an administrator.

b. Click **Control Panel > System**.

c.   In the **System** window, click **Device Manager**.

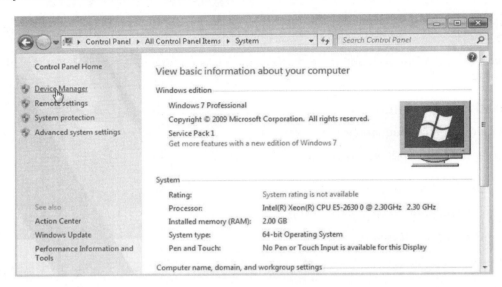

d.   The **Device Manager** window opens.

What information is listed in the Device Manager window? Why would you use it?

_____

_____

Step 2:   Display the monitor settings on your computer.

As an administrator, there are times when you will need to resolve monitor issues on a computer. Device Manager makes it easy to locate and install new drivers for your devices. You will use Device Manager to review the device driver information for your computer's monitor, and to review driver options available to you.

Note: Check with your instructor before making any device changes on the computer.

a.   Click the arrow to the left of **Monitors**.

b.   Right-click the **Monitor** device, **Generic Non-PnP Monitor** in the example, and select **Properties** from the dropdown menu.

c.   The **Generic Non-PnP Monitor Properties** window opens. Select the **Driver** tab. This tab displays the software driver information that is currently installed for this monitor.

What additional information does Driver Details provide?

_____

_____

d. Click **Update Driver**.

What two options do you have for updating the driver?

_____

_____

e. From the **Update Driver Software** window, click **Cancel** to return to the **Monitor Properties** window. What does the Roll Back Driver button do? Why is it grayed out in the example?

_____

_____

f. Close all open windows.

Lab 6.1.2.14 - Device Manager in Windows 8

Introduction

In this lab, you will open Device Manager to display devices listed on your computer. You will also display the monitor settings.

Recommended Equipment

The following equipment is required for this exercise:

- A computer running Windows 8

Step 1:   Open Device Manager.

a.   Log on to the computer as an administrator.

b.   Click **Control Panel > System**.

c. In the **System** window, click **Advanced system settings**.

d. The **Device Manager** window opens.

What information is listed in the Device Manager window? Why would you use it?

_____

_____

Step 2:   Display the monitor settings on your computer.

As an administrator, there are times when you will need to resolve monitor issues on a computer. Device Manager makes it easy to locate and install new drivers for your devices. You will use Device Manager to review the device driver information for your computer's monitor, and to review driver options available to you.

Note: Check with your instructor before making any device changes on the computer.

a.   Click the arrow to the left of **Monitors**.

b. Right-click the device, **Generic Non-PnP Monitor** in the example, and select **Properties** from the dropdown menu.

c. The **Generic Non-PnP Monitor Properties** window opens. Select the **Driver** tab. This window displays the software driver information that is currently installed for this monitor.

What additional information does Driver Details provide?

_____

_____

d.   Click **Update Driver**.

What two options do you have for updating the driver?

_____

_____

e.   From the **Update Driver Software** window, click **Cancel** to return to the **Monitor Properties** window.

What does the Roll Back Driver button do? Why is it grayed out in the example?

_____

_____

Close all open windows.

Lab 6.1.2.16 - Region and Language Options in Windows 7 and Vista

Introduction

In this lab, you will examine regional and language settings in Windows 7 and Windows Vista.

Recommended Equipment

- A computer running Windows 7 or Vista

Step 1: Open with the Region and Language settings on your PC.

a. Log on to the computer.

b. Click **Control Panel > Region and Language**.

c.   The **Region and Language** window opens.

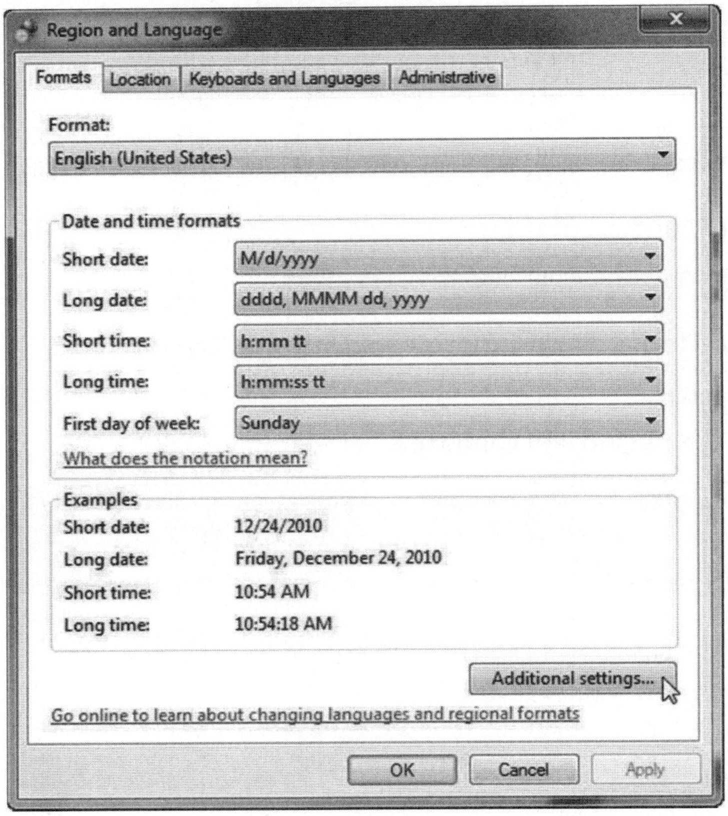

What regional format is being used?

_____

_____

d.   Click **Additional settings**. The **Customize Format** window opens.

What are the tabs that can be customized?

_____

e.   Click **Cancel**.

f.   Select **Belarusian (Belarus)** in the **Format** drop-down menu. Notice the changes to the output in the Examples area of how data is displayed using this format.

   Note: In Windows Vista, select **Belarusian (Belarus)** in the **Current Format** drop-down menu.

g. Choose the original setting from the **Format** drop-down box. Click the **Keyboards and Languages** tab, and click the **Change keyboards… button.**

h.   The **Text Services and Input Languages** window opens. Click **Add**.

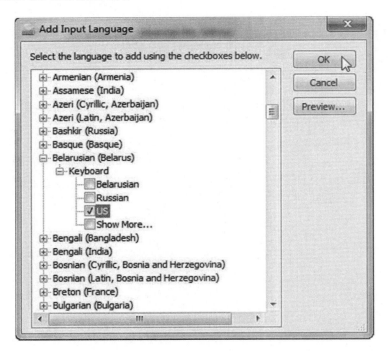

i.   The **Add Input Language** window opens. Scroll down the list of options and click **Belarusian (Belarus)
     > Keyboard**. Check **US** and click **OK**.

j.   In the **Text Services and Input Languages** window, click **Apply** to accept the changes.

What is the default input language?

_____

k.   Close all open windows.

Step 2: Set the Language bar to appear on the Taskbar.

a.   Right-click the **Taskbar**.

b.   Select **Toolbars > Language bar** to ensure that the Language bar is shown in the Taskbar.

c. Right-click the **Language bar** in the Taskbar. Click **Settings**.

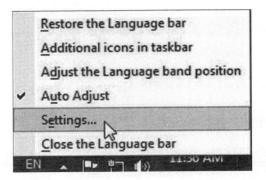

d. The **Text Service and Input Languages** window opens. Select the keyboard that was added. Bengali (Bangladesh), and then click **Remove > OK.**

e. Close all open windows.

Lab 6.1.2.16 - Region and Language Options in Windows 8

Introduction

In this lab, you will examine regional and language settings in Windows 8.

Recommended Equipment

- A computer running Windows 8

Step 1:   Open the Language and Region tools.

a.   Log on to the computer.

b.   Click **Control Panel > Language**.

c.   The **Language** window opens. Click **Change date, time, or number formats**.

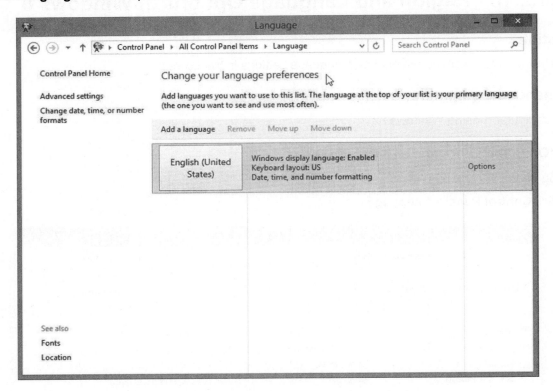

What regional format is being used?

d. The **Region** window opens. Select **Belarusian (Belarus)** from the **Format** drop-down box. Notice how the formats have changed.

What are the tabs that can be customized?

_____

e. Click **Cancel**.

Step 2: Add a keyboard.

a. Click **Add a language**.

b. The **Add a language** window opens. **Scroll** through the list of languages. Notice the changes to the output in the boxes of how data is displayed using different formats.

c. Click **Belarusian > Add**.

Step 3:   **Work with the Taskbar Language button.**

   a.   A language button is now displayed on the taskbar. Click the **language** button.

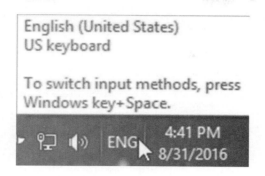

   b.   Click **Belarusian**.

   c.   Click the **Language** button again, and change the keyboard back to the default.

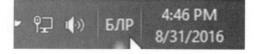

Step 4:   Remove the keyboard.

a. In the **Language** window, select the new keyboard and click **Remove**.

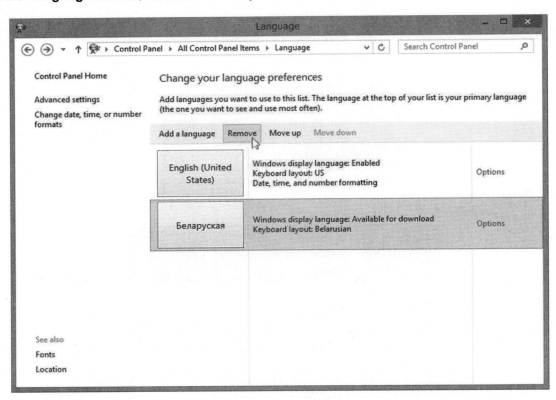

b. Close all open windows.

Reflection

Why would someone wish to change the input language of the operating system?

_____

_____

_____

Lab 6.1.3.6 - Monitor and Manage System Resources in Windows 7 and Vista

Introduction

In this lab, you will use administrative tools to monitor and manage system resources.

Recommended Equipment

The following equipment is required for this exercise:

- A computer running Windows 7 or Vista with Internet access

Step 1:   Stopping and starting a service.

You will explore what happens when a service is stopped then started.

a. Log on to Windows as an administrator.

Note: Some antivirus or antispyware programs must be uninstalled on the computer for Windows Defender to work.

b. To see if Windows Defender is turned off, click **Start.** In the **Search programs and files** field, type **Defender** and select **Windows Defender**.

If the **This program is turned off** message is displayed, click the **click here to turn it on** link.

Note: Windows Defender should start, if not, uninstall any antivirus or antispyware programs and re-open Windows Defender.

c. Click **Control Panel > Administrative Tools > Computer Management.**

d. The Computer Management window opens. Click the **arrow** to the left of **Services and Applications**, and select **Services**.

e. Resize and position the **Windows Defender** and **Computer Manageme**nt windows so they can be seen at the same time.

Can Windows Defender check for updates? _____

f. Scroll the **Computer Management** window so you see the **Windows Defender** service.

What is the status of the service? _____

g. Right-click the **Windows Defender** service, and select **Stop**.

Note: The reason this service will be stopped is so that you can easily see the results. When stopping a service, to free up system resources the service uses, it is important to understand how the overall system operation will be affected.

h. The **Service Control** window opens and closes. Select the Windows Defender window to make it active.

What is the status of the Windows Defender service?

i. Start the Windows Defender service by clicking **Start now**.

Note: Windows Vista requires that you start Windows Defender from the **Computer Management** window. Right-click the **Windows Defender** service, and click **Start**.

Can Windows Defender check for updates? _____

j. Close the **Windows Defender** window but keep the **Computer Management** window open.

k. Expand **Event Viewer > Windows Logs**, then select **System**.

l. Select the second event in the list.

Look below the General tab. Explain what has happened to the Windows Defender service.

_____

m. Click the up arrow button on the keyboard or select the event above the one you just viewed.

n. Close all open windows.

Step 2:   Starting and stopping the Routing and Remote Access service.

You will explore what happens when a service is stopped then started.

a. Navigate to the **Network and Sharing Center** window by clicking **Network > Network and Sharing Center**.

Note: If Network is not shown in the Start menu, complete the following: Right-click **Start > Properties > Start Menu** tab. Click **Customize**, and then scroll down the list to **Network**. Place a check mark next to Network, and then click **OK > OK**.

b.   Click **Change adapter settings** in the left pane. Reduce the size of the **Network Connections** window and leave it open.

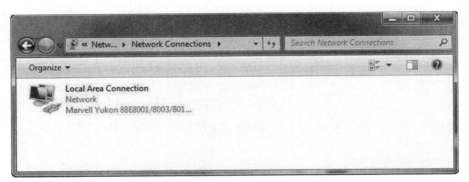

Note: For Windows Vista, click **Manage network connections**.

c.   Open the **Control Panel**.

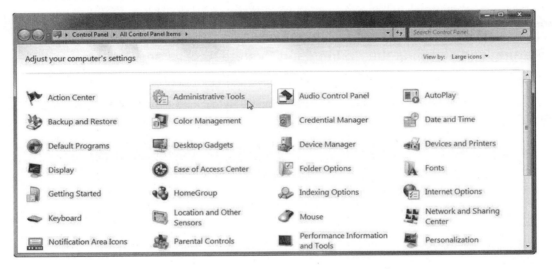

d.   Click the **Administrative Tools** icon.

e. The **Administrative Tools** window opens. Double-click the **Performance Monitor** icon. The **Performance Monitor** window opens. Make sure **Performance Monitor** in the left pane is highlighted. Click the **Freeze Display** icon to stop the recording.

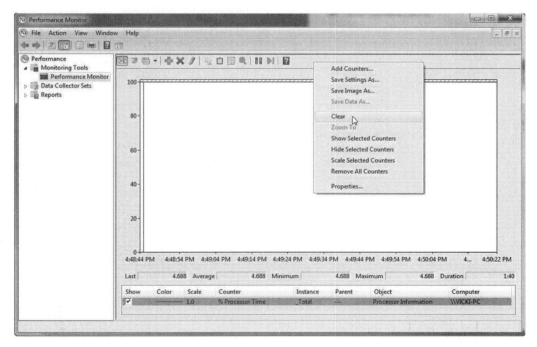

Note: In Windows Vista, the tool is called **Reliability and Performance Monitor**.

f. Right-click the **Performance Monitor** menu bar and select **Clear** to clear the graph. Leave this window open.

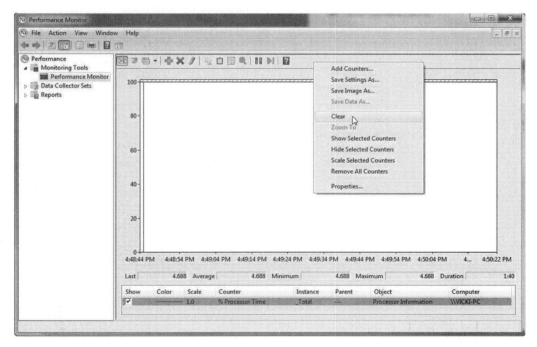

g. Navigate to the **Administrative Tools** window by clicking **Control Panel > Administrative Tools**.

h. Double-click the **Services** icon.

i. Expand the width of the **Services** window so you have a clear view of the content. Scroll down in the right pane until you see the service Routing and Remote Access. Double-click **Routing and Remote Access**.

j.   The **Routing and Remote Access Properties (Local Computer)** window opens. In the **Startup type** dropdown field, select **Manual** and then click **Apply.**

Note: The Start button is now active; do not click the button yet. Leave this window open.

k. Position the **Network Connections**, **Routing and Remote Access Properties (Local Computer)**, and **Performance Monitor** windows so you can clearly see them at the same time.

l.   Click the **Performance Monitor** window to make it active. Click the **Unfreeze Display** icon to start the recording.

m.   Click the **Routing and Remote Access Properties (Local Computer)** window to make it active. To start the service, click **Start**. A window with a progress bar opens.

n. The **Routing and Remote Access Properties (Local Computer)** window now shows the Stop and
    Pause button active. Leave this window open.

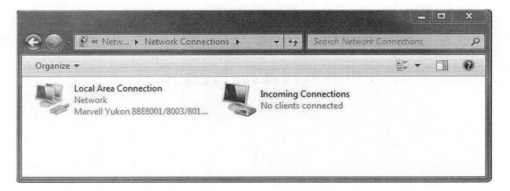

o. Click the **Network Connections** window to make it active.

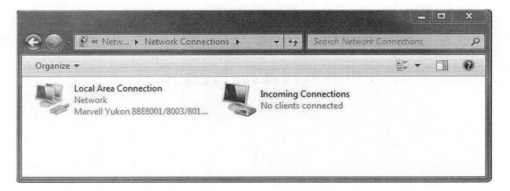

p. Press the function key **F5** to refresh the content.

    What changes appear in the right pane after starting the **Routing and Remote Access** service?

    _____

q. Click the **Routing and Remote Access Properties (Local Computer)** window to make it active and click **Stop**.

r. Click the **Network Connections** window to make it active.

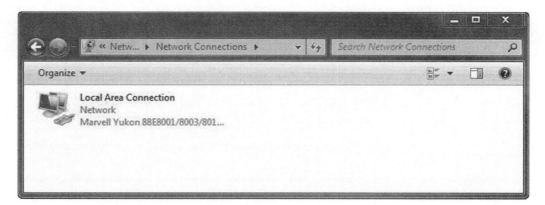

What changes appear in the right pane after stopping the Routing and Remote Access service?

_____

s. Click the **Performance Monitor** window to make it active and click the **Freeze Display** icon to stop the recording.

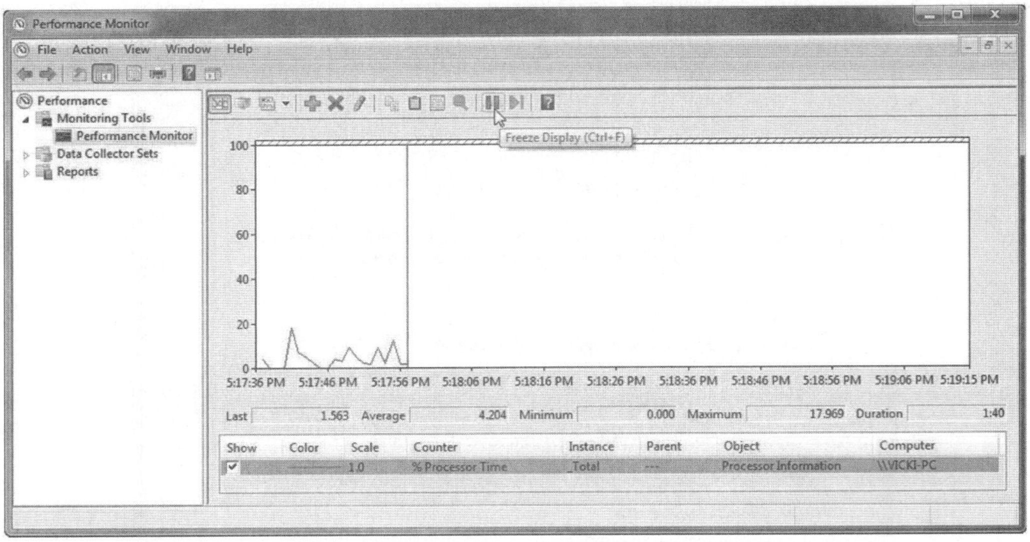

Which counter is being recorded the most in the graph (hint: look at the graph color and counter color)?

_____

t. Click the **Change graph type** drop-down menu, and select **Report**.

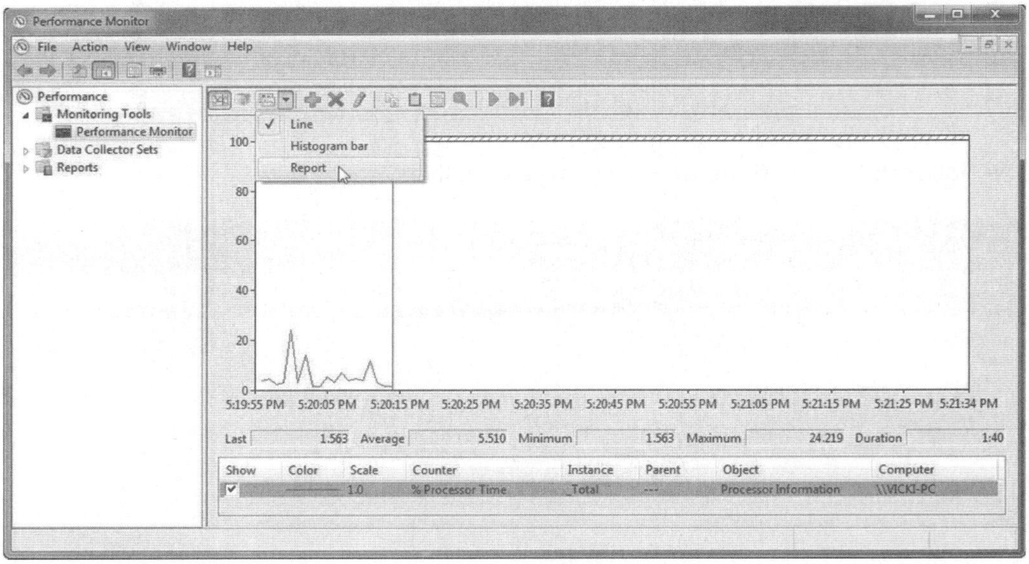

u. The display changes to report view.

What values are displayed by the counter?

_____

v. Click the **Routing and Remote Access Properties (Local Computer)** window to make it active. In the Startup type field, select **Disabled** and click **OK**.

w. Click the **Services** window to make it active.

What is the Status and Startup Type for Routing and Remote Access?

x. Click the **Performance Monitor** window to make it active. Click the **Unfreeze Display** icon to start the recording.

y. Close all open windows.

Step 3:   Work in the Computer Manager utility.

a. Click **Control Panel > Administrative Tools**.

b. Double-click the **Computer Management** icon.

c. The **Computer Management** window opens. Expand the three categories by clicking on the **arrow** next to: **System Tools**, **Storage**, and **Services and Applications**.

d. Click the arrow next to **Event Viewer** and then click the arrow next to **Windows Logs**. Select **System** and double-click the first event in the window.

e. The **Event Properties** window opens for the first event. Click the **down arrow** key to locate an event for **Routing and Remote Access**. You should find four events that describe the order for starting and stopping the **Routing and Remote Access** service.

What are the descriptions for each of the four events?

_____

_____

_____

_____

f.   Close all open windows.

Step 4:   Configuring Administrative tools.

For the rest of this lab, you will configure advanced Administrative Tool features and monitor how this affects the computer.

a.   Click **Control Panel > Administrative Tools > Performance Monitor**. The Performance Monitor window opens.

   Note: In Windows Vista, the utility is called **Reliability and Performance Monitor**.

b. Expand **Data Collector Sets.** Right-click **User Defined**, and select **New** > **Data Collector Set**.

c. The **Create new Data Collector Set** window opens. In the Name field, type **Memory Logs**. Select the **Create manually (Advanced)** radio button, and click **Next**.

d.   The **What type of data do you want to include?** screen opens. Check the **Performance counter** box and then click **Next**.

e.   The **Which performance counters would you like to log?** screen opens. Click **Add**.

f. From the list of available counters, locate and expand **Memory**. Select **Available MBytes** and click **Add>>**.

g. You should see the **Available MBytes** counter added in the right pane. Click **OK**.

h.   Set the Sample interval field to **4** seconds. Click **Next**.

i.   In the **Where would you like the data to be saved?** screen, click **Browse**.

j. The **Browse For Folder** window opens. Select **drive (C:) > PerfLogs > OK**.

k. The **Where would you like the data to be saved?** window opens with the directory information that you selected in the previous step. Click **Next**.

l.   The **Create the data collector set?** screen opens. Click **Finish**.

m.   Expand **User Defined**, and select **Memory Logs.** Right-click **Data Collector01** and select **Properties**.

n.   The **DataCollector01 Properties** window opens. Change the **Log format:** field to **Comma Separated.**

o.   Click the **File** tab.

DataCollector01 Properties   x

Performance Counters | File

Log file name:

DataCollector01

File name format:

[   ] [>]

☐ Prefix file with computer name

Log mode
  ☐ Overwrite
  ☐ Append
  ☐ Circular (requires a non-zero maximum file size)

Example file name:
C:\PerfLogs\VICKI-PC_20101224-000001\DataCollector01.csv

[OK]   [Cancel]   [Apply]   [Help]

What is the full path name to the example file?

_____

p.   Click **OK**.

q. Select the **Memory Logs** icon in the left pane of the **Performance Monitor** window. Click the **green arrow** icon to start the data collection set. Notice a green arrow is placed on top of the **Memory Logs** icon.

r. To force the computer to use some of the available memory, open and close a browser.

s.   Click the **black square** icon to stop the data collection set.

What change do you notice for the Memory Logs icon?

_____

t.   Click **Start > Computer**, and click **drive C: > PerfLogs.** Locate the folder that starts with your PC's name followed by a timestamp, **VICKI-PC_20101224-00001** in the example. Double-click the folder to open it, and then double-click the **DataCollector01.csv** file.

Note: In Vista, the folder will be named with a number, for example **000001**.

Note: If the **Windows cannot open the file**: message is displayed, select the radio button **Select a program from a list of installed programs > OK > Notepad > OK**.

What does the column farthest to the right show?

_____

u. Close the **DataCollector01.csv** file and the window with the PerfLogs folder.

v. Select the **Performance Monitor** window. Right-click **Memory Logs > Delete.**

w. The **Performance Monitor > Confirm Delete** window opens. Click **Yes**.

x. Open drive **C: > PerfLogs** folder. Right-click on the folder that was created to hold the Memory log file, then click **Delete**.

y. The Delete Folder window opens. Click **Yes**.

z. Close all open windows.

Lab 6.1.3.6 - Monitor and Manage System Resources in Windows 8

Introduction

In this lab, you will use administrative tools to monitor and manage system resources.

Recommended Equipment

- A computer running Windows 8 with Internet access

Step 1:   How to stop and start a service in Windows.

You will explore what happens when a service is stopped and then started.

a. Log on to Windows as an administrator.

   Note: Some antivirus or antispyware programs must be uninstalled on the computer for Windows Defender to work.

b. To see if Windows Defender is turned off, click **Start** in the **Search programs and files** field, type **Defender**, and select **Windows Defender**. **Windows Defender** should be running.

   Note: In Windows 8.0, click **Search**, type **Defender,** and select **Windows Defender**.

   Note: If **Windows Defender** is not running, a warning window will open and **Windows Defender** will not start. To start Windows Defender, click **Control Panel > Action Center**. In **the Virus protection (Important)** section of the **Action Center** window, click **Turn on now**.

c. Without closing **Windows Defender**, open the **Services** console. Click **Control Panel > Administrative Tools > Computer Management**.

d. The **Computer Management** window opens. Under Services and Applications, select **Services**.

e.   Close the **Windows Explorer** window but keep the **Windows Defender** and **Computer Management** windows open. Resize and position both windows so they can be seen at the same time.

Can Windows Defender check for updates? (Use the **Update tab** to answer the question.) _____

f.   Scroll the **Computer Management** window so you see the **Windows Defender Service**.

What is the status of the service?   _____

Note: While most of the Windows services can be managed through the Services console, it is not possible to stop **Windows Defender** from Windows 8's **Services** console.

g. To turn off **Windows Defender**, make the **Windows Defender** window active. Select the **Settings** tab, and select **Administrator**. Uncheck the **Turn on this app** checkbox, and click **Save changes**.

h. A warning window will open. Click **Close**. Notice that the **Windows Defender** application closes completely.

Note: The reason this service will be stopped is so you can easily see the results. When stopping a service to free up system resources the service uses, it is important to understand how the overall system operation will be affected.

Note: Although Windows Defender Service cannot be controlled through the **Computer Management Services** window, Windows Defender's status is still monitored and displayed. It may be necessary to refresh the **Computer Management** window by pressing **F5**.

i. Now that **Windows Defender** service is stopped, try to run **Windows Defender** again by clicking **Search**, typing **Defender**, and selecting **Windows Defender**.

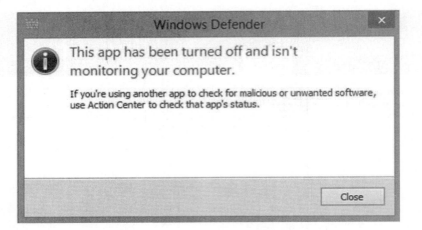

What must be done so Windows Defender can run?

_____

j. Use **Action Center** to start the Windows Defender service. Click **Control Panel > Action Center**. In the **Virus protection (Important)** section, click **Turn on now**.

k. The **Windows Defender** window will open, as the service should now be running again. Close the **Windows Defender** window but make sure the Computer Management window is open.

l. Expand **Event Viewer** > **Windows Logs** > select **System**.

m. Select the second **Service Control Manager** event in the list.

Look below the General tab and explain what has happened to the Windows Defender service.

_____

_____

n. Click the up arrow button on the keyboard or select the event above the one you just viewed.

Look below the General tab and explain what has happened to the Windows Defender service.

_____

_____

o.   Close all open windows.

Step 2:   Understanding the impact of services.

In this section, you will stop **Windows Base Filtering Engine (BFE)**, analyze the impact in the system, and restart BFE. BFE is responsible for managing the firewall and a number of other security policies in Windows. BFE is an important Windows service, as many other services depend on it.

a.   Ensure **Windows Defender** is running by clicking **Control Panel > Windows Defender**.

b.   Open the Computer Management utility. Click **Control Panel > Administrative Tools > Computer Management**. Select **Service** and locate the **Base Filtering Engine** service.

c. Stop the BFE service by right-clicking it and selecting **Stop.** Alternatively, you can use the stop button on the upper toolbar of the **Services Console** while the BFE service is selected.

d. Windows will present a warning message to remind you about all the services that depend on BFE. Click **Yes** to stop BFE and its dependent services.

Note: The services listed may differ from this warning message.

e. Windows should not let you stop BFE if the **Windows Defender** service is displayed in the **Stop Other Services** window. Since **Windows Defender** cannot be stopped via the **Services Console**, BFE cannot be stopped via the **Services Console.**

Note: If this error window does not appear, skip to **substep h**.

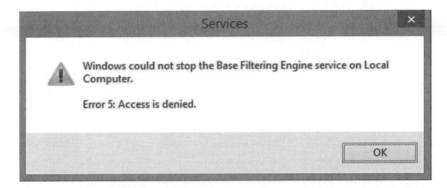

f.   To stop BFE, **Windows Defender** must be stopped first. Open **Windows Defender** and click **stop** on the **Settings** tab. Refer to the beginning of this lab for details.

g.   Now that **Windows Defender** is stopped, open the **Services Console** and stop BFE. Right-click the BFE service and select **Stop.**

What does the status column of the **Services Console** indicate for the BFE service?

_____

h. Since a number of security related services depend on BFE, alerts are issued and can be reviewed in
Action Center.

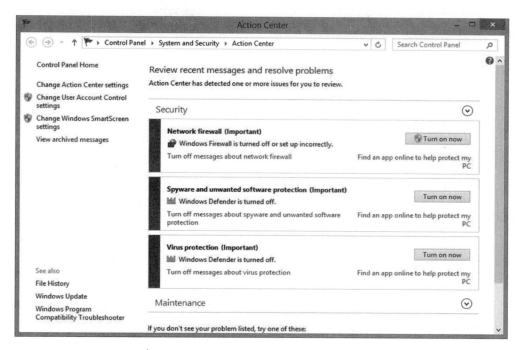

Note: The issues listed may differ in the **Action Center**.

Why is it important to exercise care when managing services?

_____

_____

i. Restart any stopped service from the **Action Center** by selecting the service and clicking **Turn on now**.

Step 3:   Configure advanced features in Administrative Tools.

For the rest of this lab, you will configure advanced Administrative Tool features and monitor how this affects
the computer.

a. From **Windows Explorer,** right-click **This PC** and select **Manage**. The **Computer Management** window
opens.

b.   Expand **System Tools > Performance >Data Collector Sets.** Right-click **User Defined**, and then click **New** > **Data Collector Set**.

c.   The **Create new Data Collector Set** window opens. In the Name field, type **Memory Logs**. Select the **Create manually (Advanced)** radio button and click **Next**.

d. The **What type of data do you want to include?** window opens. Check the **Performance counter** box
    and click **Next**.

e. The **Which performance counters would you like to log?** window opens. Click **Add**.

f. From the list of available counters, locate and expand **Memory**. Select **Available MBytes > Add** and click **OK.**

g. Set the **Sample interval**: field to **4** seconds. Click **Next**.

h. The **Where would you like the data to be saved?** window opens. Click **Browse….**

i. Select Local Disk (**C:),** and then select the **\PerfLogs** folder. Click **OK**.

j. Verify the correct root directory path is selected, and click **Next**.

k. The **Create the data collector set?** window opens. Click **Finish**.

l.   Expand **User Defined** and select **Memory Logs.** Right-click **Data Collector01** and select **Properties**.

m.   The **DataCollector01 Properties** window opens. Change the **Log format:** field to **Comma Separated**.

n.   Click the **File** tab.

What is the full path name to the example file name?

_____

o.   Click **OK**.

p. Select the **Memory Logs** icon in the left pane of the **Performance Monitor** window. Click the **green arrow** icon to start the data collection set. Notice a green arrow is placed on top of the **Memory Logs** icon.

q. To force the computer to use some of the available memory, open and close a browser.

r.   Click the **black square** icon to stop the data collection set.

What change do you notice for the Memory Logs icon?

s.   Open **Windows Explorer**, and click **Local Disk (C:) > PerfLogs.** Click on the folder that was created to store the memory log and double-click the **DataCollector01.csv** file.

Note: Click **Continue** on the Windows warning messages.

t.   If the **Windows cannot open the file:** message is displayed, select the radio button **Select a program from a list of installed programs > OK > Notepad > OK**.

What does the column farthest to the right show?

_____

u.   Close the **DataCollector01.csv** file and **Windows Explorer**.

v.   Select the **Performance Monitor** window.

w.   Right-click **Memory Logs > Delete** and click **Yes**.

x.   Open **Windows Explorer** and click the **Local Drive C: > PerfLogs** folder. Right-click the folder that was created to store the memory logs, and click **Delete**.

y.   Close all open windows.

Lab 6.1.4.2 - Hard Drive Maintenance in Windows 7 and Vista

Introduction

In this lab, you will examine the results of using Disk Check and Disk Defragmenter on a hard drive.

Recommended Equipment

- A computer running Windows 7 or Vista.
- Two or more partitions on the hard drive.

Step 1: Run the Error-Checking tool on a disk volume.

a. Log on to Windows as an administrator.

b. Click **Start > Computer**. Right-click **New Volume (G:) > Properties > Tools > Check Now**.

Note: Substitute the volume name and drive (G:) for those used in your computer.

c. Make sure there are no check marks in either checkbox. Click **Start**.

d.   The **Your device or disk was successfully scanned** window opens. Click the expand button next to **See details**.

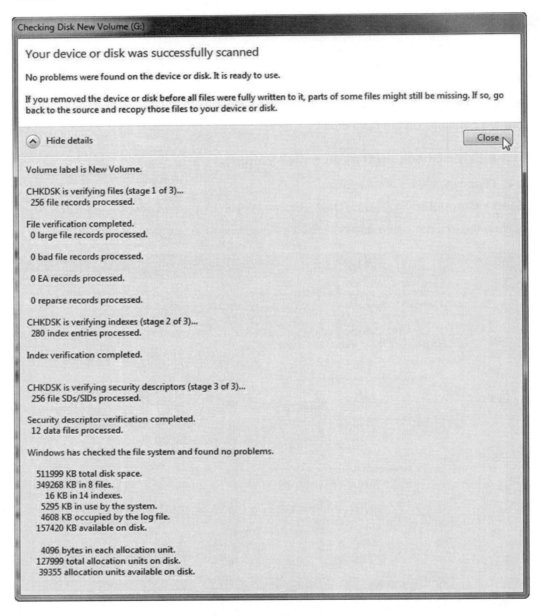

How many stages were processed? _____

e.   Click **Close**.

f.   Select the **Tools** tab, and then click **Check Now**.

g. Remove the check mark next to **Automatically fix file system errors**. Place a check mark in the
checkbox next to **Scan for and attempt recovery of bad sectors** and click **Start**.

Check Disk New Volume (G:)
Check disk options
☐ Automatically fix file system errors
☑ Scan for and attempt recovery of bad sectors

Start   Cancel

h. The **Your device or disk was successfully scanned** window opens. Click the expand button next to
See details.

Checking Disk New Volume (G:)

Your device or disk was successfully scanned

No problems were found on the device or disk. It is ready to use.

If you removed the device or disk before all files were fully written to it, parts of some files might still be missing. If so, go back
to the source and recopy those files to your device or disk.

⌃ Hide details   Close

Volume label is New Volume.

CHKDSK is verifying files (stage 1 of 5)...
  256 file records processed.

File verification completed.
  0 large file records processed.

  0 bad file records processed.

  0 EA records processed.

  0 reparse records processed.

CHKDSK is verifying indexes (stage 2 of 5)...
  280 index entries processed.

Index verification completed.

CHKDSK is verifying security descriptors (stage 3 of 5)...
  256 file SDs/SIDs processed.

Security descriptor verification completed.
  12 data files processed.

CHKDSK is verifying free space (stage 5 of 5)...
  39355 free clusters processed.

Free space verification is complete.
Windows has checked the file system and found no problems.

    511999 KB total disk space.
    349268 KB in 8 files.
       16 KB in 14 indexes.
     5295 KB in use by the system.
     4608 KB occupied by the log file.
    157420 KB available on disk.

     4096 bytes in each allocation unit.
    127999 total allocation units on disk.
     39355 allocation units available on disk.

What stages were processed? _____

i.   Click **Close**.

j.   Select the **Tools** tab **> Check Now**.

k.   Place a check mark in both checkboxes. Click **Start**.

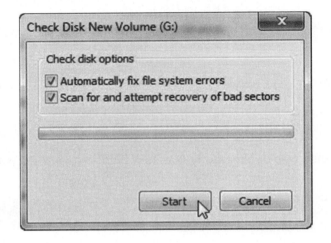

l. The **Your device or disk was successfully scanned** window opens. Click the expand button next to **See details**.

Checking Disk New Volume (G:)

Your device or disk was successfully scanned

No problems were found on the device or disk. It is ready to use.

If you removed the device or disk before all files were fully written to it, parts of some files might still be missing. If so, go back to the source and recopy those files to your device or disk.

(^) Hide details   Close

Volume dismounted. All opened handles to this volume are now invalid.
Volume label is New Volume.

CHKDSK is verifying files (stage 1 of 5)...
  256 file records processed.

File verification completed.
  0 large file records processed.

  0 bad file records processed.

  0 EA records processed.

  0 reparse records processed.

CHKDSK is verifying indexes (stage 2 of 5)...
  280 index entries processed.

Index verification completed.

CHKDSK is verifying security descriptors (stage 3 of 5)...
  256 file SDs/SIDs processed.

Security descriptor verification completed.
  12 data files processed.

CHKDSK is verifying file data (stage 4 of 5)...
  240 files processed.

File data verification completed.
CHKDSK is verifying free space (stage 5 of 5)...
  121275 free clusters processed.

Free space verification is complete.
Windows has checked the file system and found no problems.

   511999 KB total disk space.
    21588 KB in 7 files.
       16 KB in 14 indexes.
     5291 KB in use by the system.
     4608 KB occupied by the log file.
   485104 KB available on disk.

     4096 bytes in each allocation unit.
   127999 total allocation units on disk.
   121276 allocation units available on disk.

What stages were processed? _____

What is being verified in each of the stages?

_____

_____

_____

Were any problems found with the volume? _____

If so, what are they?

_____

_____

m. Click **Close** and close all open windows.

Step 2:   Check the Event Viewer for the Chkdsk log.

a. Click **Start > Control Panel > Administrative Tools > Event Viewer**.

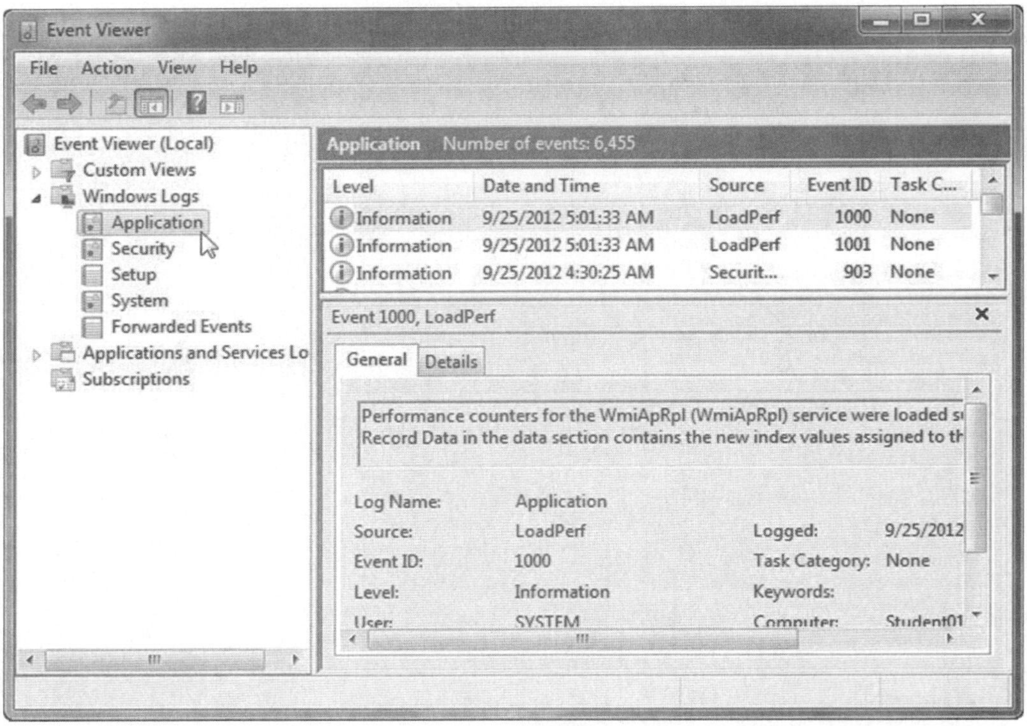

b. In the left pane, expand **Windows Logs** and click **Application**. Double-click the top event in the middle pane.

c. If the displayed event is not Chkdsk, click the **black down arrow** until the Chkdsk event appears.

Which stages are shown as completed?

_____

d.   Close all open windows.

Step 3:   Disk defragmenter.

Note: Do not perform this step if your computer has an SSD drive. It is unnecessary to defragment SSD drives.

a.   Click **Start > Computer,** then right-click **drive (C:)** and select **Properties.** Click **Tools > Defragment Now**.

b.   The **Disk Defragmenter** window opens, click **Defragment disk**.

Note: In Windows Vista, an option window opens, click **Defragment now….** In the **Disks to defragment:** window, check only **(C:) > OK**.

c.   Click **Local Disk (C:) > Analyze disk**.

What percentage of the disk is fragmented?

_____

d. You should be able to watch the progress of the defragmentation process in the **Disk Defragmenter** window.

Note: Windows Vista Disk Defragmenter does not show the progress of the defragmentation process.

What is the first process during defragmenting (see Progress column)?

_____

What are the three tasks performed for each pass (see Progress column)?

_____

How many passes did it take to defragment drive C:?

_____

e. When defragmenting is completed, click **Close**.

f. Close all windows.

Note: It is not possible to view the detail of the defragmented hard drive through the GUI version of defragmenter.

Lab 6.1.4.2 - Hard Drive Maintenance in Windows 8

Introduction

In this lab, you will examine the results of using Disk Check and Disk Defragmenter on a hard drive.

Recommended Equipment

- A computer running Windows 8
- Two or more partitions on the hard drive

Step 1:   Run the Error-Checking tool on a disk volume.

a.   Log on to Windows as an administrator.

b.   Open **Windows Explorer**. Right-click **New Volume (G:) > Properties > Tools > Check Now**.

Note: Substitute the volume name and drive (G:) for those used in your computer.

c.   Because Windows monitors the drives and runs automatic scheduled scans, you may see a message saying that **You don't need to scan this drive**. Click **Scan drive**.

d. The **Your drive was successfully scanned** window opens. Click **Show details**.

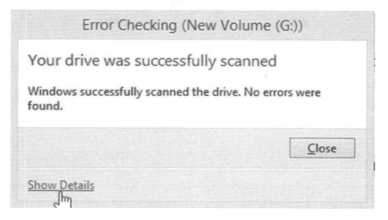

e. The **Event Viewer** opens to display the **Chkdsk** event. Double-click the **Information** event in the middle pane.

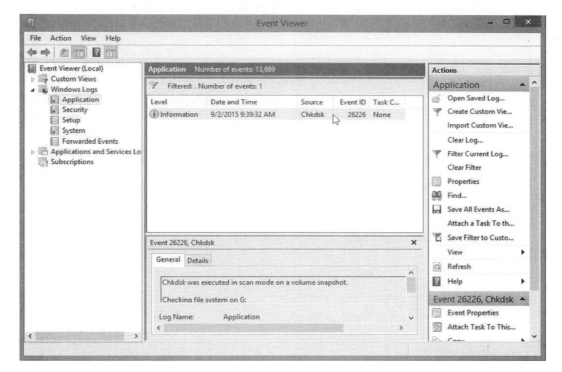

How many stages were processed?

_____

Were any problems found with the volume? _____

If so, what are they?

_____

_____

f.   Click **Close**.

g.   Close all open windows.

Step 2:   Use the Disk defragmenter tool.

Note: Do not perform this step if your computer has an SSD drive. It is unnecessary to defragment SSD drives.

a.   Open **Windows Explorer**. Right-click **drive (C:) > Properties**. Click the **Tools** tab **> Optimize**.

b.   The **Optimize Drives** window opens. Click **(C:) > Analyze**.

What percentage of the disk is fragmented?

c.   Click **Optimize** to start defragmenting the disk.

What is the first process during defragmenting (see **Current status** column)?

_____

What are the four tasks performed for each pass (see **Current status** column)?

_____

How many passes did it take to defragment drive C:?

_____

d.   When defragmenting is complete, click **Close**.

e.   Close all windows.

Note: It is not possible to view the detail of the defragmented hard drive through the GUI version of defragmenter.

Lab 6.1.4.4 - Managing System Files in Windows

Introduction

In this lab, you will use Windows utilities to gather information about the computer.

Recommended Equipment

- A computer running Windows

Step 1:   Customize the Start menu in Windows.

a.   Log on to the computer as an administrator.

Note: If you are using Windows 8, skip to **Step 2**.

b.   To add **Run** to the Start menu, right-click **Start** and select **Properties > Start Menu** tab **> Customize….**

c.   Scroll down until you see the **Run** command. Click in the box next to select the **Run command** and click **OK**.

d.   Click **Apply > OK** to close the **Taskbar and Start Menu Properties** window.

Step 2:   Review the system information.

a.   Open **System Information** by clicking **Start > Run and** type **msinfo32**. Click **OK**.

   Note: In Windows 8, search for **msinfo32** by using the **Search Charm**.

b. Click the **plus sign** next to **Hardware Resources**, **Components**, and **Software Environment**. Expand the window so you can see all the content.

c. Under the **System Summary** heading, locate and list the following:

Processor: _____

BIOS Version/Date: _____

Total Physical Memory: _____

d. Under the **Hardware Resources** heading, locate and list the following:

DMA channels and the device using the resources.

_____

_____

e. Under the **Components** heading and **Software** heading, look around to see what information is provided in these areas.

f. Close the **System Information** window.

Step 3: Review the System Configuration.

a. Open **System Configuration** by clicking **Start > Run**, and type **msconfig**. Click **OK**.

Note: In Windows 8, search for **msconfig** by using the **Search Charm**.

Note: Do not make any changes in this utility without instructor permission.

b. Click the **General** tab.

What are the startup options?

_____

c. Click the **Boot** tab. This tab is for modifying boot options.

d. Click the **Services** tab. This tab lists the computers services and status.

Can you enable and disable services at this tab? _____

e. Click the **Startup** tab. This tab lists the programs that are automatically loaded every time you turn on your computer.

Note: In Windows 8, the **Startup** tab indicates that the **Task Manager** is used to manage startup items. There is also a link to **Startup** tab of the **Task Manager** on this tab.

f. Click the **Tools** tab.

What can you do in this tab?

_____

g. Click **Cancel** to close the **System Configuration** window.

Step 4: Review DirectX Diagnostics.

a. Open the **DirectX Diagnostic Tool** by clicking **Start > Run**, and type **dxdiag**. Click **OK**.

Note: In Windows 8, search for **dxdiag** by using the **Search Charm**.

b. If you are asked to have DirectX check driver signatures, click **No**.

Note: When the **DirectX Diagnostic Tool** first opens, it may take a minute to load all information. Your **DirectX Diagnostic Tool** may not appear exactly as shown in this lab.

c. Make sure the **System** tab is active.

What does this tool report?

_____

d. Click **Next Page** until you are at the **Display** tab.

What information is listed on this page?

_____

e.   Click **Next Page** until you are at the **Sound** tab.

What information is listed on this page?

_____

f.   Click **Next Page** until you are on the **Input** tab.

What information is listed on this page?

_____

g.   Click **Exit**.

Reflection

1.   Why would it be beneficial to turn off a service in the system configuration?

_____

_____

2.   When would you use the Startup tab of the system configuration tool?

_____

_____

Lab 6.1.5.4 - Common Windows CLI Commands

Introduction

In this lab, you will use CLI commands to manage files and folders in Windows.

Recommended Equipment

- A computer running Windows

Step 1:   Access the Windows command prompt.

a.   Log on to a computer as a user with administrative privileges. The account **ITEUser** is used as the example user account throughout this lab.

b.   To access the Windows command prompt in Windows 8, navigate to the **Start** screen and type **Command Prompt**. Click **Command Prompt**.

In Windows 7, click **Start** and type **Command Prompt** in the **Search programs and files** field. Click **Command Prompt** to continue.

In Windows Vista, click **Start** and type **Command Prompt** in the **Start Search** field. Click **Command Prompt** to continue.

Step 2:   Display command help from the command prompt.

You can display command line help using the **help** command. For more information on a specific command, type the command followed by **/?**.

a.   At the command prompt, type **help** and press **Enter**. A list of commands is displayed.

Using the information displayed by the help command, explain the functions of the following commands.

Command	Function
CD	
CHKDSK	
COPY	
DEL	
DIR	
DISKPART	
EXIT	
FORMAT	
GPRESULT	
MD	
TASKLIST	
RD	
ROBOCOPY	
SHUTDOWN	
XCOPY	

b. Type **md /?** at the prompt to display additional information and switches that can be used with this command.

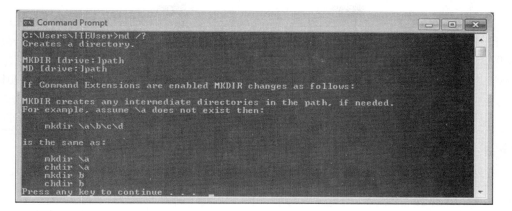

Step 3:   Create and change directories.

In this step, you will use the change directory (**cd**), make directory (**md**), and directory (**dir**) commands.

Note: A directory is another word for folder. Directory and folder are used interchangeably throughout this lab.

a. Type **cd** at the command prompt. What is the current directory?

_____

b. Type **dir** at the command prompt to list the files and folders that are in the current folder.

c. In the current directory, use the **md** command to create three new folders: **ITEfolder1**, **ITEfolder2**, and **ITEfolder3**. Type **md ITEfolder1** and press **Enter**. Create **ITEfolder2** and **ITEfolder3**.

d. Type **dir** to verify the folders have been created.

e. Type **cd ITEfolder3** at the command prompt and press **Enter**. Which folder are you in now?

_____

f. Within the **ITEfolder3** folder, create a folder named **ITEfolder4**. Use the **dir** command to verify the folder creation.

g. Type **cd ..** to change the current directory. Each **..** is a shortcut to move up one level in the directory tree. After issuing the **cd ..** command, what is your directory now?

_____

What would be the current directory if you issue this command at C:\Users\ITEfolder3?

_____

Step 4:   Create text files.

a. Navigate to the **C:\Users\ITEUser\ITEfolder1** directory. Type **cd ITEfolder1** at the prompt.

b. Type **echo This is doc1.txt > doc1.txt** at the command prompt. The **echo** command is used to display a message at the command prompt. The **>** is used to redirect the message from the screen to a file. For example, in the first line, the message **This is doc1.txt** is redirected into a new file named **doc1.txt**. Use the **echo** command and **>** redirect to create these files: **doc2.txt**, **file1.txt**, and **file2.txt**.

c. Use the **dir** command to verify the files are in the **ITEfolder1** folder.

Step 5:   Copy, delete, and move files.

a. At the command prompt, type **move doc2.txt C:\Users\ITEUser\ITEfolder2** to move the file **doc2.txt** to the **C:\Users\ITEUser\ITEfolder2** directory.

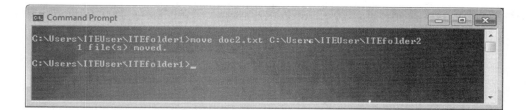

b. Type **dir** at the prompt to verify that **doc2.txt** is no longer in the current directory.

c. Type **cd C:\Users\ITEUser\ITEfolder2** to change the directory to **ITEfolder2**. Type **dir** at the prompt to verify **doc2.txt** has been moved.

d. Type **copy doc2.txt doc2_copy.txt** to create a copy of **doc2.txt**. Type **dir** at the prompt to verify a copy of the file has been created.

e. Now use the **move** command to move **doc2_copy.txt** to **ITEfolder1**. Type **move doc2_copy.txt ..\ITEfolder1**.

f. A copy of **doc2.txt** can be created and renamed with the **copy** command. Type **copy doc2.txt ..\ITEfoler1\doc2_new.txt** at the prompt.

g. Type **dir ..\ITEfolder1** to view the content in **ITEfolder1** without leaving the current directory.

```
Command Prompt
c:\Users\ITEUser\ITEfolder2>dir ..\ITEfolder1
 Volume in drive C has no label.
 Volume Serial Number is DCA8-CC2E

 Directory of c:\Users\ITEUser\ITEfolder1

09/20/2015  07:24 PM    <DIR>          .
09/20/2015  07:24 PM    <DIR>          ..
09/20/2015  07:19 PM                19 doc1.txt
09/20/2015  07:20 PM                19 doc2_copy.txt
09/20/2015  07:20 PM                19 doc2_new.txt
09/20/2015  07:20 PM                20 file1.txt
09/20/2015  07:20 PM                20 file2.txt
               5 File(s)             97 bytes
               2 Dir(s)   4,691,791,872 bytes free

c:\Users\ITEUser\ITEfolder2>
```

h. Change the current directory to **ITEfolder1**. Type **cd ..\ITEfolder1** at the prompt.

i. Move **file1.txt** and **file2.txt** into **ITEfolder3**. To move all the files that contain the word **file** into **ITEfolder3** with one command, use a **wildcard** (*) character to represent one or more characters. Type **move file*.txt ..\ITEfolder3**.

```
Command Prompt
C:\Users\ITEUser\ITEfolder1>move file*.txt ..\ITEfolder3
C:\Users\ITEUser\ITEfolder1\file1.txt
C:\Users\ITEUser\ITEfolder1\file2.txt
        2 file(s) moved.

C:\Users\ITEUser\ITEfolder1>_
```

j. Now delete **doc2_copy.txt** from the **ITEfolder1** directory. Type **del doc2_copy.txt**. Use the **dir** command to verify the file deletion.

Step 6:   Use the xcopy command.

In this step, the **xcopy** command is used to copy all the content in a directory and delete the empty directory.

a. Verify the content of ITEfolder3. Type **dir ..\ITEfolder3**.

```
Command Prompt
C:\Users\ITEUser\ITEfolder1>dir ..\ITEfolder3
 Volume in drive C has no label.
 Volume Serial Number is AA01-BC29

 Directory of C:\Users\ITEUser\ITEfolder3

09/07/2015  07:34 PM    <DIR>          .
09/07/2015  07:34 PM    <DIR>          ..
09/07/2015  07:18 PM                20 file1.txt
09/07/2015  07:18 PM                20 file2.txt
09/07/2015  07:13 PM    <DIR>          ITEfolder4
               2 File(s)             40 bytes
               3 Dir(s)  10,408,062,976 bytes free

C:\Users\ITEUser\ITEfolder1>_
```

b. Verify the content in **ITEfolder1**. Move all the files in this folder to ITEfolder2. Type **move doc*.txt ..\ITEfolder2** to move the files.

c. Type **xcopy ..\ITEfolder3 .** at the prompt to copy the content of **ITEfolder3** to **ITEfolder1**. Note the **.** at the end of the command. It is a shortcut for the current directory.

```
Command Prompt                                                    —  □  ✕
C:\Users\ITEUser\ITEfolder1>xcopy ..\ITEfolder3 .
..\ITEfolder3\file1.txt
..\ITEfolder3\file2.txt
2 File(s) copied

C:\Users\ITEUser\ITEfolder1>_
```

d.   At the prompt, type **dir** to display the content of **ITEfolder1**. Only the files in the **ITEfolder3** were copied into **ITEfolder1**. The directory **ITEfolder4** was not copied into **ITEfolder3**.

```
Command Prompt                                                    —  □  ✕
C:\Users\ITEUser\ITEfolder1>dir
 Volume in drive C has no label.
 Volume Serial Number is AA01-BC29

 Directory of C:\Users\ITEUser\ITEfolder1

09/07/2015  08:19 PM    <DIR>          .
09/07/2015  08:19 PM    <DIR>          ..
09/07/2015  07:18 PM                20 file1.txt
09/07/2015  07:18 PM                20 file2.txt
               2 File(s)             40 bytes
               2 Dir(s)   10,408,062,976 bytes free

C:\Users\ITEUser\ITEfolder1>_
```

e.   Use **help xcopy** to determine which switch would allow the **xcopy** command to copy **all** the files and directories.

f.   Because **ITEfolder4** is an empty folder, **/E** is needed to copy all the content of **ITEfolder3** and the empty subfolder.

Type **xcopy /E ..\ITEfolder3 .** at the prompt to copy the files. When prompted, type **a** to allow overwriting the existing files.

```
Command Prompt                                                    —  □  ✕
C:\Users\ITEUser\ITEfolder1>xcopy /E ..\ITEfolder3 .
Overwrite C:\Users\ITEUser\ITEfolder1\file1.txt (Yes/No/All)? a
..\ITEfolder3\file1.txt
..\ITEfolder3\file2.txt
2 File(s) copied

C:\Users\ITEUser\ITEfolder1>_
```

g.   Verify the **ITEfolder4** was also copied in **ITEfolder1**.

```
Command Prompt                                                    —  □  ✕
C:\Users\ITEUser\ITEfolder1>dir
 Volume in drive C has no label.
 Volume Serial Number is AA01-BC29

 Directory of C:\Users\ITEUser\ITEfolder1

09/07/2015  08:20 PM    <DIR>          .
09/07/2015  08:20 PM    <DIR>          ..
09/07/2015  07:18 PM                20 file1.txt
09/07/2015  07:18 PM                20 file2.txt
09/07/2015  08:15 PM    <DIR>          ITEfolder4
               2 File(s)             40 bytes
               3 Dir(s)   10,408,062,976 bytes free

C:\Users\ITEUser\ITEfolder1>_
```

Step 7:   Delete directories.

In this step, you will delete an empty and a non-empty directory using the **rd** command.

a. Navigate to the **C:\Users\ITEUser\ITEfolder3** directory.

b. Use the **rd ITEfolder4** to delete the empty directory. Verify the directory removal using the **dir** command.

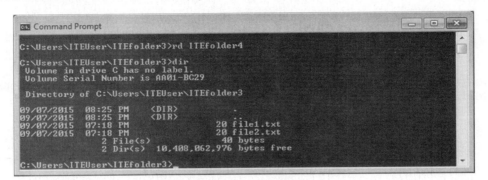

c. Navigate to **C:\Users\ITEUser** folder.

d. Use the **rd ITEfolder2** to delete the non-empty directory. The message indicates that the directory is not empty and cannot be deleted.

e. Use **rd /?** command to determine the switch that allows the deletion of a non-empty directory.

f. Type **rd /S ITEfolder2** to delete this folder. When prompted, type **y** to delete the directory. Use **dir** to verify that **ITEfolder2** was deleted.

g. Type **exit** to close the command prompt window.

Reflection

What are the advantages of using CLI vs. GUI?

Lab 6.1.5.6 - System Utilities in Windows

Introduction

In this lab, you will use Windows utilities to configure operating system settings.

Recommended Equipment

The following equipment is required for this exercise:

- A computer running Windows

Step 1:   Open the management console.

a.   Open the Microsoft Management Console. Click **Start**, type **mmc**, and press **Enter**.

Note: In Windows 8, type **mmc** in the **Search Charm**.

b.   The **Console1 - [Console Root]** window opens. To build your own custom console, click **File > Add/Remove Snap-in**.

c.   The **Add or Remove Snap-ins** window opens. To add a folder snap-in, to organize your snap-ins, scroll down until you see the **Folder** snap-in. Select **Folder** and click **Add>**.

d.   To add the **Link to Web Address** snap-in, scroll down and select **Link to Web Address**. Click **Add>**.

e. The **Link to Web Address** wizard opens. In the **Path or URL:** box, type **http://www.cisco.com**. Click **Next>**.

f. In the **Friendly name for the Link to Web Address snap-in** box, type **Cisco**. Click **Finish**.

Step 2:   Create a custom management console.

a.   To add snap-ins to the folder snap-in, click **Advanced**.

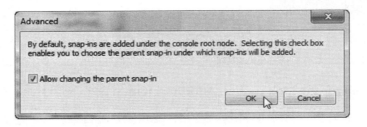

b.   The **Advanced** window opens. Check the box next to **Allow changing the parent snap-in**. Click **OK**.

c.   A drop-down menu appears for **Parent snap-in**. In the **Parent snap-in** box, select **Folder**.

d. Add the following snap-ins: **Computer Management**, **Device Manager**, and **Disk Management**.

   Note: When you are asked what computer the snap-in will manage, select the default by clicking **Finish**. Click **OK** to accept all changes.

e. The **Console1** window opens. Right-click the **Folder** icon and select **Rename**. Change the name of the folder to **Management Tools**.

f. To save the custom console, click **File > Save As**. Change the file name to your name. Example: **John's Console**. Change the **Save in** box to **Desktop**. Click **Save**.

g. Close all open windows.

h. On the desktop, double-click the **Console** icon to re-open the console with your snap-ins.

i. Review the **Management Tools** folder by double-clicking on the tools. Close the **Console** window when you finish your review.

Step 3:   Change your desktop background settings.

a.   To open the **Choose your desktop background** window, right-click the **Desktop**, select **Personalize**, and click **Desktop Background**.

What is the background picture?

_____

b.   Click the **Picture location** drop-down button and select **Solid Colors**. Select a **blue** color.

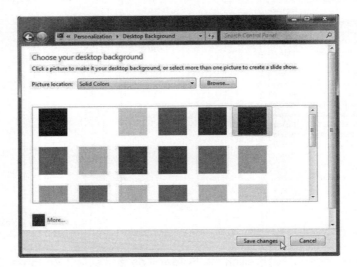

c.   Click **Save changes**. The computer screen should now have a blue background. If not, ask the instructor for assistance.

d.   Close all open windows.

Step 4:   Open the Registry Editor.

a.   To open the **Registry Editor**, click **Start** and type **regedit.** Press **Enter**.

Note: Do not make any changes in the Registry Editor without instructor permission.

b. Select the **HKEY_CURRENT_USER** entry. To search for the **Background** key, click **Edit > Find...**, and type **Background**. Click **Find Next**.

Note: In Windows 8, expand the **HKEY_CURRENT_USER** entry by clicking the arrow to the left. Select **Control Panel** from the list.

c. The **Background** value is located. Leave this window open.

In which folder is the background located? _____

What is the data value of the background (hint – it has three numbers that correspond to red, green, and blue)?

Step 5: Export a registry key.

We will now export the **HKEY_CURRENT_USER\Control Panel\Colors** folder.

a. In the left pane, select the **Colors** folder and click **File > Export**.

b. Save the file to the desktop with the name **BlueBKG**.

c. At the desktop, right-click the **BlueBKG.reg** icon and select **Edit**.

d.   Notepad opens displaying the contents of **BlueBKG.reg**.

What is the data value of the **Background**?

_____

e.   Close the **BlueBKG.reg – Notepad** window.

f.   Open the **Choose your desktop background** page in Personalize appearance and sounds by right-clicking the **Desktop > Personalize > Desktop Background**.

g.   Click the **Location** drop-down button and select **Solid Colors**. Select a **red** color.

h.   Click **Save** changes. Close the **Personalization** window.

i.   The desktop should be red. Click the **Registry Editor** window.

j. On your keyboard, press **F5** to refresh the **Registry Editor** window.

What is the data value of the background? Answers may vary based on the shade of red selected in Display Properties.

_____

Step 6: Import a registry file.

We will now import the **BlueBKG.reg** file.

a. Click the **Registry Editor** window.

b. Click **File > Import**. Locate and click the **BlueBKG.reg** file and then click **Open**.

c. The **Registry Editor** informational message opens, letting you know that keys and values have been successfully added to the registry. Click **OK**.

d. Select the **Registry Editor** window.

What is the data value of the background?

_____

What is the color of the desktop? _____

e. Restart the computer.

What is the color of the desktop? _____

f. Reset **Display Properties Background** to the original settings.

g. Close all open windows.

h. Delete the custom console and BlueBKG file on the desktop.

Reflection

1. Why would it be beneficial to add snap-ins to the mmc that are for other computers on the network?

_____

_____

_____

2. After restarting the computer, why was the desktop color changed?

_____

_____

_____

_____

Lab 6.3.1.2 - Managing the Startup Folder in Windows 7 and Vista

Introduction

In this lab, you will customize the Startup folder and the Run key in the registry.

Recommended Equipment

- A computer running Windows 7 or Vista

Step 1:   Creating a shortcut for Internet Explorer.

a.   Click **Start** > **All Programs,** right-click **Internet Explorer**, and click **Send To** > **Desktop (create shortcut)**.

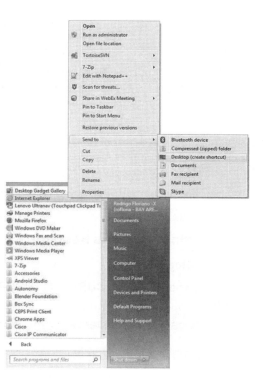

Step 2:   Adding the shortcut to the Startup menu.

a.   To open the Startup folder, click **Start > All Programs**, right-click the **Startup** folder, and select **Open**.

b.   Drag the **Internet Explorer** shortcut icon to the right pane of the **Startup** folder.

c.   Restart Windows.

d.   Log on to Windows as an administrator.

What happens when you log in?

_____

e.   Close **Internet Explorer**.

Step 3:   Manage Startup applications using Windows Registry.

a.   Click **Start,** type **regedit**, and press **Enter**.

b.   The **Registry Editor** window opens. Expand **HKEY_CURRENT_USER > Software > Microsoft > Windows > CurrentVersion> Run.**

Note: Incorrect changes to the registry can cause system errors and/or system instability.

c. Right-click anywhere in the white space on the right side of the window. Select **New** and click **String Value**. A new **String Value** is created.

d. Click anywhere in the white space of the window.

e. Right-click **New Value #1** > **Rename**. Type **Notepad** and press **Enter**.

f.   Right-click **Notepad** > **Modify**. Type **C:\Windows\system32\notepad.exe** in the **Value data** field. Click **OK**.

g.   Close the **Registry Editor** window.

h.   Restart Windows.

i.   Log on to Windows as an administrator.

      What happens when you log in?

      _____

j.   Close all open Windows.

Step 4:   Removing programs from the Startup folder and registry.

a.   Click **Start > All Programs > Startup**. Right-click **Internet Explorer** and select **Delete.** Click **Yes** on the **Delete File** window.

b. To remove **Notepad** from the **Run** folder in the **Registry**, click **Start**, type **regedit**, and press **Enter**.

c. Expand the **HKEY_CURRENT_USER** > **Software** > **Microsoft** > **Windows** > **CurrentVersion**> **Run**.

d. Right-click **Notepad** and select **Delete.** Click **Yes** for the **Confirm Value Delete**.

e. Restart Windows.

f. Log on to Windows as an administrator.

What happens when you log in?

_____

g. Close all open windows.

Reflection

Why would a user want to stop programs from starting automatically?

_____

_____

_____

_____

Lab 6.3.1.2 - Managing the Startup Folder in Windows 8

Introduction

In this lab, you will customize the **Startup folder** and the **Run Key** in the **Registry** to manage what applications are started automatically when **Windows** starts. You will also use the **Startup** tab to manage the programs already added to the **Startup folder**.

Recommended Equipment

- A computer running Windows 8

Step 1:   Customize the Startup folder.

a. To add a program to the **Startup Folder**, you must first locate it and create a shortcut. Open **File Explorer** and navigate to **C:\Program Files\Internet Explorer**.

b. Locate the **Internet Explorer** executable file, **iexplorer.exe**. Right-click the **iexplorer.exe** executable, click **Send to**, and select **Desktop (create shortcut).** This will create a shortcut to **Internet Explorer** on the **Desktop.**

Note: Depending on your computer settings, the file extension may not be shown.

c. Close the **File Explorer** window.

d. To access the **Startup folder** in **Windows 8**, click **Search**, type **run**, and press **Enter**.

e. The **Run** window opens. Type **shell:startup** and press **Enter**.

f. The **Startup** window opens. Move the **Internet Explorer** shortcut, previously created in the desktop, to the **Startup folder** by dragging it on the **Windows Explorer** window.

Now that the Internet Explorer shortcut has been added to the Startup folder, what should happen after the PC is rebooted?

_____

g. Restart the computer.

Did **Internet Explorer** automatically open after the boot process was complete?

_____

h. Close Internet Explorer.

Step 2: Review computer setting in Task Manager.

a. Open the **Task Manager** by right-clicking the **taskbar** at the bottom of the desktop. Select **Task Manager** from the menu.

Note: Only **Desktop applications** can be added to the **Startup tab**. Windows 8 Modern UI apps (**Windows Apps**) are not allowed to start automatically with Windows.

b. To access more features, click **More details** at the bottom of the **Task Manager** window. You should see the **Processes** tab of **Task Manager**.

c. Click the **Startup** tab. A list of applications is displayed that will be started automatically when Windows starts. Notice that **Internet Explorer** is listed.

d. Close all windows.

Step 3:   Managing Startup applications using Windows Registry.

The **Windows Registry** is a tree-like structure that can be used to configure many different aspects of **Windows**.

a.   To edit the **registry,** open **regedit.** Click **Search,** type **regedit**, and press **Enter.**

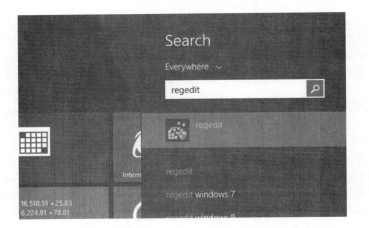

b.   The **Registry Editor** window opens. Expand **HKEY_CURRENT_USER > Software > Microsoft > Windows > CurrentVersion > Run**.

   Note: Incorrect changes to the registry can cause system errors and/or system instability.

c.   Right-click anywhere in the white space in the right pane of the **Registry Editor** window.

d.   Select **New** and click **String Value**.

e. A new **String Value** is created.

f. Click anywhere in the white space of the window. Right-click **New Value #1**, and select **Rename**.

g.   Type **Notepad** for the new name and press **Enter**.

h.   Right-click **Notepad** and select **Modify…**.

i.   Type **C:\Windows\System32\notepad.exe** in the **Value name:** field and click **OK**.

j.   Close the **Registry Editor** window.

k.   Restart the computer.

What happens when you log in?

_____

l.   Close all open Windows.

Step 4:   Removing applications from Startup.

You can use the Startup tab to manage what applications continue to run automatically in future reboots.

a.   Right click the **taskbar** and select **Task Manager.**

b.   Click **More details** and select the **Startup** tab. The **Startup** tab now shows **Internet Explorer** and **Notepad**.

c.   Stop **Internet Explorer** from automatically starting after reboots by right-clicking **Internet Explorer** and selecting **Disable**. While Internet Explorer is still listed under the **Startup** tab, it will no longer be automatically started after a reboot.

d.   Do the same for **Notepad** by right-clicking **Notepad** and selecting **Disable**.

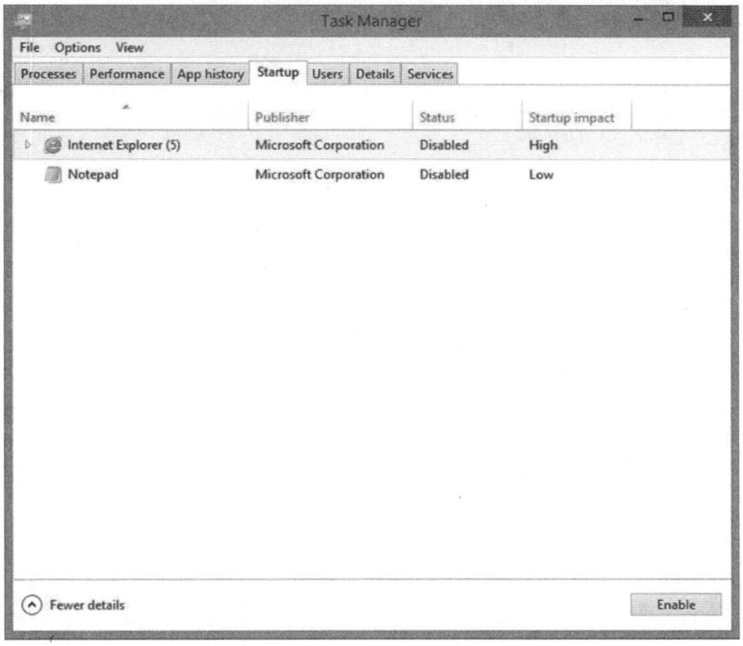

What does the **Startup impact** column indicate?

_____

Reflection

Why would a user want to stop programs from starting automatically?

_____

_____

_____

_____

Lab 6.3.1.5 - Task Scheduler in Windows 7 and Vista

Introduction

In this lab, you will schedule a task using the Windows 7 Task Scheduler utility. You will then make changes to your task and test your task by running it.

Recommended Equipment

- A computer running Windows 7 or Vista

Step 1: Open the Task Scheduler utility.

a. Log on to Windows as an administrator.

b. Click **Control Panel > Administrative Tools > Task Scheduler**.

Step 2: Run the Create Basic Task Wizard.

a. Click **Create Basic Task** in the Actions pane.

b. On the **Create a Basic Task** screen of the **Create Basic Task Wizard** window, type **Disk Cleanup** in the **Name:** field, and click **Next**.

c. On the **Task Trigger** screen, select the **Weekly** radio button. Click **Next**.

d.   On the **Weekly** screen, use the scroll buttons in the **Start:** field to set the time to **6:00:00 PM**. Set the **Recur every _ weeks on:** field to **1**. Check the **Friday** checkbox. Click **Next**.

Note: The date field will display today's date. It is not necessary to change the date.

e.   On the **Action** screen, make sure **Start a program** is selected. Click **Next**.

f.   On the **Start a program** screen, click **Browse**.

g.   Type **cle** in the **File name:** field, select **cleanmgr.exe**, and click **Open**.

h.   The **Start a Program** screen re-opens with **C:\Windows\System32\cleanmgr.exe** added to the **Program/script:** field. Click **Next**.

i.   Review the **Summary** screen and click **Finish**.

Step 3:   Review and make changes to your scheduled task.

a.   In the left pane of the **Task Scheduler** window, select **Task Schedule Library**.

Note: You may need to click **Refresh** to see the new **Disk Cleanup** task that was created.

b.   Select the task **Disk Cleanup** and, in the right pane, click **Properties**.

c. The **Disk Cleanup Properties (Local Computer)** window opens. In the **Configure for:** drop-down menu, select **Windows® 7, Windows Server™ 2008 R2**. Click **OK**.

Note: For Windows Vista, keep **Windows Vista, Windows Server 2000** selected in the **Configure for:** field.

d. Click the **Actions** tab. Select the **Start a program** row, and then click **Edit**.

e.   The **Edit Action** window opens. Type **/d c:** in the **Add Arguments (optional):** field. Click **OK**.

Note: The /d c: argument tells the cleanmgr.exe program to clean the C: drive.

f.   To close the **Disk Cleanup Properties (Local Computer)** window, click **OK**.

Step 4:   Run the scheduled task now.

a.   Select the **Disk Cleanup** task, and click **Run** in the right pane of the **Task Scheduler** window.

Note: The **Disk Cleanup Options** window opens in Vista. Select **Files from all users on this computer**.

b.   Click the **Disk Cleanup** icon that appears on the **Task Bar**.

c. The **Disk Cleanup** window is brought to the foreground. This window displays the status of the **Disk Cleanup** process.

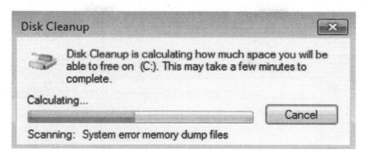

Note: It may take a few minutes for Disk Cleanup to complete.

d. Once the Disk Cleanup process completes, the **Disk Cleanup for Local Disk (C:)** window opens. Click **Cancel**.

Note: Clicking **OK** will delete the files selected in the **Files to delete:** box. **Check with your instructor before clicking OK.** Clicking OK will open the **Disk Cleanup** verification window asking if you are sure you want to permanently delete these files. It is not necessary to delete these files to complete this lab. If you are sure you want to delete these files permanently, click **Delete Files**.

Step 5:   Delete a scheduled task.

a.   To delete the **Disk Cleanup** task that you created, select the **Disk Cleanup** task, and click **Delete** in the right pane of the **Task Scheduler** window.

b.   The **Task Scheduler verification** window opens asking if you want to delete this task. Click **Yes.**

c.   Make sure the Disk Cleanup task you created is removed from the **Task Scheduler** window. Close **Task Scheduler**.

Reflection

What other weekly tasks would be useful to run in Task Scheduler?

_____

_____

_____

_____

_____

Lab 6.3.1.5 - Task Scheduler in Windows 8

Introduction

In this lab, you will schedule a task using the Windows 8 Task Scheduler utility. You will then make changes to your task and test your task by running it.

Recommended Equipment

- A computer running Windows 8

Step 1:   Open the Task Scheduler utility.

a.   Log on to Windows as an administrator.

b.   Click **Control Panel > Administrative Tools > Task Scheduler**.

Step 2:   Run the Create Basic Task Wizard.

a.   Click **Create Basic Task** in the Actions pane.

b. On the **Create a Basic Task** screen of the **Create Basic Task Wizard** window, type **Disk Cleanup** in the **Name:** field, and then click **Next**.

c. On the **Task Trigger** screen, select the **Weekly** radio button. Click **Next**.

d.   On the **Weekly** screen, use the scroll buttons in the **Start:** field to set the time to **6:00:00 PM**. Set the **Recur every _ weeks on:** field to **1**. Check the **Friday** checkbox. Click **Next**.

Note: The date field will display today's date. It is not necessary to change the date.

e.   On the **Action** screen, make sure **Start a program** is selected. Click **Next**.

f.   On the **Start a program** screen, click **Browse**.

g.   Type **cle** in the **File name:** field, select **cleanmgr.exe**, and click **Open**.

h. The **Start a Program** screen re-opens with **C:\Windows\System32\cleanmgr.exe** added to the **Program/script:** field. Click **Next**.

i. Review the **Summary** screen, and click **Finish**.

Step 3:   Review and make changes to your scheduled task.

a.   In the left pane of the **Task Scheduler** window, select **Task Schedule Library**.

Note: You may need to click **Refresh** to see the new **Disk Cleanup** task you created.

b.   Select the task **Disk Cleanup** and then click **Properties** in the right pane.

c.   The **Disk Cleanup Properties (Local Computer)** window opens. In the **Configure for:** drop-down menu,
select **Windows 8.1**. Click **OK**.

Note: For Windows 8.0, select **Windows 8** in the **Configure for:** field.

d.   Click the **Actions** tab. Select the **Start a program** row, and then click **Edit**.

e. The **Edit Action** window opens. Type **/d c:** in the **Add Arguments (optional):** field. Click **OK**.

Note: The **/d c:** argument tells the cleanmgr.exe program to clean the C: drive.

f. To close the **Disk Cleanup Properties (Local Computer)** window, click **OK**.

Step 4:   Run the scheduled task now.

a. Select the **Disk Cleanup** task, and click **Run** in the right pane of the **Task Scheduler** window.

b. Click the **Disk Cleanup** icon that appears on the **Task Bar**.

c. The **Disk Cleanup** window is brought to the foreground. This window displays the status of the **Disk Cleanup** process.

Note: It may take a few minutes for Disk Cleanup to complete.

d. Once the Disk Cleanup process completes, the **Disk Cleanup for Local Disk (C:)** window opens. Click **Cancel**.

Note: Clicking **OK** will delete the files selected in the **Files to delete:** box. **Check with your instructor before clicking OK.** Clicking OK will open the **Disk Cleanup** verification window asking if you are sure you want to permanently delete these files. It is not necessary to delete these files to complete this lab. If you are sure you want to delete these files permanently, click **Delete Files**.

Step 5:   Delete a scheduled task.

a.   To delete the **Disk Cleanup** task you created, select the **Disk Cleanup** task and click **Delete** in the right
pane of the **Task Scheduler** window.

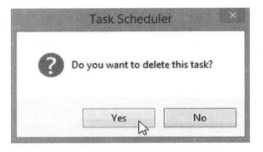

b.   The **Task Scheduler verification** window opens asking if you want to delete this task. Click **Yes.**

c.   Verify the **Disk Cleanup** task you created is removed from the **Task Scheduler** window. Close **Task
Scheduler**.

Reflection

What other weekly tasks would be useful to run in Task Scheduler?

_____

_____

_____

_____

_____

Lab 6.3.1.7 - System Restore in Windows 7 and Vista

Introduction

In this lab, you will create a restore point and then use it to restore your computer.

Recommended Equipment

- A computer running Windows 7 or Vista

Step 1:   Create a restore point.

a.   Click **Control Panel > System > System protection**.

b. Click the **System Protection** tab in the **System Properties** window and click **Create**.

c. In the **Create a restore point** description field of the **System Protection** window, type **Application Installed**. Click **Create**.

d. The **System Protection** window displays the progress of the creation of the restore point. When the message **The restore point was created successfully** displays, click **Close**.

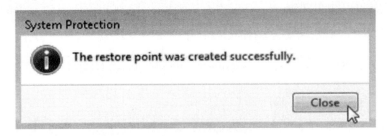

e. Click **OK** to close the **System Properties** window.

Step 2:   Work in the System Restore utility.

a. Click **Start > All Programs > Accessories > System Tools > System Restore**.

b. When the **System Restore** window opens, click **Next**.

c. The **System Restore** window displays a list of restore points.

What type of restore point was created in step 1?

_____

d. Close all open windows.

Step 3:   Make changes to your computer.

a.   Click **Control Panel > Programs and Features > Turn Windows features on or off**.

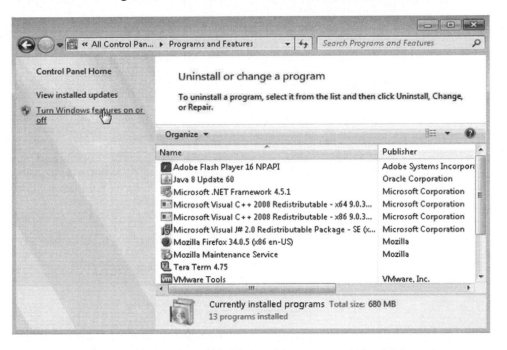

b.   The **Windows Features** window opens. Click the **Internet Information Services** checkbox, and click **OK**.

c. A progress window opens displaying the progress bar of **changes to features**. This window will close on its own when the configuration changes are complete.

d. Once the changes have completed and the progress window closes, close all remaining open windows.

Step 4:   Open Windows Explorer browser to display the default localhost page.

a. Open **Internet Explorer** and type http://localhost and press **Enter**. The IIS default page will open. This page indicates that the IIS Server is running on your computer.

b. Close the browser.

Step 5:   Create a new document and store it in the Documents folder.

a. To open the Notepad application, click **Start,** type **notepad**, and press **Enter**.

b. In the **Untitled – Notepad** window, type the sentence **This is a test for a Restore Point** and click **File > Save As…**.

c.   In the **Save As** window, click **Documents,** and type **Restore Point Test file** in the **File Name:** field. Click **Save**.

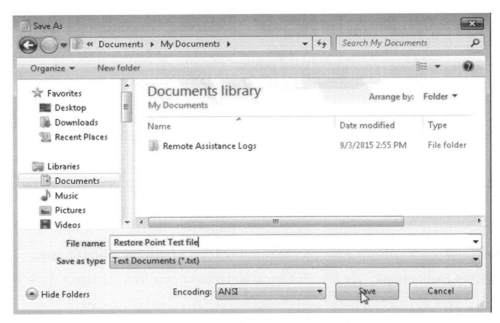

d.   Close **Notepad**.

Step 6:   Verify that you successfully installed the IIS service.

a.   Click **Control Panel > Administrative Tools > Internet Information Services (IIS) Manager**.

b.   Being able to open the **Internet Information Services (IIS) Manager** utility indicates that the IIS Server installed successfully. Close all open windows.

Step 7:   Restore the computer using the restore point you created in Step 1.

   a.   Click **Start > All Programs > Accessories > System Tools > System Restore** to open the **System Restore** window.

   b.   Select the **Recommended restore** radio button, and click **Next**.

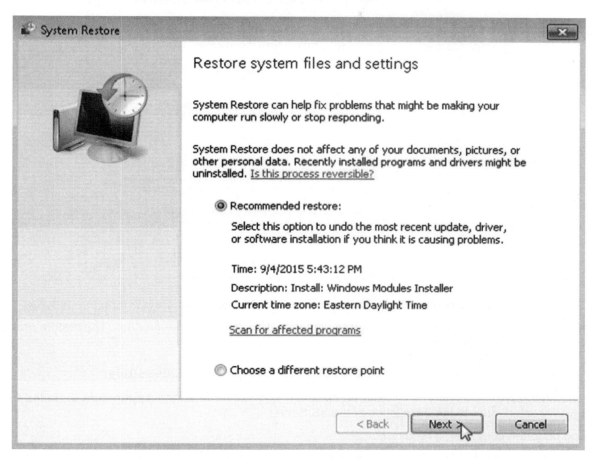

c.   The **Confirm your restore point window** opens. Click **Finish**.

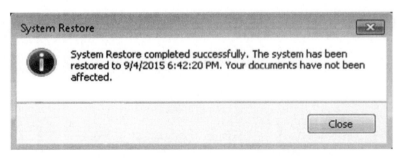

d.   The **System Restore** confirmation window opens. Click **Yes** to start the system restore process.

Note: Windows will restart the computer to complete the system restore process. The restore process can take several minutes.

Step 8:   Verify that the system restore process has completed successfully.

The operating system has now been restored back to how it looked when the **Application Installed** restore point was created, prior to the installation of the IIS Server.

a.   Log on to the computer, if required.

b.   You should see a **System Restore** window open informing you that the system restore completed successfully. Click **Close**.

c.   Click **Control Panel > Administrative Tools**.

Is the IIS Manager application listed?

_____

d.   Open the **Internet Explorer** browser, type http://localhost and press **Enter**.

Does the IIS Server page display?

_____

e.   Close **Internet Explorer**.

f.   Navigate to the **Documents** folder. Open the **Restore Point Test file.txt** file.

Is the Restore Point Test File.txt document in the Documents folder? If so, does it still have the sentence that you added in Step 5?

_____

g.   Close all open windows.

Reflection

When would be a good time to create a manual restore point? Why?

_____

_____

_____

_____

Lab 6.3.1.7 - System Restore in Windows 8

Introduction

In this lab, you will create a restore point and use it to restore your computer.

Recommended Equipment

- A computer running Windows 8

Step 1:   Create a restore point.

a.   Click **Control Panel > Recovery.**

b. Select **Configure System Restore** in the **Recovery** window.

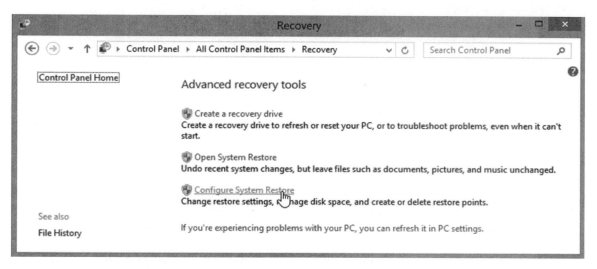

c. Click the **System Protection** tab in the **System Properties** window and then click **Create**.

d. In the **Create a restore point** description field of the **System Protection** window, type **Application Installed**. Click **Create**.

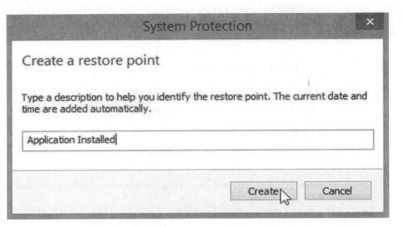

e. You will be notified in the **Systems Protection** window when the restore point has been created successfully. Once this message appears, click **Close**.

f. Click **OK** to close the **System Properties** window.

Step 2:   Work in the System Restore utility.

a. In the **Recovery** window, click **Open System Restore**.

b. The **System Restore** window opens, click **Next**.

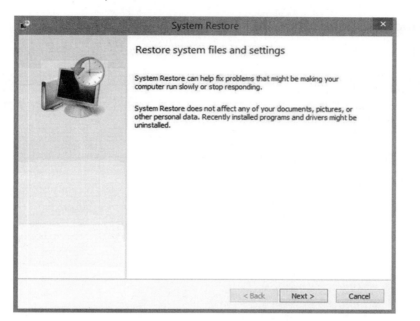

c. A list of restore points is displayed in the **System Restore** window.

What type of restore point did you create in step 1?

_____

d. Close all open windows.

Step 3: Make changes to your computer.

a. Click **Control Panel > Programs and Features > Turn Windows features on or off**.

b. The **Windows Features** window opens. Click the **Internet Information Services** checkbox, and click **OK**.

c.   The **Windows Features** window opens with an **Applying Changes** message. When the message displays **Windows completed the requested changes**, click **Close**.

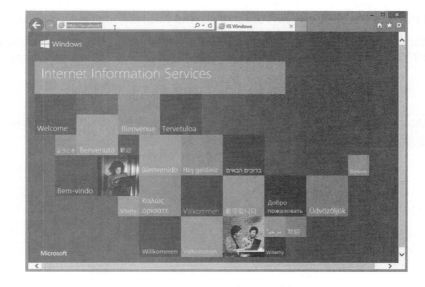

d.   Close all remaining open windows.

Step 4:   Open the Windows Explorer browser to display the default localhost page.

a.   Open **Internet Explorer**, type http://localhost, and press **Enter**. The IIS default page will open.

Note: The IIS initial page on Windows 8.0 appears differently than the example.

b.   Close the browser.

Step 5:   Create a new document and store it in the Documents folder.

a. To open the Notepad application, click **Start**, type **notepad**, and press **Enter**.

b. In the **Untitled – Notepad** window, type **This is a test for a Restore Point**, then click **File > Save As…**.

c. In the **Save As** window, click **Documents** and type **Restore Point Test file** in the **File Name:** field. Click **Save**.

d. Close **Notepad**.

Step 6:   Verify that you successfully installed the IIS service.

a. Click **Control Panel** > **Administrative Tools** > **Internet Information Services (IIS) Manager**.

b. If the **Internet Information Services (IIS) Manager** window opens asking **Do you want to get started with Microsoft Web Platform to stay connected with latest Web Platform Components?**, click **No**.

Note: Being able to open **Internet Information Services (IIS) Manager** window verifies that the IIS Server is installed on the computer.

c.   Close all open windows.

Step 7:   Restore the computer back to the restore point you created in step 1.

a.   Click **Control Panel > Recovery > Open System Restore**.

b.   In the **System Restore** window, select the **Application Installed** restore point that was created in step 1 and click **Next**.

c. The **Confirm your restore point window** opens. Click **Finish**.

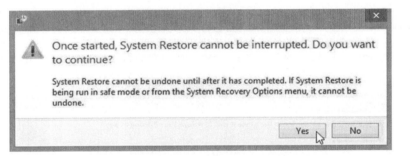

d. A warning message window opens telling you that the **System Restore** process should not be interrupted once it begins, and asks if you want to continue. Click **Yes** to start the System Restore process.

Note: Windows will restart the computer to complete the System Restore process.

Step 8: Verify that the System Restore process completed successfully.

The operating system restores to the point before the IIS application was installed. This can take several minutes to complete.

a. Logon to the computer if required.

b. The **System Restore** window opens informing you that the System Restore completed successfully. Click **Close**.

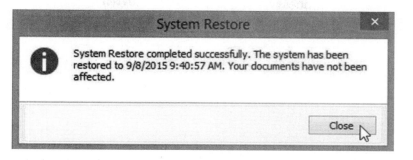

Note: You may need to click the desktop tile after Windows 8.0 reboots to see the **System Restore completed successfully** message.

c. From the **Control Panel,** click **Administrative Tools**.

Is the IIS Manager application listed?

_____

d. Open the **Internet Explorer** browser, type http://localhost and press **Enter**.

Did the IIS Server page display?

_____

e. Close **Internet Explorer**.

f. Open **File Explorer**, and navigate to the **Documents** folder.

Is the **Restore Point Test File.txt** in this folder? If so, are the contents the same in this document? Why?

_____

g. Close all open windows.

Reflection

When would be a good time to create a manual restore point? Why?

_____

_____

_____

_____

Chapter 7: Networking Concepts

Lab 7.3.2.6 - Build and Test Network Cables

Introduction

In this lab, you will build and test straight-through and crossover Unshielded Twisted-Pair (UTP) Ethernet network cables.

Note: With a straight-through cable, the color of wire used by pin 1 on one end is the same color used by pin 1 on the other end, and similarly for the remaining seven pins. The cable will be constructed using either TIA/EIA T568A or T568B standards for Ethernet. This determines which color wire is to be used on each pin. Straight-through cables are normally used to connect a host directly to a router, switch, or a wall plate in an office area.

With a crossover cable, the second and third pairs on the connector at one end of the cable are reversed at the other end. The pin-outs for the cable are the T568A standard on one end and the T568B standard on the other end. Crossover cables are normally used to connect switches or they can be used to connect two hosts directly together.

Recommended Equipment

- Two 2 to 3 ft. (0.6 to 0.9 meter) lengths of UTP cable, Category 5 or 5e
- A minimum of four RJ-45 connectors (more may be needed if miswiring occurs)
- An RJ-45 crimping tool
- Two computers with operating systems installed.
- Wire cutters
- Wire stripper
- Ethernet wire map tester
- Ethernet cable meter (optional)
- Ethernet certification meter (optional)

Wire Diagrams

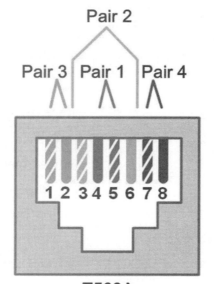

T568A

T568A Wiring Standard			
Pin No.	Pair No.	Wire Color	Function
1	3	White/Green	Transmit
2	3	Green	Transmit
3	2	White/Orange	Receive
4	1	Blue	Not used
5	1	White/Blue	Not used
6	2	Orange	Receive
7	4	White/Brown	Not used
8	4	Brown	Not used

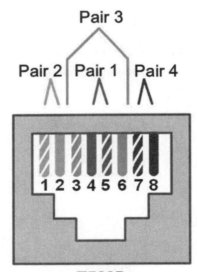

T568B Wiring Standard			
Pin No.	Pair No.	Wire Color	Function
1	2	White/Orange	Transmit
2	2	Orange	Transmit
3	3	White/Green	Receive
4	1	Blue	Not used
5	1	White/Blue	Not used
6	3	Green	Receive
7	4	White/Brown	Not used
8	4	Brown	Not used

Step 1:   Obtain and prepare the cable.

a. Determine the length of cable required. This could be the distance from a computer to a switch or between a device and an RJ-45 outlet jack. Add 12 in. (30.5 cm.) to the total distance. The TIA/EIA standard states the maximum length is 16.4 ft. (5 m). Standard Ethernet cable lengths are usually 2 ft (0.6 m.), 6 ft. (1.8 m.), or 10 ft. (3m).

Which length of cable did you choose and why did you choose this length?

_____

_____

b. Cut a piece of cable to the desired length. Stranded UTP cable is commonly used for patch cables (the cables between an end network device such as a PC and an RJ-45 connector) because it is more durable when bent repeatedly. It is called stranded because each of the wires within the cable is made up of many strands of fine copper wire, rather than a single solid wire. Solid wire is used for cable runs that are between the RJ-45 jack and a wiring closet.

c. Using wire strippers, remove 2 in (5 cm.) of the cable jacket from both ends of the cable.

Step 2:   Prepare and insert the wires.

a. Determine which wiring standard will be used. Circle the standard.

   T568A   **T568B**

b. Locate the correct table or figure from the **Wire Diagrams** based on the wiring standard used.

c. Spread the cable pairs and arrange them roughly in the desired order based on the standard chosen.

d. Untwist a short length of the pairs and arrange them in the exact order needed by the standard, moving left to right starting with pin 1. **It is very important to untwist as little as possible. The twists are important because they provide noise cancellation**.

e. Straighten and flatten the wires between your thumb and forefinger.

f. Ensure the cable wires are still in the correct order as the standard.

g. Cut the cable in a straight line to within 0.5 to .75 in. (1.25 to 1.9 cm.) from the edge of the cable jacket. If it is longer than this, the cable will be susceptible to crosstalk (the interference of bits from one wire with an adjacent wire).

h. The key (the prong that sticks out from the RJ-45 connector) should be on the underside pointing downward when inserting the wires. Ensure the wires are in order from left to right starting with pin 1. Insert the wires firmly into the RJ-45 connector until all wires are pushed to the end of the connector.

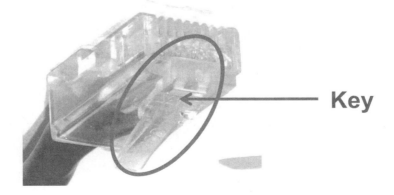

Key

Step 3:   Inspect, crimp, and re-inspect the connector.

a.   Visually inspect the cable and ensure the right colors are aligned to the correct pins.

b.   Visually inspect the end of the connector. The eight wires should be pressed firmly against the end of the RJ-45 connector. Some of the cable jacket should be inside the first portion of the connector. This provides strain relief for the cable. If the cable jacket is not far enough inside the connector, it may eventually cause the cable to fail.

c.   If everything is correctly aligned and inserted properly, place the RJ-45 connector and cable into the crimper. The crimper will push two plungers down on the RJ-45 connector.

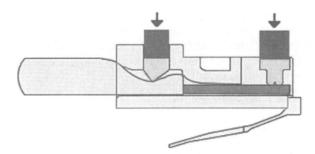

d.   Visually re-inspect the connector. If improperly installed, cut the end off and repeat the process.

Step 4:   Terminate the other cable end.

a.   Attach an RJ-45 connector to the other end of the cable.

b.   Visually re-inspect the connector. If improperly installed, cut the end off and repeat the process.

Which standard is used for patch cables in your school?

_____

Step 5:   Test the cable with a wiremap tester.

Turn on the tester and plug the cable into the jacks labeled with the wiring standard you used.

Note: If the tester does not have different jacks for different standards, refer to the documentation of the tester to determine how to test your cable.

All green lights on both parts of the tester should sequence to indicate that each wire is terminated correctly and in the proper order.

Any other lights indicate a wiring fault. Refer to the documentation of the tester to find which type of fault the cable has.

What did the lights indicate when you connected your cable? Write down the faults and pairs where the faults occurred if your cable did not pass.

_____

_____

_____

Step 6:   Test the cable using a cable meter or cable certification meter (Optional).

If your lab has a cable meter or cable certification meter, use it to validate your findings from the wiremap tester. If possible, use the meter to determine the exact length of the cable.

What were the findings from the cable meter or cable certification meter?

_____

_____

_____

Step 7:   Connect a computer using the cable.

a.   Connect a PC to another computer, router, or switch.

b.   Visually check the LED status lights on the NIC. If they are on (usually green or amber), the cable is functional.

c.   Open a command prompt on one of the computers.

d.   Type **ipconfig**.

e.   Write down the default gateway IP address.

_____

f.   From the command prompt, type **ping** *default gateway IP address*. If the cable is functional, the ping should be successful (provided that no other network problem exists and the default gateway router is connected and functional).

Was the ping successful? _____

If the ping fails, repeat the lab.

Step 8:   Build the crossover cable.

Build a cable using the T568A wiring standard on one end and the T568B wiring standard on the other.

How are these wiring standards different?

_____

Step 9:   Test the crossover cable.

Turn on the tester and plug the ends of the cable into the same wiring standard indicated on both parts of the tester. This is the same procedure as testing a straight-through cable.

What does the tester indicate?

_____

_____

If possible, test the crossover cable using a cable meter or cable certification meter. What does the meter indicate about the cable?

_____

_____

_____

Lab 7.4.1.11 - Configure a NIC to Use DHCP in Windows

Introduction

In this lab, you will configure an Ethernet NIC to use DHCP to obtain an IP address and test connectivity between two computers.

Recommended Equipment

- Wireless router
- Two computers running Windows
- Ethernet patch cables (straight-through cable)

Step 1:   Connect the hosts to the router.

a.   For **Host A**, plug one end of the Ethernet patch cable into **Port 1** of the router.

b.   For **Host A**, plug the other end of the Ethernet patch cable into the **network** port on the computer.

c.   For **Host B**, plug one end of the Ethernet patch cable into **Port 2** on the back of the router.

d.   For **Host B**, plug the other end of the Ethernet patch cable into the **network** port on the computer.

e.   Plug in the power cable of the router, if it is not already plugged in.

f.   Turn on both computers and log on to Windows on **Host A** as an **administrator**.

g.   Click **Control Panel > Network and Sharing Center**. The **Network and Sharing Center** window opens.

Step 2:   Set Host A's NIC to use DHCP.

a.   Click **Local Area Connection > Properties**. The **Local Area Connection Properties** window opens.

What is the name and model number of the NIC in the **Connect using:** field?

_____

What are the items listed in the **This connection uses the following items:** field?

_____

b.   Click **Internet Protocol Version 4 (TCP/IPv4) > Properties**. The **Internet Protocol Version 4 (TCP/IPv4) Properties** window opens.

What is listed for the IP address, Subnet mask, and Default gateway in the fields of the **Use the following IP address:** area?

_____

c. Select the **Obtain an IP address automatically** radio button, if it is not already selected.

d. Select the **Obtain DNS server address automatically** radio button, if it is not already selected.

e. Click **OK** to close the **Internet Protocol Version 4 (TCP/IPv4) Properties** window.

f. Click **OK** to close the **Local Area Connection Properties** window.

g. Click **Close** to close the **Local Area Connection Status** window.

Step 3:   Record Host A's IP address information.

a. Check the lights on the back of the NIC. These lights will blink when there is network activity.

b. Open a command window.

c. Type **ipconfig /all**, and then press the **Enter** key.

```
C:\Windows\system32\cmd.exe

Microsoft Windows [Version 6.1.7600]
Copyright (c) 2009 Microsoft Corporation.  All rights reserved.

C:\Users\Vicki>ipconfig /all

Windows IP Configuration

    Host Name . . . . . . . . . . . . : Vicki-PC
    Primary Dns Suffix  . . . . . . . :
    Node Type . . . . . . . . . . . . : Hybrid
    IP Routing Enabled. . . . . . . . : No
    WINS Proxy Enabled. . . . . . . . : No
    DNS Suffix Search List. . . . . . : va.shawcable.net

Ethernet adapter Local Area Connection:

    Connection-specific DNS Suffix  . : va.shawcable.net
    Description . . . . . . . . . . . : Marvell Yukon 88E8001/8003/8010 PCI Gigab
it Ethernet Controller
    Physical Address. . . . . . . . . : 00-11-2F-BD-08-C4
    DHCP Enabled. . . . . . . . . . . : Yes
    Autoconfiguration Enabled . . . . : Yes
    Link-local IPv6 Address . . . . . : fe80::54c7:9580:7107:3514%11(Preferred)
    IPv4 Address. . . . . . . . . . . : 192.168.1.112(Preferred)
    Subnet Mask . . . . . . . . . . . : 255.255.255.0
    Lease Obtained. . . . . . . . . . : Sunday, November 21, 2010 11:12:38 AM
    Lease Expires . . . . . . . . . . : Monday, November 22, 2010 11:12:38 AM
    Default Gateway . . . . . . . . . : 192.168.1.1
    DHCP Server . . . . . . . . . . . : 192.168.1.1
    DHCPv6 IAID . . . . . . . . . . . : 234885423
    DHCPv6 Client DUID. . . . . . . . : 00-01-00-01-14-67-04-99-00-11-2F-BD-08-C4

    DNS Servers . . . . . . . . . . . : 64.59.144.18
                                        64.59.144.19
                                        64.59.150.133
    NetBIOS over Tcpip. . . . . . . . : Enabled
```

What is the IP address of the computer? _____

What is the subnet mask of the computer? _____

What is the default gateway of the computer? _____

What are the DNS servers for the computer? _____

What is the MAC address of the computer? _____

Is DHCP enabled? _____

What is the IP address of the DHCP server? _____

On what date was the lease obtained? _____

On what date does the lease expire? _____

d.   Type **ping** *your IP address*. For example, **ping 192.168.1.112**.

```
C:\Windows\system32\cmd.exe                              _  □  X

C:\Users\Vicki>ping 192.168.1.112

Pinging 192.168.1.112 with 32 bytes of data:
Reply from 192.168.1.112: bytes=32 time<1ms TTL=128
Reply from 192.168.1.112: bytes=32 time<1ms TTL=128
Reply from 192.168.1.112: bytes=32 time<1ms TTL=128
Reply from 192.168.1.112: bytes=32 time<1ms TTL=128

Ping statistics for 192.168.1.112:
    Packets: Sent = 4, Received = 4, Lost = 0 (0% loss),
Approximate round trip times in milli-seconds:
    Minimum = 0ms, Maximum = 0ms, Average = 0ms

C:\Users\Vicki>
```

Record one of the replies from your ping command.

_____

If the ping was not successful, ask the instructor for assistance.

Step 4: Record Host B's IP address information.

a.   Log in to **Host B** as an administrator and ensure the **Obtain an IP address automatically** and the **Obtain DNS server address automatically** radio buttons are selected.

b.   Click **OK > OK**.

c.   Open a command window.

d.   Type **ipconfig /all**.

What is the IP address of the computer? _____

What is the subnet mask of the computer? _____

What is the default gateway of the computer? _____

What are the DNS servers for the computer? _____

What is the IP address of the DHCP server? _____

Step 5: Set static IP address information.

a.   Select the radio buttons **Use the following IP address** and **Use the following DNS server address**.

b.   Enter in the IP address information for the NIC from the previous step.

c.   Click **OK > OK**.

d.   Open a command window.

e.   Type **ping** *IP address for Host B*.

If the ping was not successful, ask the instructor for assistance.

Step 6: Verify connectivity.

a.   From **Host B**, type **ping** *IP address for Host A*.

Was the ping successful? _____

b.   From **Host A,** type **ping** *IP address for Host B*.

Was the ping successful? _____

c.   Return all network configurations to their original settings, unless stated otherwise by the instructor.

d.   Set the NIC to **Obtain an IP address automatically** and **Obtain DNS server address automatically**.

e.   Click **OK** > **OK**.

Chapter 8: Applied Networking

Lab 8.1.2.10 - Connect to a Router for the First Time

Introduction

In this lab, you will configure basic settings on a wireless router.

Recommended Equipment

- A computer with Windows installed
- An Ethernet NIC installed
- Wireless router
- Ethernet patch cable

Step 1:   Connect the computer to the router.

a. Ask the instructor for the following information that is used during the lab.

Router Address Information:

IP address: _____

Subnet mask: _____

Router name: _____

DHCP Server Setting Information:

Start IP address: _____

Maximum number of users: _____

Static DNS 1 (optional): _____

Router Access:

Router Password: _____

Note: Only use configurations assigned by the instructor.

b. Plug in the power of the wireless router. Boot the computer and log in as an administrator.

c. Connect the computer to one of the **Ethernet** ports on the wireless router with an Ethernet patch cable.

Note: If this is the first time connecting to the lab router, follow these instructions to set a network location. This will be explained later in the course.

d.   In the **Set Network Location** window, select **Public network**.

e.   Click **Close** to accept the network location Public.

f. Open a command prompt and type **ipconfig /renew**.

What is the default gateway for the computer?

_____

Step 2: Log in to the router.

a. Open **Internet Explorer**. Type the IP address of your default gateway in the **Address** field, and then press **Enter**.

b. In the **Windows Security** window, type **admin** in the **Password:** field and then click **OK**.

Note: If this user name and password combination does not work, ask your instructor or refer to the documentation of the router for the correct user name and password for your router.

c. The **Setup screen** appears.

In the **Internet Setup** section, what is the **Internet Connection Type** assigned to the router?

_____

d. Make sure the **Internet Connection Type** is set to **Automatic Configuration – DHCP**.

e. Locate the **Network Setup** section. Verify that the **DHCP Server** is enabled.

What is the Router IP address and the subnet mask?

_____

Record the DHCP Server Settings:

Start IP Address: _____

Maximum Number: _____

IP Address Range: _____

f. Enter the **Router Address** and **DHCP Server Setting** information provided by the instructor: **IP Address**, **Subnet Mask**, **Start IP Address**, and **Maximum Number of Users**.

g. Click **Save Settings**.

h. The router may need to reboot at this time. If necessary, reboot the router and log back in.

Step 3:   Find the IP address information of the computer.

a. Open a command prompt.

b. Type **ipconfig /all**, and record the following information.

Computer IP information:

IP address: _____

Subnet mask: _____

Gateway: _____

DNS (optional): _____

c. Click **Start > Control Panel > Network and Sharing Center > Change adapter settings**.

Note: In Windows Vista, click **Start > Control Panel > Network and Sharing Center > Manage network connections**.

d. In the **Network Connections** window, right-click the correct Ethernet adapter and select **Properties**. Click **Internet Protocol Version 4 (TCP/IPv4)** and select **Properties**.

e.   Use the recorded information to configure the NIC with static IP information. Click **OK**, and click **Close**.

Step 4:   Change QoS settings.

a.   Click the **Applications & Gaming** tab and then select **QoS**.

b.   Make sure **WMM Support** is enabled. Click **Save Settings > Continue**, if any changes were made.

Step 5:   Change router password.

a.   Click the **Administration** tab and then select **Management**.

b. Type **Network** in the Router **Password:** and **Re-enter to confirm:** fields.

c. Click **Save Settings > Continue**.

d. Log back into the router using the new IP address and password.

What IP address did you enter into the URL field of the browser?

_____

What password did you use to access the router GUI?

_____

Step 6:   Reset the router to the original configuration.

a. Unless stated otherwise by the instructor, restore the router back to factory default if the option is available.

If default restoration is not available, return the configurations to the following settings or settings provided by the instructor.

Router Address Information:

- o   IP address: 192.168.1.1
- o   Subnet mask: 255.255.255.0
- o   Router name: .... Router

DHCP Server Setting Information:

- o   Start IP address: 192.168.1.100
- o   Maximum number of users: .. 50
- o   Static DNS 1 (optional): .... 0.0.0.0 or leave it blank

Router Access:

- o   Router Password: .... Admin

b.   Navigate to the **Internet Protocol Version 4 (TCP/IPv4) Properties** window on the computer. Select **Obtain an IP address automatically** and **Obtain DNS server address automatically**. Click **OK**, and click **Close**.

c.   Close the browser, log off the computer, and turn off the router.

Lab 8.1.2.12 - Configure Wireless Router in Windows

Introduction

In this lab, you will configure and test the wireless settings on a wireless router.

Recommended Equipment

- A computer with Windows installed
- A Wireless NIC installed
- An Ethernet NIC installed
- A wireless Router
- Ethernet patch cable

Note: All wireless settings in this lab are for a 2.4 GHz wireless connection. Follow the same steps for setting up a 5 GHz wireless connection or when setting up both 2.4 GHz and 5 GHz connections.

Step 1:   Gathering information.

Ask the instructor for the following information:

Router IP Information (IP address and subnet mask): _____

Router name: _____

DHCP Server Information (start IP address and maximum number of hosts): _____

Static DNS 1 (optional): _____

SSID: _____

Channel number: _____

Router Username/Password: _____

Wireless Security (passphase key): _____

Note: Only use configurations assigned by the instructor.

Step 2:   Connecting to the wireless router.

a.   Plug in the power of the wireless router. Boot the computer and log in as an administrator.

b.   Connect the computer to one of the **Ethernet** ports on the wireless router with an Ethernet patch cable.

Note: If this is the first time connecting to the lab router, you must set the network location in Windows.

c.   Open the command prompt. Type **ipconfig /renew** to force the computer to request an IP address from the wireless router via DHCP.

What is the IP address of the default gateway for the computer?

_____

What device took the role of default gateway?

_____

_____

Step 3:   Logging into the wireless router.

a.   Open a web browser, type the IP address of your default gateway in the URL field, and then press **Enter**.

b.   The **Windows Security** window opens. Type the password provided by the instructor in the **Password** field and then click **OK**.

Step 4:   Configuring basic IP information.

a.   The Setup screen opens. Using the information provided by the instructor in **Step 1**, fill in the fields under
Router Address and **DHCP Server Setting.** The information includes **IP Address**, **Subnet Mask**,
Router Name, **Start IP Address**, and **Maximum Number of Users**. Click **Save Settings** to save the
changes.

b.   The **Your settings have been successfully saved. A system reboot is in progress and may take up
to 60 seconds** message is displayed.

c. Click **Continue** and wait for the wireless router boot process to complete before proceeding. After the router reboots, you may need to log back into it using the router IP address that was configured in this step.

Step 5: Configuring wireless settings.

a. In a web browser, enter the router IP address that you had configured in step 4 in the URL field. When prompted, enter the username and password.

b. Click the **Wireless** tab.

c. Click the **Network Mode** drop-down menu for the **5 GHz Wireless Settings**.

What 802.11 technologies are supported?

_____

d. Click the **Channel** drop-down menu under **5 GHz Wireless Settings**.

What channels are listed?

_____

e. Disable **Network Mode** for the **5 GHz Wireless settings**.

f. Click the **Network Mode** drop-down menu under 2.4GHz Wireless Settings.

What 802.11 technologies are supported?

g. Choose **Mixed** in the **Network Mode** drop-down menu.

What is the default SSID for the wireless router?

h. Type **Cisco#** in the **Network Name (SSID)** field, where # is the number assigned by the instructor.

i. Click the **Channel** drop-down menu for the **2.4GHz Wireless Settings**.

What channels are listed?

j. Select the Channel number that was provided by the instructor.

k. Click **Save Settings > Continue**, then close the browser.

Step 6:   Connecting the computer to the wireless network.

a.   Unplug the Ethernet cable from the computer.

b.   View wireless networks associated with the wireless adapter configured for the computer by following the path:

Start > Control Panel > Network and Sharing Center > Connect to a network

A list of available wireless networks is displayed.

What wireless network(s) are available?

_____

c. Choose **Cisco#**, where # is the number assigned by the instructor, make sure **Connect automatically** is selected, and then click the **Connect** button.

d. When the **Set Network Location** window opens, select **Public network > Close**.

Step 7: Hiding the SSID.

a. Open a browser. Type the IP address of your default gateway in the URL field, and then press **Enter**.

b. The **Windows Security** window opens. Type the password provided by the instructor in the **Password**: field.

c. The Setup screen opens. Navigate to **Basic Wireless Settings**. Select **Disable** for the 2.4 GHz SSID broadcast.

d. Click **Save Settings > Continue**.

Why would you disable SSID broadcast?

_____

e. Close all open windows.

f. View wireless networks associated with the wireless adapter configured to the computer by following the path:

Start > Control Panel > Network and Sharing Center > Connect to a network

What wireless network(s) are available?

_____

g. Because the wireless router is not broadcasting the SSID, the wireless network name does not appear in the wireless networks list detected by **Windows**. To connect **Windows** to a wireless network that does not broadcast its SSID, the SSID you must know the wireless network's SSID.

h. Go back to **Network and Sharing Center**. If **Network and Sharing Center** is no longer open, open it again.

i.   Click **Manage wireless networks**.

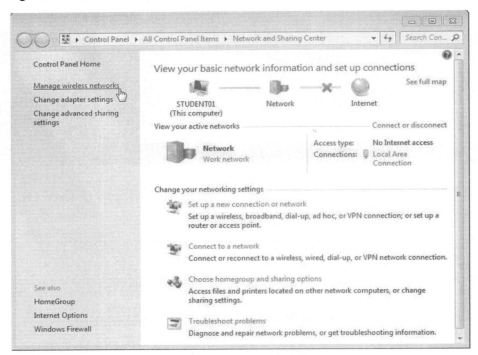

j.   When the **Manage Wireless Networks** window opens, double click **Cisco#**, where # is the number assigned to you.

Note: The wireless router is currently configured to not broadcast the wireless network SSID. The reason why it appears in this list is that the **Cisco#** network was added to this computer before.

k. Select the check box **Connect even if the network is not broadcasting its name (SSID)**, then click **OK**.

l. View wireless networks associated with the wireless adapter configured for the computer.

What wireless network(s) are available?

Step 8:   Adding security to the wireless network.

a.   Connect to **Cisco#**, where # is the number assigned by the instructor and log into the router using a web browser.

b.   Click the **Wireless** tab and then select **Wireless Security**.

c.   In the **Security Mode** drop-down box, for the **2.4GHz Wireless Security**, select **WPA2 Personal**.

d.   Type **ITEv6.0!** for the Passphrase and click **Save Settings > Continue**.

You should have lost connection to the wireless router. Why did that happen?

_____

_____

_____

Step 9:   Connecting the computer to a secure wireless network.

a.   View wireless networks associated with the wireless adapter configured to the computer.

b.   Choose **Cisco#**, where # is the number assigned by the instructor, make sure **Connect automatically** is selected, and then click the **Connect** button.

c. When the **Connect to a Network** window opens, type **ITEv6.0!** for the **Security key**, and then click **OK**.

Step 10: Cleaning up.

a. Connect the computer to one of the **Ethernet** ports on the wireless router with an Ethernet patch cable.

b. Return configurations by restoring to factory default or using the following settings:

Router Address Information:
- o IP address 192.168.1.1
- o Subnet mask 255.255.255.0
- o Router name Linksys

DHCP Server Setting Information:
- o Start IP address 192.168.1.100
- o Maximum number of users 50
- o Static DNS 1 (optional): 0.0.0.0 or leave it blank

SSID Values:
- o Network Name (SSID): Linksys
- o SSID Broadcast: Disabled

Channel Number:
- o Channel: Auto

Router Access:
- o Router Password: admin

Wireless Security:
- o Security Mode: Disable

c. Close the browser and logoff the computer.

Lab 8.1.2.14 - Test the Wireless NIC in Windows

Introduction

In this lab, you will check the status of your wireless connection, investigate the availability of wireless networks, and test connectivity.

Recommended Equipment

- A computer running Windows
- A wireless NIC installed
- An Ethernet NIC installed
- A wireless router
- Internet connectivity

Step 1:   Ping the loopback.

a.   Disconnect the Ethernet cable from your computer.

What are the names of the wireless connections that are available?

_____

b.   Connect to the classroom wireless network. Ask your instructor for the SSID and log on credentials if necessary.

c.   Open a command window.

d.   Ping **127.0.0.1** to test the loopback.

How many replies did you receive? _____

Why would you perform this test?

_____

Step 2:   Ping the default gateway.

a.   Use the **ipconfig** command.

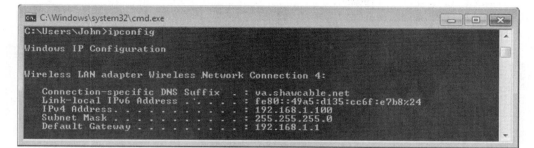

What is the IP address of the default gateway? _____

b.   **Ping** the **default gateway**. A successful ping indicates that there is a connection between the computer and the default gateway.

```
C:\Windows\system32\cmd.exe                                         [_][□][x]
C:\Users\John>ping 192.168.1.1

Pinging 192.168.1.1 with 32 bytes of data:
Reply from 192.168.1.1: bytes=32 time=2ms TTL=64
Reply from 192.168.1.1: bytes=32 time<1ms TTL=64
Reply from 192.168.1.1: bytes=32 time=1ms TTL=64
Reply from 192.168.1.1: bytes=32 time<1ms TTL=64

Ping statistics for 192.168.1.1:
    Packets: Sent = 4, Received = 4, Lost = 0 (0% loss),
Approximate round trip times in milli-seconds:
    Minimum = 0ms, Maximum = 2ms, Average = 0ms

C:\Users\John>
```

Step 3:   Find computers on the network.

a.   Type **net view** to make sure that you can see the other computers on the network. This indicates that there are no problems with the network between your computer and other computers on the same network.

```
Administrator: C:\Windows\system32\cmd.exe                          [_][□][x]
C:\Users\Administrator>net view
Server Name            Remark
---------------------------------------------------------------------------
\\BRAXTON-PC
\\STUDENT01
The command completed successfully.

C:\Users\Administrator>
```

List the computer names that are displayed.

_____

b. Use the **tracert** command along with your school's Web site or the Cisco Networking Academy Web site. Example: type **tracert www.netacad.com**.

```
Administrator: C:\Windows\system32\cmd.exe

C:\>tracert www.netacad.com

Tracing route to liferay-prod-1009279580.us-east-1.elb.amazonaws.com [107.21.30.
124]
over a maximum of 30 hops:

  1     3 ms     3 ms     5 ms  rcdn-dmzbb-891.cisco.com [10.99.57.17]
  2    37 ms    36 ms    37 ms  rcdn-access-hub-tun10.cisco.com [10.88.208.1]
  3    32 ms    36 ms    36 ms  rcdn9-sdfd-access-gw1-gig3-2.cisco.com [10.101.9
.89]
  4    37 ms    37 ms    36 ms  rcdn9-cd2-sbb-gw2-eth7-25.cisco.com [72.163.16.1
89]
  5    37 ms    37 ms    38 ms  rcdn9-cd1-corp-gw1-ten0-1-0.cisco.com [72.163.16
.54]
  6    37 ms    37 ms    38 ms  rcdn9-cd1-dmzbb-gw1-vla777.cisco.com [72.163.0.7
7]
  7    37 ms    38 ms    38 ms  rcdn9-cd1-isp-gw1-ten0-0-0.cisco.com [72.163.0.6
]
  8    38 ms    38 ms    37 ms  rcdn9-sdfc-isp-ssu2-ten1-1.cisco.com [72.163.0.8
6]
  9    40 ms    37 ms    38 ms  rcdn9-sdfa-isp-ssu1-vla851.cisco.com [72.163.0.9
8]
 10    38 ms    36 ms    38 ms  rcdn9-cd1-isp-gw1-ten0-1-0.cisco.com [72.163.0.8
1]
 11    38 ms    39 ms    39 ms  xe-10-0-3.edge9.Dallas1.Level3.net [4.30.74.45]
 12    48 ms    48 ms    49 ms  vlan60.csw1.Dallas1.Level3.net [4.69.145.62]
 13    38 ms    38 ms    38 ms  ae-63-63.ebr3.Dallas1.Level3.net [4.69.151.134]
 14    57 ms    58 ms    58 ms  ae-7-7.ebr3.Atlanta2.Level3.net [4.69.134.22]
 15    71 ms    71 ms    71 ms  ae-2-2.ebr1.Washington1.Level3.net [4.69.132.86]
 16    72 ms    85 ms    77 ms  ae-91-91.csw4.Washington1.Level3.net [4.69.134.1
42]
 17   166 ms   150 ms    71 ms  ae-4-90.edge2.Washington1.Level3.net [4.69.149.2
06]
 18   164 ms    75 ms   140 ms  AMAZON.COM.edge2.Washington1.Level3.net [4.79.22
.74]
```

What IP address was returned?

_____

How many devices (hops) are displayed?

_____

Why would you perform this test?

_____

c. Use the **nslookup** command with the IP address you just discovered. Type **nslookup 72.163.6.233**.

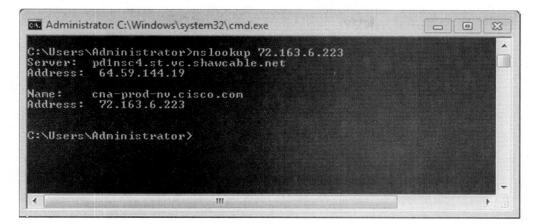

What name was returned?

_____

Why would you perform this test?

_____

Step 4:   Test your Internet connection.

a. Open a web browser.

b. Type **www.cisco.com** in the **Address** field, and then press **Enter**.

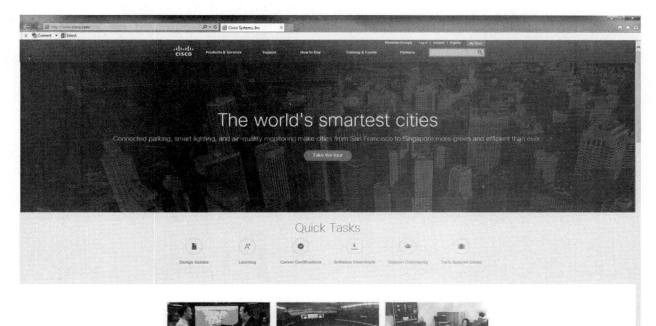

c.   Click **Control Panel > Network and Sharing Center >**. **Change adapter settings.**

Note: In Windows Vista, click **Control Panel > Network and Sharing Center >**. **Manage network connections.**

d.   Right-click the **Wireless Network Connection** icon **> Status**.

The **Wireless Network Connection Status** window opens.

What is the state of the media?

_____

What is the signal quality?

_____

e.   Click **Close**.

Reflection

1.   What information does a positive response from the default gateway provide for you when the computer has no Internet connection?

_____

_____

2.   If you receive a positive response from the default gateway, but you have no Internet access, where is the problem?

_____

_____

Lab 8.1.3.9 - Share Resources in Windows

Introduction

In this lab, you will create and share a folder, set permissions for the shares, create a **Homegroup** and a **Workgroup** to share resources, and map a network drive.

Due to **Windows Vista** lack of **Homegroup** support, networks running **Windows Vista** or earlier must be configured as a **Workgroup** before resources can be easily shared. When working with **Windows 7** or later, **Homegroup** is recommended.

In Part 1 of this lab, you will configure the computers to share resources by verifying that the computer that is sharing the resources is in the Home or Private network.

Part 2 of this lab focuses on Windows 7 and 8; you will create and share a folder, set permission for the shared folder, create a **Homegroup,** and map a network drive. Part 3 of this lab focuses on Workgroup using Windows Vista or later.

Note: The steps for sharing a folder, setting permissions for the shared folders and mapping network drives are similar for Windows 7 and Vista; they will be only be shown for Windows 7, as a result of this similarity.

Recommended Equipment

- Two or more computers running Windows Vista, 7, or 8 that are connected to each, either directly or through a switch.

To better identify which steps are performed on which computer, the lab will refer to them as **computer01**, **computer02**, or both. Switch to the other computer only when directed to do so within the instructions.

Two users were created for this lab: **User1** was created on **computer01,** and **User2** was created on **computer02**.

Part 1:   Setting Up Windows for Sharing

In this part, you will set up Windows computer for sharing. In order for the computer to share its resources using the default sharing setting provided by Windows, the network settings need to be set to private network.

Step 1:   Set up Windows 8.1 for sharing.

a.   Before you can share files and folders in Windows 8.1, set the network connection to **Private**. On **computer01**, follow the path:

Start Screen > type **pc settings >** click **PC Settings**

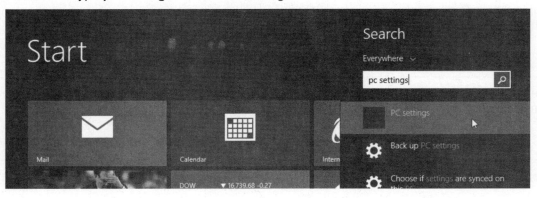

b.   The **PC Settings** window opens. Select **Network.**

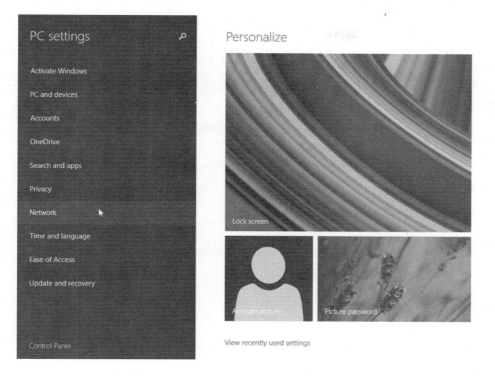

c.   The **Network** window opens. Select **Connections >** the network connection you want to change.

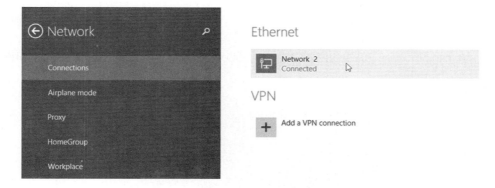

d.   Under **Find devices and content**, turn the **Find PCs, devices and content on this network...** switch to **On**.

e. To confirm the chosen network connection is now set to **Private**, open the **Network and Sharing Center** by following the path:

Control Panel > Network and Sharing Center

The network should now be listed as **Private**.

Now that the network connection setting is set to **Private network**, you should be able to share resources with other Windows computers in the same private network.

Step 2:   Set up Windows 8.0 for sharing.

a. For Windows 8, click the network icon (![icon]) in the bottom right of the desktop. The **Networks** side bar opens.

b. Right-click the desired network name and click **Turn sharing on or off**.

c. Click **Yes, turn on sharing and connect to devices** to turn on sharing.

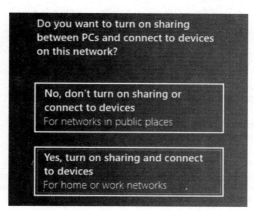

d. Navigate to the **Control Panel > Network and Sharing Center >** verify that you are in private network.

Step 3: Change the network type to Home Network in Windows 7.

a. On **computer01**, click **Start > Control Panel > Network and Sharing Center >** click **Public network**, **Work network** or **Home network**.

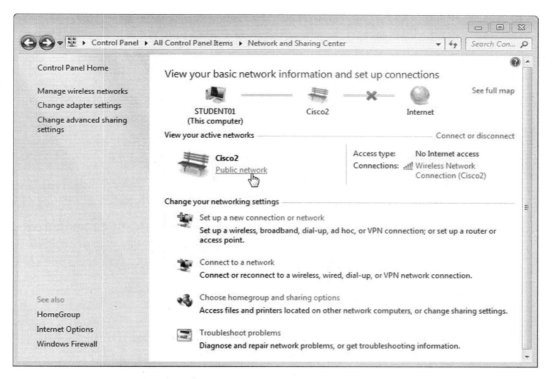

b. The **Set Network Location** window opens. Click **Home network**. If it is already set to **Home network**, click **Cancel** to continue.

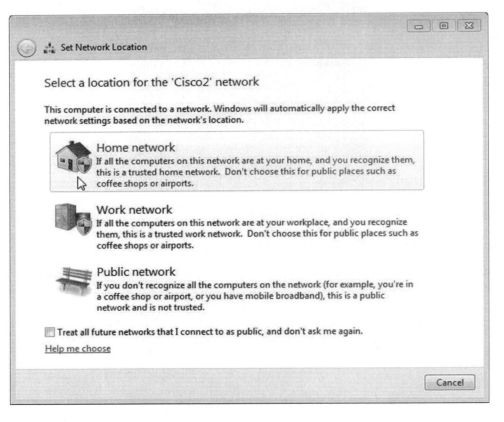

c. Click **Close**. Verify that the network location is set to **Home network**.

d. If the **Create a Homegroup** window displays, click **Cancel** for now. A homegroup will be created later in the lab.

Step 4:   Change the network type to private network in Windows Vista.

a. On the Windows Vista computer, click **Start > Control Panel > Network and Sharing Center**.

b.   Click **Customize** to set network settings.

c.   Click **Private** to allow network discovery. Click **Next**. Click **OK** and click **Close**.

Part 2:   Sharing Resources in Windows 7 and 8

Step 1:   Prepare to share a folder in Windows.

a.   On **computer01**, click **Start > Control Panel > Folder Options**.

b. Click the **View** tab. Uncheck the **Use Sharing Wizard (Recommended)** checkbox, and then click **OK**.

Step 2: Create the folder to be shared.

a. On **computer01**, right-click any empty area on the **Desktop**, and then choose **New > Folder**.

b. Name the folder **Example**.

c. Open **Notepad** and type **This is an example document**.

d. Save the file in the **Example** folder with the name **Brief**, and then close **Notepad**.

Step 3: Share the folder.

a. On **computer01**, right-click the **Example** folder, and then choose **Properties** > select the **Sharing tab** > click **Advanced Sharing**.

b.   Select the **Share this folder** checkbox, and then click **OK**. Click **Close** to close the **Example Properties** window.

c.   On the computer with the shared folder, click **Start > Control Panel > System**.

What is the name of the computer?

_____

Step 4:   Access a shared folder on a remote computer.

a.   On computer02, choose Start > Search programs and files. Type **\\computer01\Example**. Notice that computer01 is the name of the computer with the Example folder, and then press Enter. In Windows 8, navigate to the Start screen, and type **\\computer01\Example** and press Enter.

Due to security, it may be necessary to enter a username and password before **computer01\Example** can be accessed from **computer02**. If this happens, make sure to enter the username and password for **computer01**, the computer that is sharing the resource. In the example window below, the username **User1**, a user created only in **computer01**, was used to gain access to the resources shared by **computer01**.

When you have successfully accessed the resource shared by **computer01**, the content in the folder **Example** is displayed.

Can you open the **Brief** file? _____

Can you delete the **Brief** file? What happens?

_____

b. Click **Cancel**.

Step 5:   Change the permissions of a shared folder.

a.   Return to **computer01**, the computer with the shared folder.

b.   Right-click the **Example** folder, and then choose **Properties** > select the **Sharing** tab > click **Advanced Sharing** > click **Permissions**.

What are the default permissions?

_____

What needs to be changed to allow any remote users to make changes in the **Example** folder?

_____

c.   Allow **Everyone** to change the contents of the **Example** folder by checking the box on the **Allow** column and **Change** row. Click **OK** to close the **Permissions** window. Click **OK** to close the **Advanced Sharing** window. Click **Close** to **Example Properties** window.

d.   Go back to **computer02** and open the **Example** folder again by following the path.

e.   **Start Screen** > type **\\computer01\Example** > press **Enter**.

Can you open the **Brief** file?

_____

Can you delete the **Brief** file? What happens?

_____

f.   Close all open windows on both **computer01** and **computer02**.

g.   Go back to **computer01** and delete the shared folder.

Step 6:   Map a network drive.

a.   On **computer02**, open **Windows Explorer** or **File Explorer** in Windows 8 by clicking the Folder icon ( ) in the **Taskbar.**

b.   In the **Windows Explorer** window or **File Explorer** window in Windows 8, right-click **Network** > select **Map network drive**.

c.   Set the Drive to "**S**" and then click **Browse….**

d.   When the window is populated, expand the other computer and select **User1 > OK**.

Note: If the window is not populated, make sure Network Discovery is turned on. To turn on Network Discovery, go to **Control Panel > Network and Sharing Center > Change advanced sharing settings > select Turn on Network Discovery** in the current profile.

e. The **What network folder would you like to map?** screen opens. Click **Finish**.

f. Close all open windows.

g. Click **Start > Computer** in Windows 7 and 8.0.

   Note: Click **Start > This PC** in Windows 8.1.

Which **Network Location** drive do you see?

_____

Step 7:   Create a homegroup.

In this step, a homegroup is created if there is no homegroup available on the network.

a.   On **computer01**, click **Start > Control Panel > HomeGroup**. Click **Create a homegroup**.

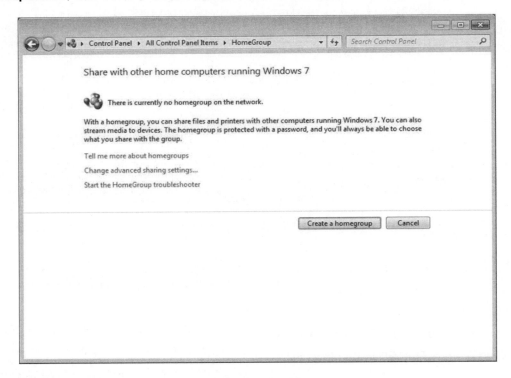

b.   Make sure **Documents** is checked, and then click **Next**.

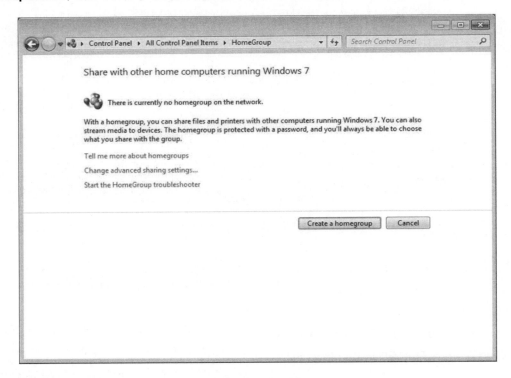

c. Record the **Homegroup** password. Notice it is case sensitive.

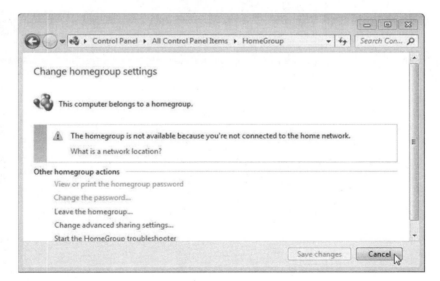

d. Click **Finish**.

Step 8: Verify the availability of a homegroup.

a. On **computer02**, click **Start > Control Panel > HomeGroup**.

Why is **Homegroup** not available?

If a homegroup is not available, click **What is a network location?** to change your Network Type in Windows 7 in the **Change homegroup settings**. Select **Home network**. Click **Close**.

In Windows 8.0, click **Change network location** to change the Network Type in the **Change homegroup settings**. Click **Yes, turn on sharing and connect to devices**.

In Windows 8.1, click **Change network location** to change the Network Type in the **Change homegroup settings**. Click **Yes**.

Step 9: Join the homegroup.

a. On **computer02**, click **Start > Control Panel > HomeGroup**. Click **Join now**. Click **Next** again for Windows 8.

b. Make sure **Documents** is checked or the permission is set to **Shared**, and then click **Next**.

c. Enter the password you recorded when the **Homegroup** was created and click **Next**.

d.   Click **Finish**.

Step 10: Create folders and files to be shared within a homegroup.

a.   On both computers, click **Start > Documents**.

b.   On **computer01,** create a folder, in **Document library**, called **Computer01**.

c.   On **computer02,** create a folder, in **Document library**, called **Computer02**.

   Note: For Windows 8.1, create folders in **This PC > Documents,** called **Computer01** and **Computer02**.

d.   For both computers, open **Notepad** and type the following text: "This file is shared in a homegroup". Next, save the file as **MyFile1** in the folder you just created on **computer01** and **MyFile2** in the folder you just created on **computer02**.

e.   Close all open windows.

Step 11: Add homegroup and network shortcuts to Start Menu for Windows 7.

On both computers, complete the following if it is not already configured on the computer.

a.   Right-click **Start > Properties > Start Menu** tab **> Customize**.

b.   Scroll down until you see both the **Homegroup** and **Network** items.

c.   Check both **Homegroup** and **Network**, if this is not already done, and then click **OK > OK**.

Step 12: Access Resources via Homegroup.

a.   On **computer02**, click **Start** then the **Homegroup** icon in the Start menu.

Locate the **Homegroup** icon, click the expand arrow next to the other computer name, click **Documents**, and then double-click **Computer01**.

In Windows 8, open **File Explorer** and locate **Homegroup** in the left panel.

You should be able to read the file, but can you delete the file located on the other computer? _____

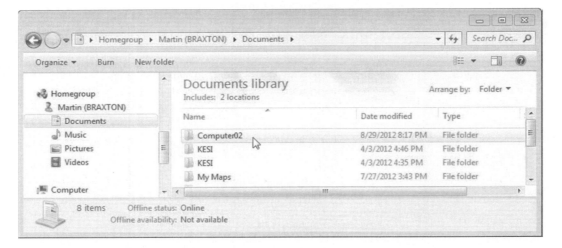

b.   Right-click on **MyFile1 > Properties > Security** tab **>** select **HomeUsers**.

What are the **Permissions for HomeUsers**? _____

c.   Click **Cancel**.

d.   Close all open windows.

Step 13: Clean up.

On both computers, return configurations to the following settings:

a.   Delete all folders and files created on the computer.

b.   Leave the **Homegroup** by following the path:

Start > Control Panel > Homegroup > Leave the homegroup > Leave the homegroup > Finish.

c.   Set the network location type back to **Public** network.

For Windows 7, **Control Panel > Network and Sharing Center > click Home network > click Public network**.

For Windows 8.0, click the Network icon in the bottom right of the desktop > right-click the desired network > click **Turn sharing on or off** > click **No, don't turn on sharing or connect to devices**.

For Windows 8.1, **Start > PC Settings > Network > Connections >** click desired network name **> Turn off sharing**.

d.   Check the box **Use sharing Wizard (Recommended)**. The checkbox can be found at:

Start > Control Panel > Folder Options > View tab

e.   Delete any mapped drives by following the path:

Start > right-click **Network > Disconnect network drive >** select network drive **> OK**

Part 3:   Creating or Joining a Workgroup

Step 1:   Create or join a workgroup.

Workgroup name: GROUP#, where # is a number used to make the name unique within the class environment. Feel free to allow the students to pick a name on their own.

Workgroup is the name of Microsoft's term for peer-to-peer local area network.

To create or join a **Workgroup**, you will need a Workgroup name. Ask your instructor for the Workgroup name to be used.

What is the Workgroup name?

_____

a. On both computers, click **Start > Control Panel > System**. Click **Change settings**.

b. The **System Properties** window opens. Click **Change....**

c.   In the **Computer Name/Domain Change** window, make sure **Workgroup** is selected and type **GROUP#**, where # is the group number assigned by the instructor. Click **OK**.

d.   Click **OK** when the **Welcome to the GROUP# workgroup** screen opens.

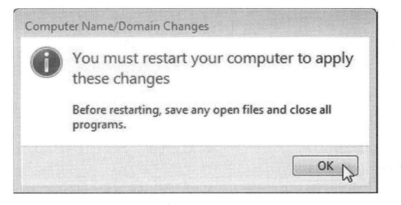

e.   Click **OK** and then **Restart Now** to restart the computer.

f.   Click **Close** in the **System Properties** window. Click **Restart Now** to restart the computer.

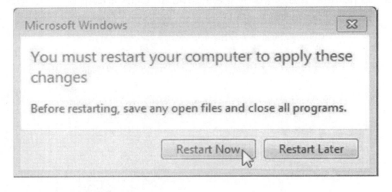

Step 2:   Verify access to network resources.

After restarting both computers, you will verify that the computers can access the shared resources within the workgroup.

a.   On both computers, click **Start > Control Panel > System**.

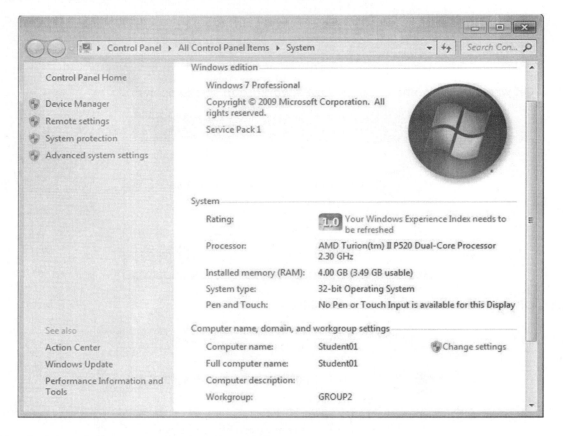

What is the workgroup name for the computer?

_____

b.   Close the **System** window.

c. In **computer01**, open the **Windows Explorer** in Windows Vista and 7 or **File Explorer** in Windows 8, click **Network** to locate the resources in **computer02**. Enter the user credentials for **computer01** if prompted.

Step 3:   Clean up.

Change the workgroup to the default Workgroup.

Start > Control Panel > System > click **Change settings > click Change >** type **Workgroup** in the Workgroup field **>** click **OK** and restart the computer.

Lab 8.1.4.3 - Remote Assistance in Windows

Introduction

In this lab, you will remotely connect to a computer, examine device drivers, and provide remote assistance.

Recommended Equipment

- Two Windows 7, Windows 8, or Vista computers connected to a LAN.
- The two computers must be part of the same Workgroup and on the same subnet.

Step 1: Create a Remote Assistance folder on the desktop of PC-2.

a. Log on to PC-2 as a member of the administrator group. Ask your instructor for the user name and password.

b. Right-click PC-2's desktop and select **New > Folder**. Name the folder **Remote Permission**.

c. Right-click the **Remote Permission** folder, then select **Properties > Sharing > Advanced Sharing.**

d. The **Advanced Sharing** window opens. Check the **Share this folder** checkbox. Click **OK**.

e.   Click the **Security** tab. Make sure the user name **ITEuser** is listed. Click **Close**. If **ITEuser** is not listed, add it. Click **Edit > Add**, type **ITEuser** and then click **Check Names**.

Step 2:   Configure Remote Assistance settings on PC-2.

a.   Click **Control Panel > System > Remote settings**.

b. The **System Properties** window opens. Check the **Allow Remote Assistance connections to this computer** checkbox, and then click **Advanced**.

c. The **Remote Assistance Settings** window opens. Make sure there is a check mark in the **Allow this computer to be controlled remotely** checkbox. Set the maximum of time invitations can remain open to **1 Hours**, place a check mark in the **Create invitations that can only be used from computers running Windows Vista or later** checkbox, and then click **OK**.

d. Click **OK** in the **System Properties** window.

e. Close all open windows.

Step 3:   Create a Remote Assistance Invitation on PC-2.

  a.   Click **Start > All Programs > Maintenance > Windows Remote Assistance**.

   Note: In Windows 8, navigate to the **Start** screen, then type **msra,** and then press **Enter**.

  b.   The **Windows Remote Assistance** window opens. Click **Invite someone you trust to help you**.

c. The **How do you want to invite your trusted helper?** screen appears. Click the **Save this invitation as a file**.

Which methods can you use to contact someone for assistance?

_____

d. The **Save As** window opens. Click **Desktop > Remote Permission** File Folder. In the **File name** field, type **Invitation 1**. Click **Save**.

Note: In Windows Vista, the **Windows Remote Assistance** window opens. Click **Browse > Desktop > Remote Permission** folder. Type **Invitation 1** in the File name field, and then click **Save**. Type **Assist** for the **Password** and **Confirm the password** fields, then click **Finish**.

e.   The **Windows Remote Assistance** window opens, displaying the invitation password for your Remote Assistance session. The invitation password in the example is **DCZSCQGYST5V**.

   Note: Do **not** close the Windows Remote Assistance window.

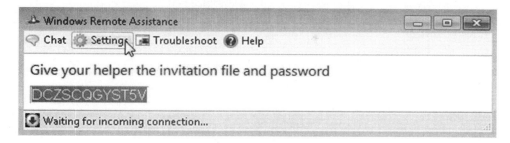

   What is the invitation password displayed on your PC? You will need this later.

_____

f.   In the Windows Remote Assistance window, click **Settings**.

g.   Make sure there is a check mark next to **Use ESC key to stop sharing control**. Set the Bandwidth usage to **Medium**. Click **OK**.

   Which features are disabled with a Medium bandwidth usage?

_____

Step 4:   On PC-1, retrieve the invitation file from PC-2.

a.   On **PC-1**, click **Start > Computer**.

   Note: For Windows 8.1, open **This PC**.

b. The **Computer** or **This PC** window opens. In the left pane, under **Network**, expand **PC-2** and then click on the **Remote Permission** folder. Double-click the **Invitation 1** file. Enter user credentials provided by your instructor if prompted.

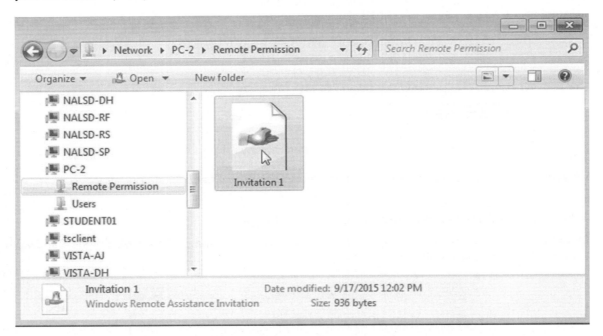

c. The **Remote Assistance** window opens, type the invitation password that you wrote down in Step 3, and then click **OK**.

    Note: In Windows Vista, you created the password **Assist**. Enter that here.

Step 5:   Allow PC-1 remote access to PC-2.

a.   On **PC-2**, the **Windows Remote Assistance** window opens requesting permission to allow **ITEuser** to connect to your computer. Click **Yes.**

b.   The title bar of the **Windows Remote Assistance** window changes to let you know that another user, ITEuser in this example, is assisting you. At this point, PC-1 has a window up that displays everything that is happening on PC-2.

Step 6:   From PC-1, request control of PC-2 using Remote Assistance.

When the user on PC-2 responds to your request to open Remote Assistance, you will have the ability to view every action taken on PC-2, from PC-1. However, if you want to take control of PC-2, you will need to request control. In the **Windows Remote Assistance – Helping ITEuser** window, click **Request control**.

Step 7:   From PC-2, allow ITEuser to share control of your desktop.

To allow the ITEuser on PC-1 to control PC-2, the user at PC-2 will need to respond to the message **Would you like to allow ITEuser to share control of your desktop?**. Check the **Allow ITEuser to respond to User Account Control prompts** checkbox, and then click **Yes.**

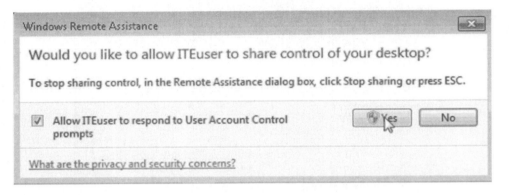

Step 8:   From PC-1, use Remote Assistance to work on PC-2.

When the user at PC-2 accepts your request for remote control, you will be able to control PC-2 as though you were at that PC.

a.   In the **Windows Remote Assistance – Helping ITEuser** window, click **Control Panel > System**.

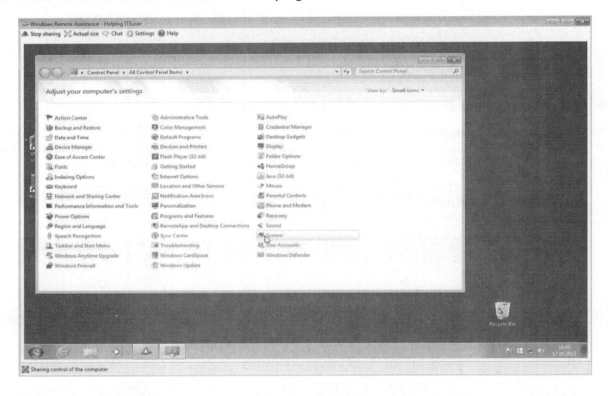

b. The **System** window opens in the **Window Remote Assistance – Helping ITEuser** window. Verify that you are working on PC-2 by reviewing the computer name. After you have verified that you are working on PC-2, close the **System** window.

c. At the top of the **Windows Remote Assistance – Helping ITEuser** window, click **Chat**.

d. A chat area appears on the left side of the **Windows Remote Assistance – Helping ITEuser** window. Type **How may I help you?** in the chat box and then click **Send**.

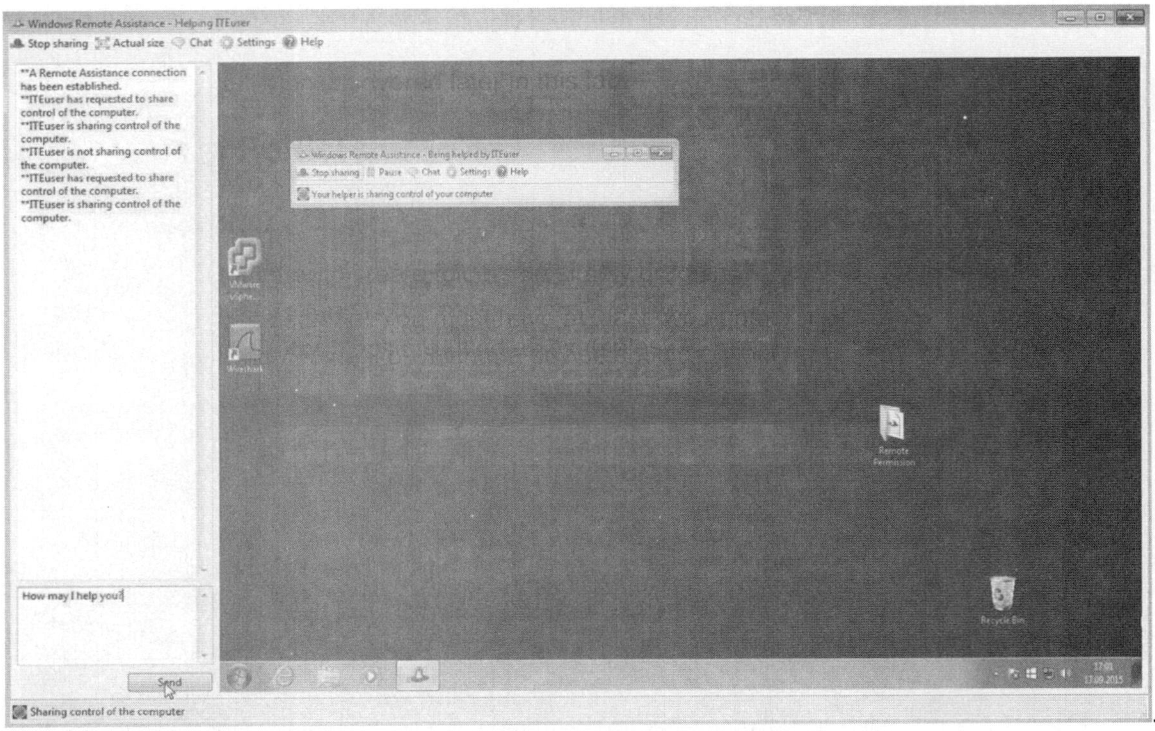

Step 9:   On PC-2, respond to the chat question from ITEuser on PC-1.

When the user on PC-1 sends a chat message to PC-2, it will appear in the **Windows Remote Assistance – Being helped by ITEuser** window. Type **Can you show me how to determine what my IPv4 Address is on this PC?**, and then click **Send**.

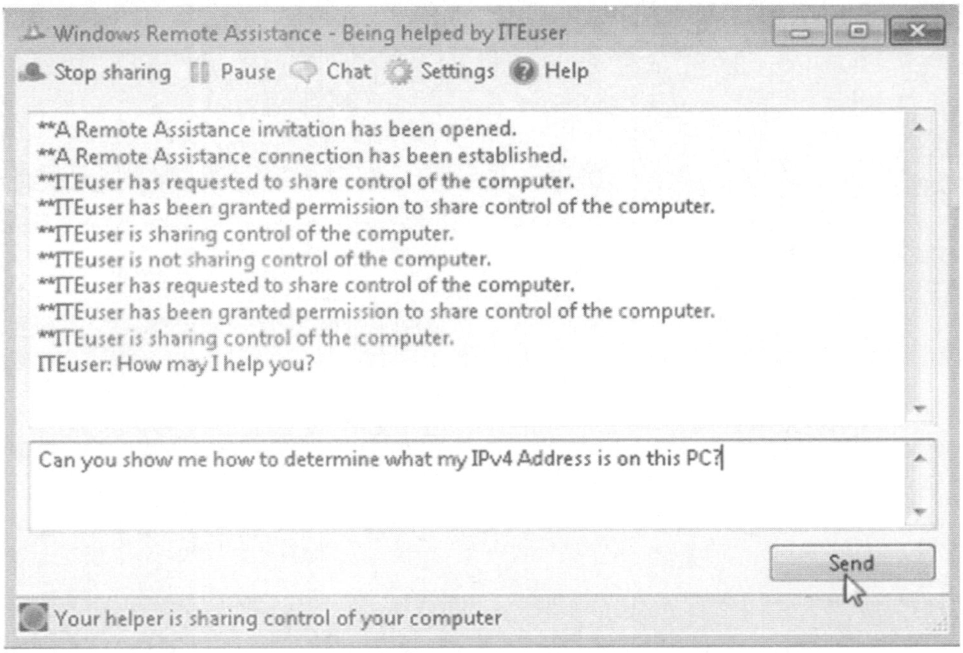

Step 10: From PC-1, show the user on PC-2 how to take the requested action.

a. You will be able to see PC-2's user typing their response in the chat window. Their response will show up in the chat area on the left side of the **Windows Remote Assistance – Helping ITEuser** window when they click send. Type **Sure!** in your chat field and click **Send**.

b. In the **Windows Remote Assistance – Helping ITEuser** window, click **Start**, type **command prompt,** and then press **Enter**.

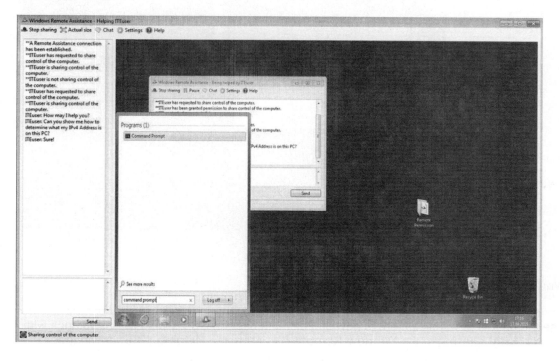

c. The **Command Prompt** window opens inside **the Windows Remote Assistance – Helping ITEuser** window. Type **ipconfig** and then press **Enter**.

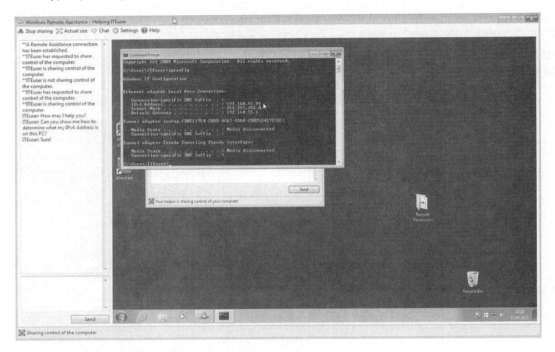

What is PC-2's IPv4 Address?

_____

d. Use the chat area to ask if there is anything else the user on PC-2 would like assistance with. If not, then click on **Stop sharing** in the **Window Remote Assistance – Helping ITEuser** window.

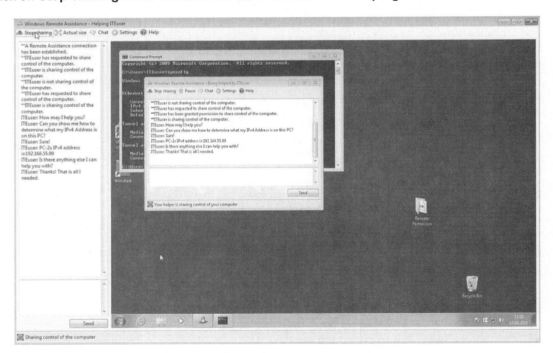

e. Close the **Windows Remote Assistance – Helping ITE** user window on PC-1.

Step 11: From PC-2, close Remote Assistance and delete the invitation folder.

a. You will receive a message that **The Remote Assistance connection has ended** in the chat window when the ITEuser disconnects. Close all open windows.

   Note: You may receive an **Are you sure you want to close Remote Assistance?** message. Click **Yes**.

b. Right-click the **Remote Permission** folder on the desktop, and select **Delete** from the menu.

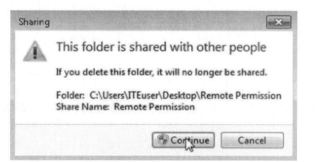

c. The **Delete folder** window opens, click **Yes**.

d. The **Sharing** window opens, click **Continue**.

Reflection

Why is it a good idea to delete the Remote Permission folder you created on the desktop of PC-2 after the Remote Assistance session has ended?

_____

_____

_____

Lab 8.1.4.4 - Remote Desktop in Windows 7 and Vista

Introduction

In this lab, you will remotely connect to another Windows 7 or Vista computer.

Recommended Equipment

The following equipment is required for this exercise:

- Two Windows 7 or Vista PCs connected to a LAN.
- The two computers must be part of the same workgroup and on the same subnet.

Step 1:   Enable Remote Desktop Connections on PC 2.

a. Log on to PC 2 as a member of the administrator group. Ask your instructor for the user name and password.

   Note: The user account must have a password to access PC 2 remotely.

b. Click **Control Panel > System > Remote settings**.

c. In the Remote Desktop area of the System Properties window, select **Allow connections only from computers running Remote Desktop with Network Level Authentication (more secure)**.

d. If a warning message opens indicating that the computer is set to go to sleep, click the **Power Options** link.

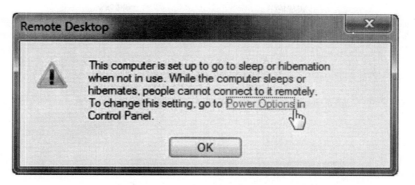

e. The Select a power plan screen opens. Click **Change plan setting**, and then select **Never** in the Turn off the display and Put the computer to sleep dropdown boxes. Click **Save changes**.

Note: If you cannot change the settings, you may need to click **Change settings that are currently unavailable** to allow you to edit the settings.

Note: This screen can also be opened by clicking **Control Panel > Power Options > Change when the computer sleeps**.

f. Click **OK** to close the warning message, if it appears.

g. In the **System Properties** window, click **Select Users**.

h. The **Remote Desktop Users** window opens.

Which user already has remote access?

_____

i. Because you will use this account to gain remote access, you do not need to add any users, click **Cancel**.

j.   Click **OK** to apply changes and close the **System Properties** window.

Step 2:   Check the firewall settings on PC 2.

a.   Click **Control Panel > Windows Firewall > Turn Windows Firewall on or off**.

b.   Verify that the **Turn on Windows Firewall** radio buttons are selected for both private and public networks. If they are not, then select **Turn on Windows Firewall**, and then click **OK**.

Note: Windows Vista only has the option to turn on or off the firewall. Verify that the **On (recommended)** radio button is selected.

Step 3:   Determine PC 2's IPv4 Address.

a. Click **Start**, and then type **command prompt** and press **Enter** to open the **Command Prompt** window.

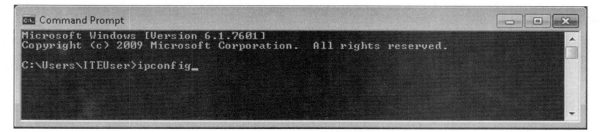

b. From the **Command Prompt** window, type **ipconfig** at the command prompt and then press **Enter**.

```
Command Prompt                                                    □ ▣ ✕
Microsoft Windows [Version 6.1.7601]
Copyright (c) 2009 Microsoft Corporation.   All rights reserved.

C:\Users\ITEUser>ipconfig_
```

c. You will need PC 2's IPv4 Address to complete Step 4. The address can be located in the output generated from the **ipconfig** command. Under the **Ethernet adapter Local Area Connection** heading, and to the right of the **IPv4 Address** row.

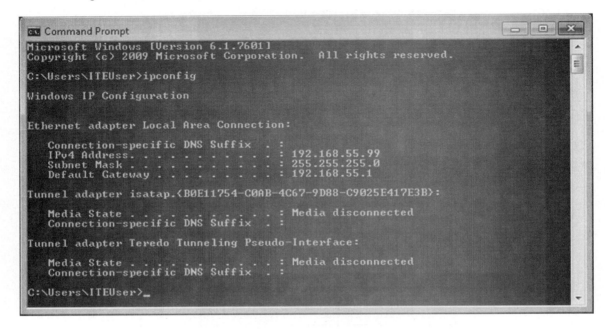

What is PC 2's IPv4 Address?

_____

d. Close all open windows and log off PC 2.

Step 4:   From PC 1, use the Remote Desktop Connection to remotely access PC 2.

a. Log on to PC 1 as an administrator or a member of the administrator group. Ask your instructor for the user name and password.

b. Click **Start > All Programs > Accessories > Remote Desktop Connection**.

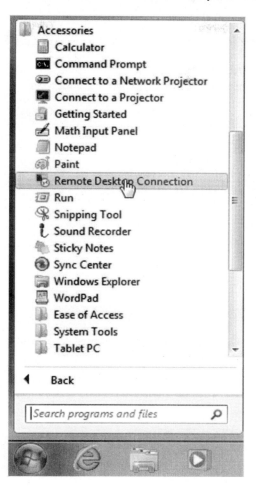

c. The **Remote Desktop Connection** window opens. Type PC 2's IPv4 Address into the Computer field and then click **Connect.**

d.   The Windows Security window opens. Enter the same user name and password that you used to login to PC 2 in Step 1. Click **OK**.

Windows Security

Enter your credentials
These credentials will be used to connect to 192.168.55.99.

ITEuser

••••••••

Domain:

☐ Remember my credentials

OK   Cancel

e.   Click **Yes** to allow the connection.

Remote Desktop Connection

The identity of the remote computer cannot be verified. Do you want to connect anyway?

The remote computer could not be authenticated due to problems with its security certificate. It may be unsafe to proceed.

Certificate name
Name in the certificate from the remote computer:
Win7-ITE

Certificate errors
The following errors were encountered while validating the remote computer's certificate:

⚠ The certificate is not from a trusted certifying authority.

Do you want to connect despite these certificate errors?

☐ Don't ask me again for connections to this computer

View certificate...   Yes   No

f.   The desktop changes and a bar appears at the top of the screen with the IPv4 Address of PC 2.

192.168.55.99

What does this bar at the top of the desktop indicate?

_____

Step 5:   Verify that you are remotely connected to PC 2.

    a.   Click **Start** and then type **command prompt** to open a **Command Prompt** window.

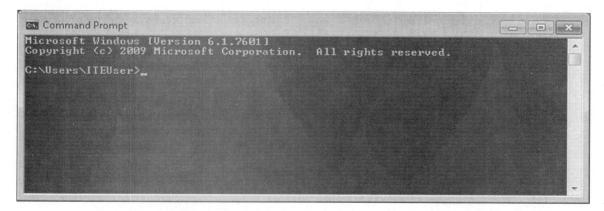

    b.   Type **ipconfig** at the command prompt and press **Enter** to view the PC's IP Address.

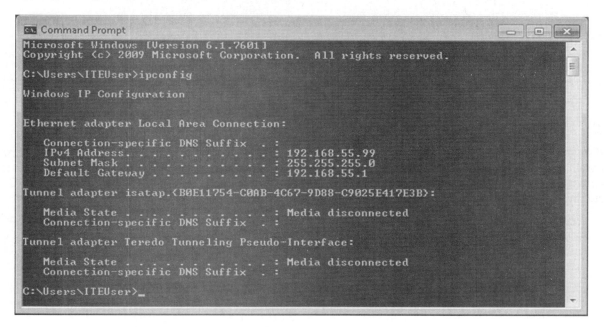

Compare the IP Address that is displayed to PC 2's IP Address that you wrote down at the end of Step 3.

Are the IP Addresses the same?

_____

c.   Click the **Minimize** button on the **Remote Desktop Connection** bar at the top of the screen.

What happens to the desktop?

_____

_____

Step 6:   Try to establish a second Remote Desktop Connection to PC 2.

When you connect to a remote PC using RDC and login to that PC with a local username and password, everything works as though you are logging into the PC locally. The problem with that is that only one user can be logged into a Windows PC at a time. That is why logging into a remote Windows PC using RDC will actually log out another RDC or local user.

a.   Working from PC 1, with the first RDC session to PC 2 still minimized, click **Start > All Programs > Accessories > Remote Desktop Connection**.

b.   Establish a second RDC session to PC 2 by typing PC 2's IPv4 Address into the Computer field again, and then clicking **Connect**.

c.   When the **Windows Security** window opens, enter the user name and password for PC 2 and click **OK**.

d.   Minimize the second session of RDC by clicking the **Minimize** button on the RDC bar at the top of the screen.

e.   Read the Remote Desktop Connection message that appears on PC 1's desktop, then click **OK**.

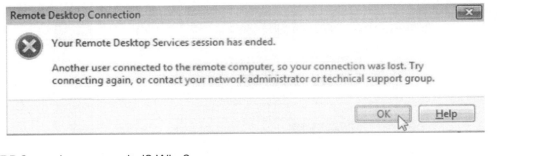

Which RDC session was ended? Why?

_____

_____

_____

f.   Maximize your RDC session to PC 2. Click on the **RDC** icon in the taskbar of **PC 1**.

g.   You should see the RDC bar displaying PC 2's IPv4 Address at the top of the screen. Click **Start > Log off**, to log out of PC 2 and close the RDC session.

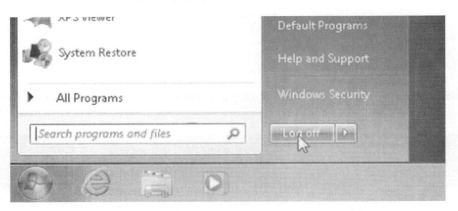

h.   Close all remaining open windows on PC 1.

Reflection

1. What happens to a local user signed into PC 2 when a remote user logs into PC 2 using RDC?

   _____

   _____

2. Why would an IT administrator use RDC?

   _____

   _____

   _____

Lab 8.1.4.4 - Remote Desktop in Windows 8

Introduction

In this lab, you will remotely connect to another Windows 8 computer.

Recommended Equipment

The following equipment is required for this exercise:

- Two Windows 8 PCs connected to a LAN.
- The two computers must be part of the same Workgroup and on the same subnet.

Step 1:   Change the power options on PC 2.

a.   Log on to PC 2 as a member of the administrator group. Ask your instructor for the user name and password.

Note: The user account must have a password to access PC 2 remotely.

b.   To open the Power Options window, click **Start > Control Panel > Power Options**.

c.   In the Preferred plans section of the **Power Options** window, click **Change plan settings** to the right of the **Balanced (recommended)** plan.

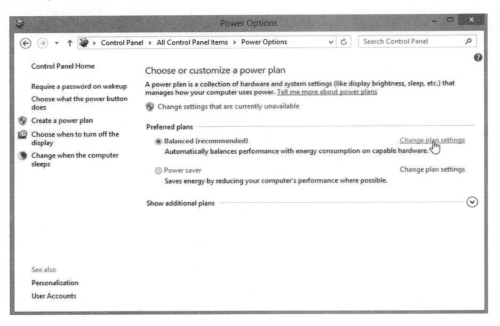

d.   The **Edit Plan Settings** window opens. Click **Change settings that are currently unavailable**. Select **Never** in the **Turn off the display:** and **Put the computer to sleep:** dropdown boxes. Click **Save changes**.

e.   Click **OK** to close the warning message, if it appears.

f.   Close all open windows.

Step 2:   Enable remote desktop connections on PC 2.

a.   Click **Control Panel > System > Remote settings**.

b.   In the Remote Desktop area of the **System Properties** window, select **Allow connections only from computers running Remote Desktop with Network Level Authentication (more secure)**.

c. In the **System Properties** window, click **Select Users**.

d. The **Remote Desktop Users** window opens.

Which user already has remote access?

_____

e.   Because you will use this account to gain remote access, you do not need to add any users. Click **Cancel**.

f.   Click **OK** to apply changes and close the System Properties window.

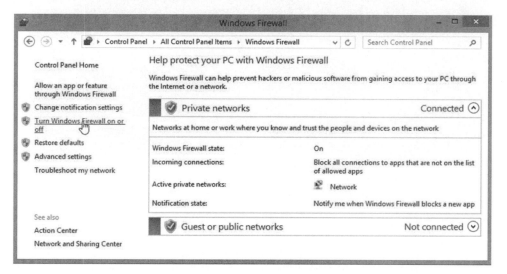

Step 3:   Check the firewall settings on PC 2.

a.   Click **Control Panel > Windows Firewall > Turn Windows Firewall on or off**.

b.   Verify that the **Turn on Windows Firewall** radio button is selected for both private and public networks. If they are not, then select **Turn on Windows Firewall**, and then click **OK**.

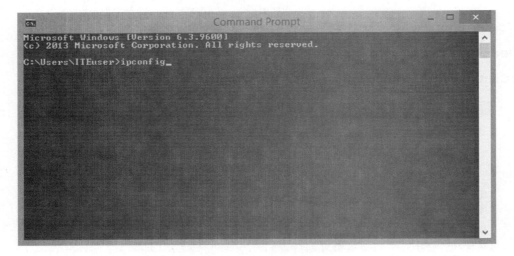

c.   Close all open windows.

Step 4:   Determine PC 2's IPv4 Address.

a.   Click **Start**, type **command prompt,** and then press **Enter** to open the **Command Prompt** window.

b.   In the **Command Prompt** window, type **ipconfig** and then press **Enter**.

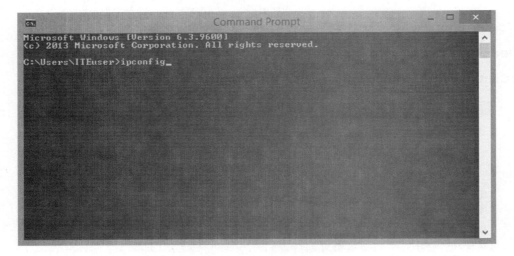

c. You will need PC 2's IPv4 Address to complete Step 5. The address can be located in the output generated from the **ipconfig** command. Under the **Ethernet adapter Local Area Connection** heading, and to the right of the **IPv4 Address** row.

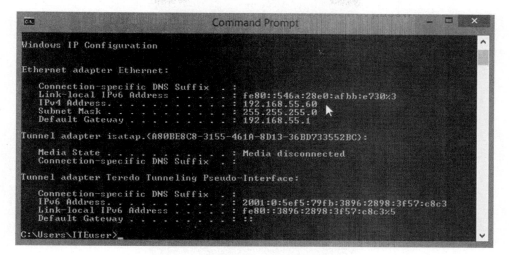

What is PC 2's IPv4 Address?

_____

d. Close all open windows and log off PC 2.

Step 5:   From PC 1, use the Remote Desktop Connection to remotely access PC 2.

a. Log on to PC 1 as an administrator or a member of the administrator group. Ask your instructor for the user name and password.

b.   Click **Start**, type **Remote**, and then select **Remote Desktop Connection** from the list.

c.   The **Remote Desktop Connection** window opens. Type PC 2's IPv4 Address into the **Computer** field and then click **Connect**.

d.   The **Windows Security** window opens. Enter the same user name and password that you used to login to PC 2 in Step 1. Click **OK**.

e.   Click **Yes** to allow the connection.

f.   The desktop changes and a bar appears at the top of the screen with the IPv4 Address of PC 2.

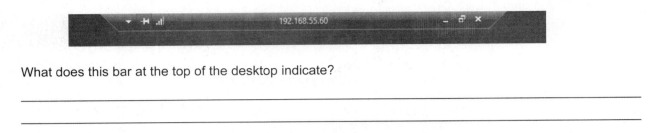

What does this bar at the top of the desktop indicate?

_____

_____

Step 6:   Verify that you are remotely connected to PC 2.

a.   Navigate to the **Start** screen and then type **command prompt** to open a **Command Prompt** window.

b.   Type **ipconfig** at the command prompt and press **Enter** to view the PC's IP Address.

```
                              Command Prompt                    _  □  ×
C:\

Windows IP Configuration

Ethernet adapter Ethernet:

   Connection-specific DNS Suffix   . :
   Link-local IPv6 Address . . . . . : fe80::546a:28e0:afbb:e730%3
   IPv4 Address. . . . . . . . . . . : 192.168.55.60
   Subnet Mask . . . . . . . . . . . : 255.255.255.0
   Default Gateway . . . . . . . . . : 192.168.55.1

Tunnel adapter isatap.{A80BE8C8-3155-461A-8D13-36BD733552BC}:

   Media State . . . . . . . . . . . : Media disconnected
   Connection-specific DNS Suffix   . :

Tunnel adapter Teredo Tunneling Pseudo-Interface:

   Connection-specific DNS Suffix   . :
   IPv6 Address. . . . . . . . . . . : 2001:0:5ef5:79fb:3896:2898:3f57:c8c3
   Link-local IPv6 Address . . . . . : fe80::3896:2898:3f57:c8c3%5
   Default Gateway . . . . . . . . . : ::

C:\Users\ITEuser>_
```

Compare the IP Address that is displayed to PC 2's IP Address that you wrote down at the end of Step 4.
Are the IP Addresses the same?

_____

c.   Click the **Minimize** button on the **Remote Desktop Connection** bar at the top of the screen.

What happens to the desktop?

_____

_____

Step 7:   Try to establish a second Remote Desktop Connection to PC 2.

When you connect to a remote PC using RDC and login to that PC with a local username and password, everything works as though you are logging into the PC locally. However, only one user can be logged into Windows at a time. That is why logging into a remote Windows PC using RDC will actually log out another RDC or local user.

a.   Working from **PC 1**, with the first RDC session to PC 2 still minimized, click **Start**, type **remote**, and then right-click on **Remote Desktop Connection** and select **Open in new window**.

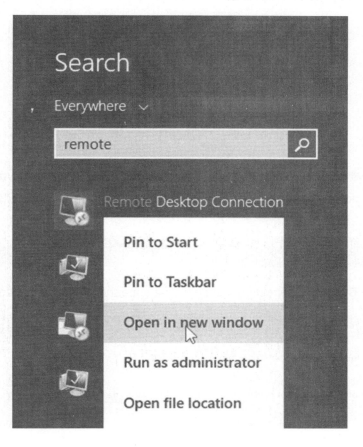

b. Establish a second RDC session to PC 2 by typing PC 2's IPv4 Address into the Computer field again, and then clicking **Connect**.

c. When the Windows Security window opens, enter the user name and password for PC 2 and click **OK**.

d. Minimize the second session of RDC by clicking the **Minimize** button on the RDC bar at the top of the screen.

e. Read the Remote Desktop Connection message that appears on PC 1's desktop, then click **OK**.

Which RDC session was ended? Why?

_____

_____

_____

f. Maximize your RDC session to PC 2. Click on the **RDC** icon in the taskbar of **PC 1**.

g. You should see the RDC bar displaying PC 2's IPv4 Address at the top of the screen. Click on the **X** icon to close the RDC session to PC 2.

h. The **Remote Desktop Connection** window opens. Read the message, and then click **OK**.

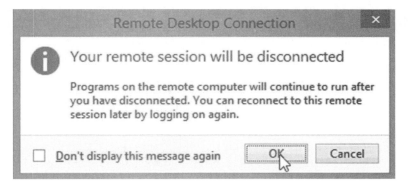

i. Close all remaining open windows on PC 1.

Reflection

1. What happens to a local user signed into PC 2 when a remote user logs into PC 2 using RDC?

_____

_____

2. Why would an IT administrator use RDC?

_____

_____

_____

Chapter 9: Laptops and Mobile Devices

Lab 9.1.1.6 - Research Docking Stations

In this lab, you will use the Internet, a newspaper, or a local store to gather information and then record the specifications for a laptop docking station. Be prepared to discuss your decisions regarding the docking station you select.

1. Research a docking station compatible with a laptop. What is the model or part number of the docking station?

   _____

2. What is the approximate cost?

   _____

3. What are the dimensions of the docking station?

   _____

   _____

4. How does the laptop connect to the docking station?

   _____

   _____

5. List some of the features available with this docking station.

   _____

   _____

   _____

6. Is this docking station compatible with other laptop models?

   _____

Lab 9.3.1.5 - Research Laptop RAM

In this lab, you will use the Internet, newspaper, or a local store to gather information about expansion memory for a laptop.

1. Research the manufacturer specifications for the memory in a laptop. List the specifications in the table below.

Memory Specifications	Laptop Expansion Memory
Form Factor	
Type	
Size (GB)	
Manufacturer	
Speed	
Slots	

2. Shop around, and in the table below, list the features and costs for expansion memory for a laptop.

Memory Specifications	Expansion Memory
Form Factor	
Type	
Size (GB)	
Manufacturer	
Speed	
Retail Cost	

3. In your research, did you find any reason to select a particular type of expansion memory over another?

_____

_____

4. Is the new expansion memory compatible with the existing memory installed in the laptop? Why is this important?

_____

_____

Lab 9.3.2.3 - Research Laptop Batteries

In this lab, you will use the Internet, newspaper, or a local store to gather information and then record the specifications for a laptop battery.

1. List the specifications for a laptop battery. Please ask your instructor for the laptop model to research.

    _____

    _____

    _____

    _____

2. Shop around, and in the table below, list the features and cost for a generic and a laptop battery from the manufacturer of the laptop.

Battery Specifications	Generic	Manufacturer
Output voltage		
Battery cell configuration ex: 6-Cell, 9-Cell		
Dimensions		
Hours of life		
Approximate cost		

3. Based on your research, which battery would you select? Be prepared to discuss your decisions regarding the battery you select.

    _____

    _____

    _____

    _____

Lab 9.3.2.5 - Research Laptop Screens

In this activity, you will use the Internet, newspaper, or a local store to gather information and then record the specifications for a laptop display onto this worksheet.

1. Research and list the specifications for a replacement laptop screen. Please ask your instructor for the laptop model to research.

Screen Specifications	Display Screen
Type	
Size	
Resolution	
Backlight Type	

2. When replacing a laptop screen, the replacement screen must match many, if not all, specifications of the original screen. Research and list which specifications must match the original display screen.

_____

_____

3. Shop around, and in the table below, list the features and cost of two replacement screens for a laptop.

Screen Specifications	Replacement #1	Replacement #2
Type		
Size		
Resolution		
Backlight Type		
Approximate Cost		
Warranty		

4. Based on your research, which replacement screen would you select? Be prepared to discuss your decisions regarding the screen you select.

_____

_____

Lab 9.3.2.7 - Research Laptop Hard Drives

In this lab, you will use the Internet, newspaper, or a local store to gather information about hard drives for a laptop.

1. Research the manufacturer specifications for the hard drive in the laptop. List the specifications in the table below.

Hard Drive Specifications	Hard Drive
Form Factor	
Type	
Size (GB)	
Port Type	
Drive Speed	

2. Shop around, and in the table below, list the features and costs of two replacement hard drives for a laptop.

Hard Drive Specifications	Replacement Hard Drive #1	Replacement Hard Drive #2
Form Factor		
Type		
Size (GB)		
Manufacturer		
Port Type		
Retail Cost		

3. In your research, did you find any reason to select a particular hard drive over another?

4. Is the new hard drive compatible with other components in the laptop? Why is this important?

Lab 9.3.2.14 - Research Building a Specialized Laptop

In this lab, you will use the Internet, a newspaper, or a local store to gather information about building a specialized laptop that supports hardware and software that allows a user to perform tasks that an off-the-shelf system cannot perform. Be prepared to discuss your selections.

For this lab, assume the customer's system will be compatible with the parts you order.

1. The customer runs an audio and video editing workstation to record music, to create music CDs and CD labels, and to create home movies. The customer wishes to upgrade the components listed in the table.

Brand and Model Number	Features	Cost
Audio Card		
Video Card		
Hard Drive		
External Monitors		

Provide reasons for the components purchased. How will they support the customer's needs?

_____

_____

_____

_____

_____

2. The customer runs computer-aided design (CAD) or computer-aided manufacturing (CAM) software and wishes to upgrade the components listed in the table.

Brand and Model Number	Features	Cost
CPU		
Video Card		
RAM		

Provide reasons for the components purchased. How will they support the customer's needs?

_____

_____

_____

_____

_____

3. The customer uses virtualization technologies to run several different operating systems to test software compatibility. The customer wishes to upgrade the components listed in the table.

Brand and Model Number	Features	Cost
RAM		
CPU		

Provide reasons for the components purchased. How will they support the customer's needs?

_____

_____

_____

_____

_____

Lab 9.6.2.2 - Research Laptop Problems

Laptops often use proprietary parts. To find information about the replacement parts, you may have to research the website of the laptop manufacturer.

Before you begin this lab, you need to know some information about the laptop.

Your instructor will provide you with the following information:

Laptop manufacturer: _____

Laptop model number: _____

Amount of RAM: _____

Size of the hard drive: _____

Use the Internet to locate the website for the laptop manufacturer. What is the URL for the website?

_____

Locate the service section of the website and look for links that focus on your laptop. It is common for websites to allow you to search by the model number. The list below shows common links that you might find, including FAQs, WIKIs, service notices, white papers, and blogs.

List the links you found specific to the laptop and include a brief description of the information in that link.

_____

_____

_____

_____

Briefly describe any service notices you found on the website. A service notice example is a driver update, a hardware issue, or a recall notice for a laptop component.

_____

_____

_____

_____

Open forums may exist for your laptop. Use an Internet search engine to locate any open forums that focus on your laptop by typing in the name and model of the laptop. Briefly describe the websites (other than the manufacturer website) that you located.

_____

_____

_____

_____

Lab 9.6.2.3 - Gather Information from the Customer

In this lab, you will act as a call center technician and create closed-ended and open-ended questions to ask a customer about a laptop problem.

A customer complains that the network connection on the laptop is intermittent. The customer states that they are using a wireless PC card for network connectivity. The customer believes that the laptop may be too far from the wireless access point; however, he does not know where the wireless access point is located.

As a technician, you need to be able to ask questions that will be recorded on a work order. In the table below, record closed-ended questions and open-ended questions that you would ask a customer.

Closed-Ended Questions	Open-Ended Questions

Lab 9.6.2.4 - Investigate Support Websites and Repair Companies

In this lab, you will investigate the services provided by a local laptop repair company, or a laptop manufacturer's support website. Use the Internet or a local phone directory to locate a local laptop repair company or laptop manufacturer's support website. Answer the following questions.

Local Laptop Repair Company

1. What different types of services does the repair company offer?

    _____

    _____

    _____

2. What brand(s) of laptop computers can be repaired at this repair company?

    _____

    _____

    _____

3. What type(s) of warranty is offered at this repair company?

    _____

    _____

    _____

4. Does the staff have industry certifications? If so, what are the certifications?

    _____

    _____

    _____

5. Is there a guaranteed completion time for repairs? If so, what are the details?

    _____

    _____

    _____

6. Does the repair company offer remote technical services?

    _____

    _____

    _____

Laptop Manufacturer Support Website

1. What steps are required for locating device drivers for a laptop?

    _____

    _____

    _____

2. What type(s) of support are offered for troubleshooting laptops?

   _____

   _____

   _____

3. Does the manufacturer website offer remote technical services? If so, what type(s)?

   _____

   _____

   _____

4. What method(s) are used to located parts?

   _____

   _____

   _____

5. What steps are required for locating manuals for a laptop?

   _____

   _____

   _____

Chapter 10: Mobile, Linux, and OS X Operating Systems

Lab 10.1.2.3 - Working with Android

Introduction

In this lab, you will place apps and widgets on the home screen and move them between different screens. You will also create folders. Finally, you will install and uninstall apps from the Android device.

Recommended Equipment

- Android tablet or smartphone running Android version 5.0

Part 1:   Apps and Widgets

Step 1:   Gain access to the device.

Turn on the device and log in with the **password**, **PIN**, or other **passcode**, if necessary.

Step 2:   Add app shortcuts to the home screen.

a.   On the **home screen**, apps can be installed using the **All Apps** icon. Touch the **All Apps** icon.

The **All Apps** screen appears.

b.   Touch and hold any app icon to create a shortcut to it on the **home screen**. As the app icon is held, the **home screen** and possible locations for the shortcut becomes visible in the background. The image below shows the **home screen** and a possible location for a shortcut as the **Calculator** app icon is held.

c.   Drag the app icon to any empty space and release it.

Step 3:   Add widgets to the home screen.

Widgets are apps that display information dynamically on the **home screen**. Different from app shortcuts represented by a single icon, widgets usually occupy a larger area of the screen and can be installed directly from a screen.

a.   To add a widget to a screen, touch and hold a blank area of a screen. The screen will reduce in size and a three-icon menu will appear.

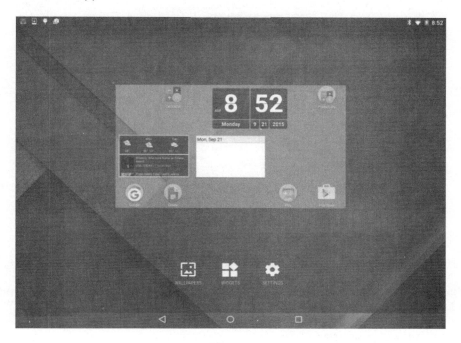

b.   Touch the **Widgets** icon. A list of installed widgets appear.

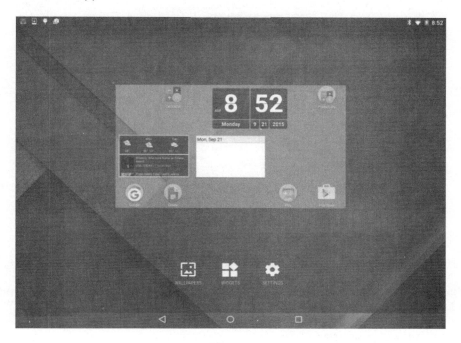

c.   Touch and hold a widget. Similarly to adding an app, the **home screen** will become visible, allowing you to choose a location for the widget. Drag the widget to any empty space and release it. In the image below, the **Google Fit Widget** is being placed on the **home screen**.

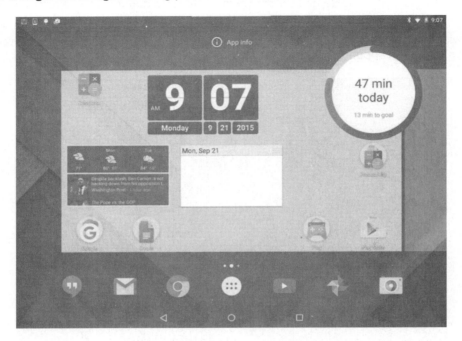

Note: Widgets and apps must be installed before they can be added to screens. Widgets and apps can be installed from the **Google Play Store**.

Step 4:   Move apps between screens.

You can move apps to other screens.

a.   Touch and hold any app icon. Drag the app to the right edge of the screen.

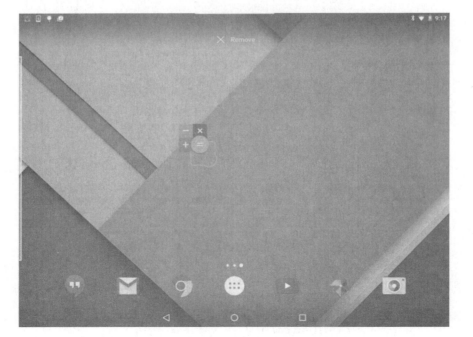

b. Drag the app icon to any empty space and release it.

Note: Widgets can also be moved to other screens in the same manner as apps.

Step 5: Remove apps or widgets from the home screen.

Apps and widgets can be removed from the **home screen**. In this example, you will remove the **Drive** app from the home screen.

a. Touch and hold the **Drive** app icon. As you hold the icon, the search box on the top of the screen is replaced by the **Remove** link. Drag the **Drive icon** onto the **Remove** link and release the app.

b.   The app is now removed from the home screen.

Note: Widgets can be removed from the home screen in the same manner.

Note: The method shown in this step simply removes the app shortcut from the home screen; the app is still installed on the device and can be easily be brought back to the home screen as seen in **Step 2** of this lab. App uninstallation is covered later in this lab.

Part 2:   Managing Folders

Step 1:   Create a folder.

Apps can be grouped together to create folders by simply dragging an app on top of another.

a.   Add another app to the screen. You must have at least two apps to create a folder. In the image below, the **Calculator** and **Photos** apps are used as examples.

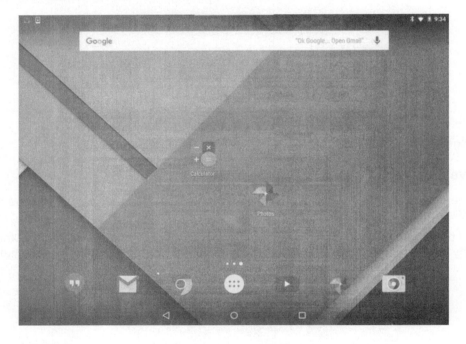

b. Touch and drag one of the apps icon onto the other.

c. Release the app. A folder is created containing both the **Calculator** and **Photos** apps.

Step 2: Rename a folder.

Folders can be named to describe the contents.

a. Touch the folder.

b. Touch the words **Unnamed folder**.

c.   Type the name **ITE Apps Folder** for the folder name.

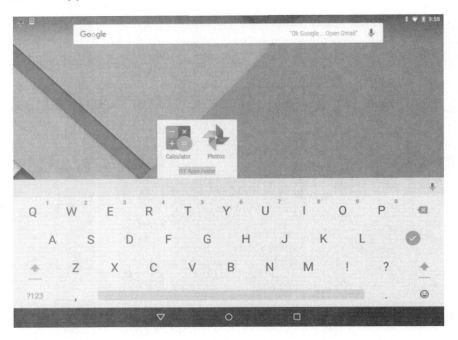

d.   Touch anywhere outside the folder to close it.

Step 3:   Remove apps from a folder.

Apps can be removed from folders.

a.   Touch and hold any app within the folder.

b.   Drag the app to an empty area of the home screen.

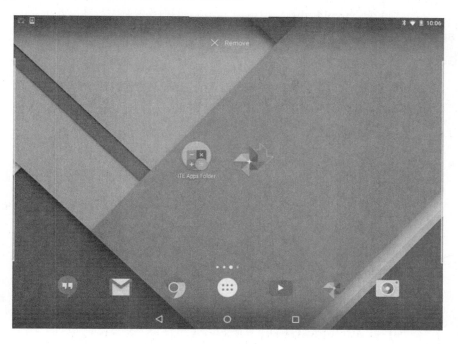

c.   Release the app.

After **Photos** is removed from the folder, what happened to the folder and the **Calculator** app?

Part 3:   Managing Apps

Step 1:   Install apps.

a.   Open the **Google Play Store** app.

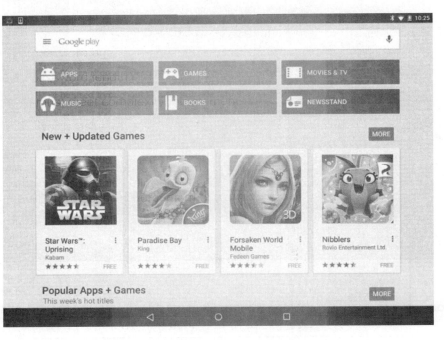

b.   Search and install **LastPass**, a free password manager for Android.

c.   Touch **LastPass Password Manager** to see details about **LastPass**.

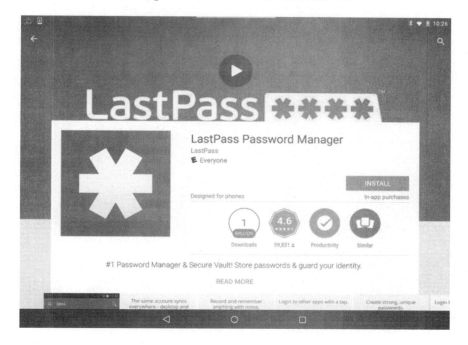

d.   Touch **INSTALL** and then **ACCEPT** on the **App Permissions** window.

e.   When the installation process finishes, the app is installed and available under **All Apps**.

Step 2:   Uninstall apps.

a.   Navigate to the **home screen**. Touch the **All Apps** icon.

b.   Touch and hold **LastPass** icon (i.e., the app you just installed in the previous step).

c.   An app menu appears. Drag the **LastPass** icon to the **Uninstall** link.

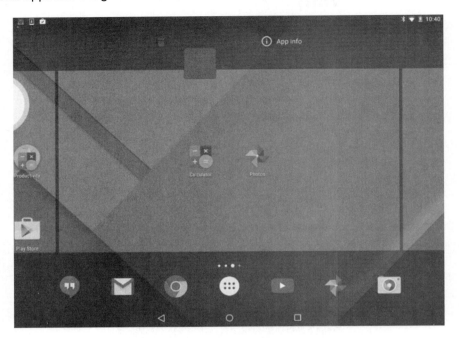

d.   Confirm you want to uninstall **LastPass** by touching **OK**.

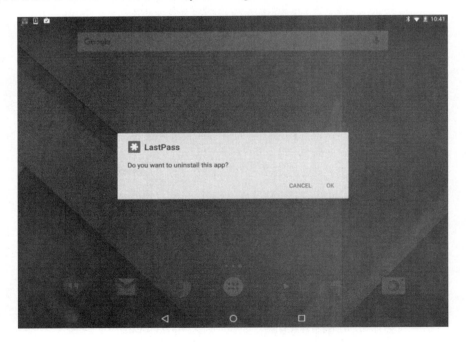

e.   The app is now uninstalled from the device.

Lab 10.1.3.3 - Working with iOS

Introduction

In this lab, you will place apps on the home screen and move them between different home screens. You will also create folders. Finally, you will install on the iOS device and uninstall them.

Recommended Equipment

- iOS tablet or smartphone running iOS version 7.0 or higher

Part 1: Apps and the Home Screen

In this part, you will access the iOS device and re-arrange the apps on the **home screen**.

a. Turn on the device and log in with the **password**, **PIN**, or other **passcode**, if necessary.

b. On the **home screen**, touch and hold any app icon until it starts to jiggle.

c. Drag the app icon to the desired location and release it.

d. Touch and hold any app icon. In this example, we will use the **Calculator** app.

e. Drag the **Calculator** app to the edge of the screen on the right to place it on a different **home screen**. This operation will also create a new home screen if there are no others.

f. Press the **Home** button when the **Calculator** is in the desired location.

Part 2:   Managing Folders

Step 1:   Create a folder.

Apps can be grouped together to create folders. A folder can be created by dragging an app on top of another.

a.   Touch and drag the **Stocks** app onto the **Calendar** app.

b. iOS will create a folder containing both apps. Release the app when the folder is created. The default folder name is determined by the types of apps placed in the folder.

c. Press the **Home** button to exit the folder editing creation mode.

Step 2: Rename folders.

Folders can be renamed to better describe their contents.

a. Open the **Finance** folder by tapping it.

b. Touch and hold the folder's name until the apps begin to jiggle. Notice the cursor is now next to the folder's name.

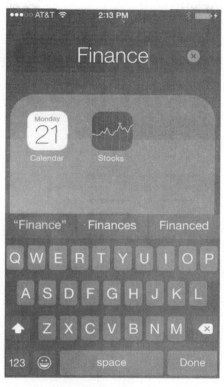

c. Delete the name **Finance** and rename it **ITE Folder**.

d. Touch anywhere outside the folder or press the **Home** button to close the folder.

Step 3: Remove apps from folders.

a. Touch the **ITE Folder** to open it.

b. Touch and hold the **Calendar** app icon within the folder. Drag the app to an empty area of the home screen outside of the folder.

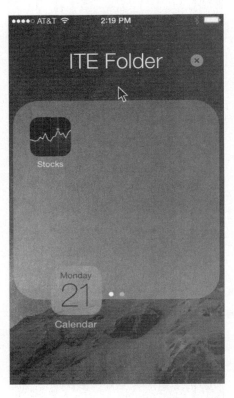

c. Release the icon. The Calendar app icon is now outside the folder.

d. Go back to the **ITE Folder** and remove **Stocks**.

What happens to the folder?

___

Part 3:   Installing Apps

To install apps on an iOS device, you must use the **App Store** app. To install an app on iOS, follow these steps:

a.   Touch the **App Store** app icon to open it.

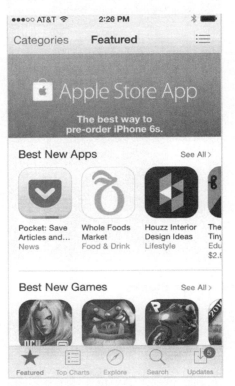

b.   Touch the **Search** tool icon at the bottom of the screen to access the app search functionality.

c.   In the search box, type **LastPass**, a free password manager for iOS.

d.   Touch **LastPass** to see details about the **LastPass** app.

e. Touch **Get** and then touch **Install** to start the installation process.

f. To begin the download, provide your Apple account password if prompted.

g. When the download and installation is finished, the progress indicator will turn into a button that reads **Open**.

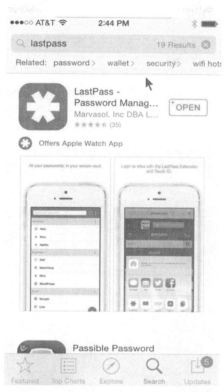

h. Press the **Home** button to return to the **home screen** and verify the app has been installed.

Note: You must set up an Apple account and provide a valid credit card number before you can install apps on iOS devices. This is a requirement put in place by Apple and is necessary even for free apps, such as **LastPass**.

Part 4: Uninstalling Apps

In this section, you will uninstall LastPass, but the process is the same for any iOS app.

a. Touch and hold the **LastPass** icon until the apps begin to jiggle. Notice that the icon has a gray circle with a black X in the upper-left corner of the icon. Apps without the X are default apps and cannot be uninstalled.

b. Confirm the deletion by touching **Delete**. The app is deleted from the device.

Lab 10.1.5.3 - Mobile Device Features

Introduction

In this lab, you will set the auto rotation, brightness, and turn GPS on and off.

Recommended Equipment

- Android tablet or smartphone running Android version 5.0 or higher
- iOS tablet or smartphone running iOS version 7.0 or higher

Part 1: Auto-Rotation

Auto-rotation is a common feature found on modern mobile devices. It allows the screen format to switch automatically between **landscape** and **portrait** modes, depending on how the user is holding the device. This section examines how to turn **auto-rotation** on or off on Android and iOS devices.

Step 1: Auto-Rotation on Android.

a. Turn on the device and log in with the password, PIN, or other passcode, if necessary.

b. Go to **All Apps > Settings > Display** (under the **Device** category).

c. Touch **When the device is rotated** and select **Stay in current orientation**.

d. Rotate the device 90 degrees clockwise. What happens to the screen?

_____

e. Rotate the device 90 degrees counter-clockwise.

f. Touch **When the device is rotated** again and select **Rotate the contents of the screen**.

g. Rotate the device 90 degrees clockwise again. What happens to the screen?

_____

h. Touch the **Home** button to return to the home screen.

Step 2: Auto Rotation on iOS.

a. Turn on the device and log in with the password, PIN, or other passcode, if necessary.

b. Swipe up from the bottom of the screen up to access **Control Center**.

c. Touch the **auto-rotation lock** icon to enable **auto-rotation lock**; it is the fifth icon in the row of icons and represented by a circular arrow going around a lock.

d. Open the **Calculator** app.

e.   Rotate the device 90 degrees clockwise. What happens to the screen?

_____

f.   Swipe up from the bottom of the screen to access the **Control Center** again.

g.   Touch the **auto-rotation lock** icon again to de-activate it.

h.   Press the **Home** button.

i.   Open the **Calculator** app.

j.   Rotate the device 90 degrees clockwise. What happens to the screen?

_____

k.   Click the **Home** button to return to the home screen.

Part 2: Brightness

Step 1:   Brightness on Android.

a.   Go to **All Apps > Settings > Display** (under the **Device** category).

b.   Touch **Brightness level**. A brightness slider appears.

c.   Move the slider all the way to the right. What happens?

_____

d.   Touch the **Adaptive brightness** toggle to enable it. The **Adaptive brightness** toggle is located right below the **Brightness level**.

What happens when **Adaptive brightness** is enabled?

_____

e.   Touch the **Adaptive brightness** checkbox.

f.   Move the slider all the way to the left. What happens?

_____

g.   Touch the **Home** button to return to the **home screen**.

Step 2:   Brightness on iOS.

a.   Go to **Settings > Display & Brightness**. The **Display & Brightness** screen appears.

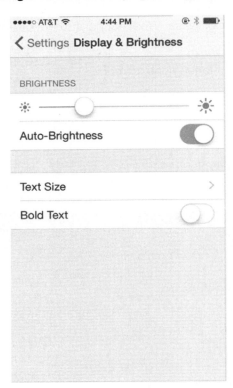

b. Turn off **Auto-Brightness** by moving the **Auto-Brightness** toggle to the **off** position.

●●●●○ AT&T 📶   4:47 PM   @ ❋ ▬▭▷

< Settings **Display & Brightness**

BRIGHTNESS

☀️ ──────⬤────────── ☀️

Auto-Brightness   ⬭

Text Size   >

Bold Text   ⬭

c. Move the slider all the way to the right. What happens?

_____

d. Turn on Auto-Brightness. What happens?

_____

e. Turn off Auto-Brightness.

f. Move the slider all the way to the left. What happens?

_____

g. Turn on Auto-Brightness. What happens?

_____

Part 3: GPS

Another common feature on modern mobile devices is **GPS** or **Location Services**. By using Global
Positioning System signals, mobile devices are able to learn and inform the user about the current location
with good accuracy.

Step 1:   GPS on Android.

a.   Go to **All apps > Settings > Location** (under **Personal**). The **Location** screen appears.

b.   Turn off Location by moving its toggle to **off**.

c.   Touch the **Home** button.

d. Open the **Maps** app by going to **All apps > Maps**.

How is the device able to determine the location?

_____

Force **Maps** to locate you with more accuracy by touching the **crosshair** icon. What happens?

_____

e. Allow Android to turn on Location by touching **YES**. Your device should now have an accurate representation for your current location.

f. Touch the **Home** button.

Step 2:   GPS on iOS.

a.   Go to **Settings > Privacy > Location Services**. The **Location Services** screen appears.

iOS allows the user to decide what apps have access to the GPS. What apps are using Location Services on your device?

_____

b.   Turn **Location Services** off. A warning message may appear stating that the Location Services will be disabled.

c.   Press the **Home** button.

d.   Touch the **Maps** app icon to open **Apple Maps**.

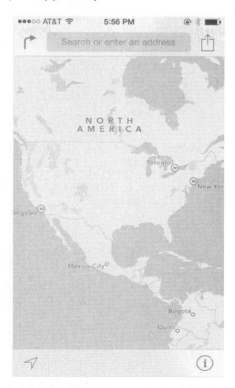

Note: You may be asked to allow **Maps** to use **Location Services**, as shown in the figure below. If this happens, touch **Allow** to add **Maps** to the list of apps that can use **Location Services.**

e.   Touch the **Current Location** icon.

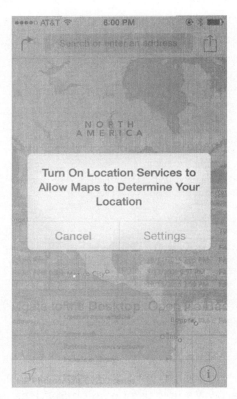

What happens?

_____

f.   Touch **Settings** in the warning box to open the Location Services setting screen. Alternatively, press the **Home** button and go to **Settings > Privacy > Location Services.**

g.   Turn Location Services on.

h.   Touch the **Home** button.

i.   Touch the **Maps** app icon.

j.   Touch the **Current Location** icon again. Was iOS able to locate you and the device? _____

k.   Click the **Home** button.

Lab 10.1.5.4 - Mobile Device Information

Introduction

In this activity, you will use the Internet, a technical journal, or a local store to gather information about an Android and an iOS device. You will then document the specifications of each Android and iOS device onto this worksheet. Be prepared to discuss your decisions regarding the devices you select.

Recommended Equipment

- PC with Internet connection

Step 1: **Select an Android and iOS device to research. Record the hardware specifications in the boxes below.**

Specifications	Android Device	iOS Device
Model		
Manufacturer		
Operating System		
Available Memory		
Camera		
Wi-Fi Connectivity		
Battery Information		

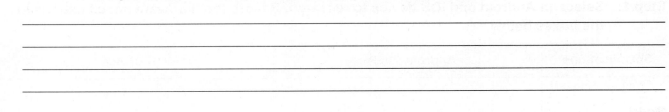

Screen Size and Resolution		
Size and Weight		

Step 2: Based on your research, which mobile device would you select? Be prepared to discuss your decisions regarding the mobile device you select.

_____

_____

_____

_____

Lab 10.2.1.2 - Passcode Locks

Introduction

For most users, these Android or iOS devices are on the go with the users, and they are usually powered on all the time. If the device is lost or stolen, the passcode can prevent unauthorized access. In this lab, you will set a passcode lock, change a passcode lock, and fail passcode authentication. You will also remove a passcode lock.

Recommended Equipment

- Android tablet or smartphone running Android version 5.0 or higher.
- iOS tablet or smartphone running iOS version 7.0 or higher.

Part 1:   Passcode Lock on Android

Step 1:   Configure passcode lock on an Android device.

a.   Turn on the device and get to the **Home screen**.

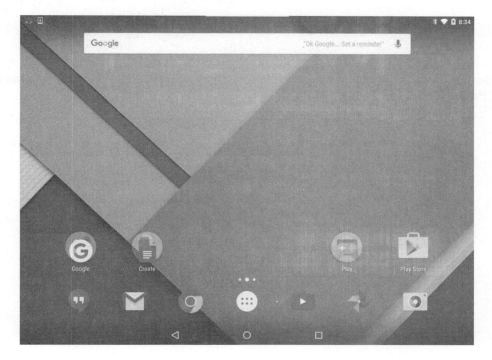

b.   Go to **All apps > Settings > Security** (under **Personal**). The **Security** screen appears.

c.   Touch **Screen Lock** to choose a method for locking the screen. Android 5.0 supports **None** (no lock), **Swipe**, **Pattern**, **PIN,** and **Password**.

d.   Touch **PIN**.

e. If the **Encryption** screen appears, Android asks if you want to use the PIN to encrypt the device. Touch **No thanks** and then touch **CONTINUE** to continue.

This is useful as the device's filesystem will be encrypted based on PIN, making it unreadable until the PIN is provided. While this feature increases security, it is out of the scope of this lab.

f. In the **Choose your PIN** screen, enter **1234**. Touch **CONTINUE**.

g. Type **1234** to confirm the **PIN**. Touch **OK**.

h.   Touch **Show all notification content** to have Android displaying all notifications on the lock screen. Touch **DONE**.

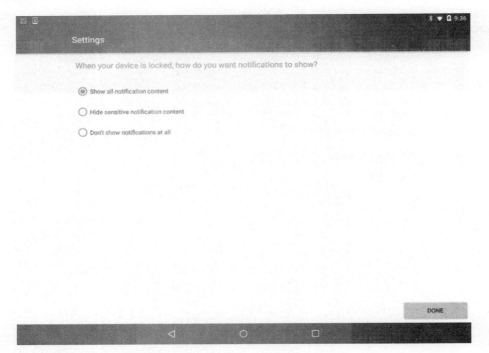

Step 2:   Use the PIN to unlock the screen.

a.   Press the **Home** button to return to the **home screen**.

b.   Press the **Power** button briefly to lock the screen. The device will go into sleep mode and the screen will go dark.

c. Press the **Power** button briefly to wake up the device. Notice that the device will now require the **PIN** before allowing access.

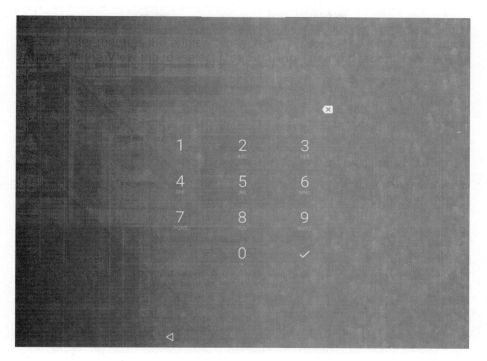

d. Enter **1234,** the previously configured **PIN**. Touch the **check mark** on the bottom-right-side of the number pad. What happens?

_____

e. Press the **Power** button briefly to lock the device.

f. Press the **Power** button briefly to wake up the device.

g. Type **4321**. Notice this is not the PIN configured in the device.

h.   Touch **check mark** on the bottom-right-side of the number pad. What happens?

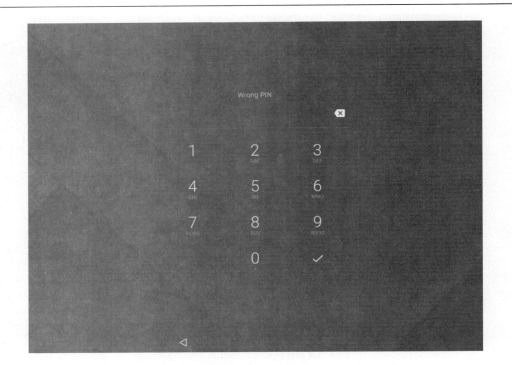

i.   Enter the incorrect **PIN** four more times. What happens?

Repeatedly incorrect PINs is an indicator that someone is trying to guess the PIN. As a security measure, Android forces the user to wait 30 seconds before attempting another guess.

j.   Touch **OK** when 30 seconds have passed. Notice that Android will keep a countdown in the background.

k.   After 30 seconds, enter the correct PIN to unlock the device.

l.   Go to **All apps > Settings > Security** (under **Personal**).

m.   Touch **Screen Lock**. What happens? Explain.

n.   Type the correct PIN.

o.   Touch **CONTINUE**.

p.   Touch **None**.

q.   Press the **Power** button briefly to lock the screen.

r.   Press the **Power** button briefly to unlock the screen. What happens?

Part 2:   Passcode Lock on iOS

Step 1:   Configure passcode lock on an iOS device.

a.   Turn on the device and get to the **Home** screen. Touch the **Settings** icon.

b.   Go to **Settings > Passcode**. The **Passcode Lock** screen appears.

Note: For some iOS versions, go to **Settings > Touch ID & Passcode**.

c.   Touch **Turn Passcode On**. The **Set Passcode** screen appears.

d.   Type **1234** as the passcode.

e.   Re-enter **1234** to confirm the passcode.

Step 2:   Use the passcode to unlock the screen.

a.   Press the **Power** button briefly to lock the device.

b.   Press the **Power** button briefly to unlock the device.

c.   Slide to unlock the device.

d. Enter the passcode **1234**. What happens?

_____

e. Press the **Power** button briefly to lock the device.

f. Press the **Power** button briefly to unlock the device.

g. Type **4321**. Notice this is not the passcode configured in the device.

h. Touch **OK**. What happens?

_____

i. Enter the incorrect PIN five more times. What happens?

_____

j. After 1 minute, enter the correct passcode.

k. Go to **Settings > Passcode**. What happens? Explain.

_____

_____

l.   Type the correct PIN. The **Passcode Lock** screen appears.

●●●●○ AT&T 🛜   10:42 AM   ✳ ▰▰▰

‹ Settings **Passcode Lock**

Turn Passcode Off

Change Passcode

Require Passcode   Immediately ›

Simple Passcode   ⬤◯

A simple passcode is a 4 digit number.

Voice Dial   ⬤◯

Music Voice Control is always enabled.

ALLOW ACCESS WHEN LOCKED:

Today   ⬤◯

Notifications View   ⬤◯

m. Touch **Turn Passcode Off**.

n.   Type the correct PIN.

o.   Press the **Power** button briefly to lock the device.

p.   Press the **Power** button briefly to unlock the device. What happens?

Lab 10.3.1.2 - Mobile Wi-Fi

Introduction

In this lab, you will turn the Wi-Fi radio on and off, forget a found Wi-Fi network, and find and connect to a Wi-Fi network.

Recommended Equipment

- Android tablet or smartphone running Android version 5.0 or higher
- iOS tablet or smartphone running iOS version 7.0 or higher

Step 1:   Configure Wi-Fi on Android device.

In this step, you will configure Wi-Fi on an Android device.

a. Turn on the device and log in with the password, pin code, or other passcode, if necessary.

b. Go to **All apps > Settings > Wi-Fi** (under **Wireless & networks**).

c.   Touch the **Wi-Fi** slider to turn it **Off**.

d.   Touch the **Wi-Fi** slider again to turn it **On**.

e.   Wait until the device is connected a wireless network before moving on to the next step.

f.   Touch the name of the network to which the device is connected. The **Wi-Fi details** window appears.

g. Touch **FORGET**. What happens?

_____

h. Touch the network to which the device used to be connected.

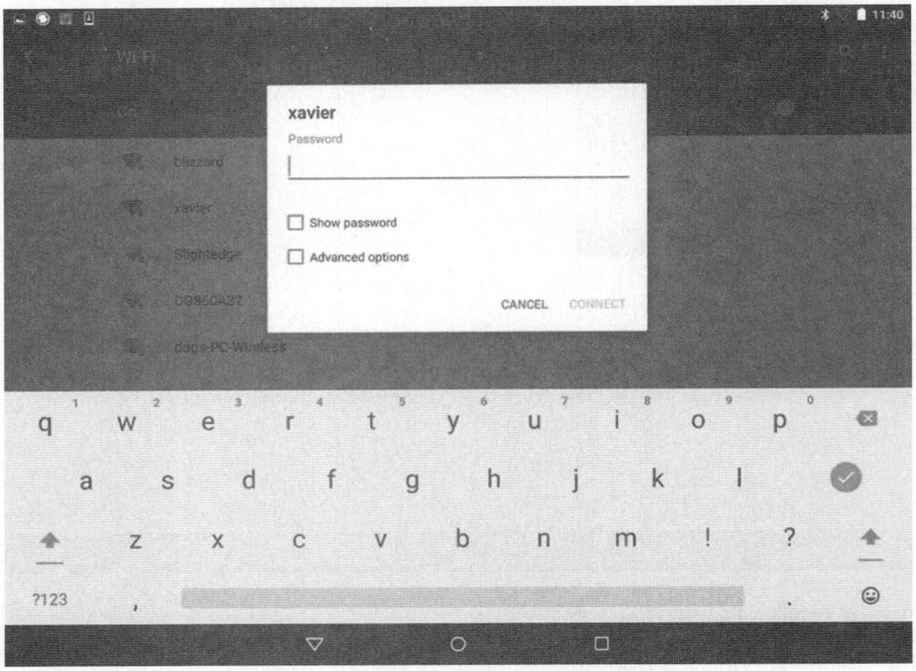

i. Type the Wi-Fi Password. Touch **CONNECT**. What happens?

_____

Step 2:   Configure Wi-Fi on an iOS device.

In this step, you will configure Wi-Fi on an iOS device.

a. Turn on the device and log in with the **password**, **PIN** code, or other **passcode**, if necessary.

b. Go to **Settings > Wi-Fi**.

c.   Touch the **Wi-Fi** slider to turn it off.

d.   Touch the **Wi-Fi** slider to turn it on.

e.   Touch the name of the network to which the device should connect to. The Wi-Fi details window opens.

f.   Touch **Forget This Network**. Confirm the deletion of the network by selecting **Forget**. What happens?

g.   Touch the network to which the device used to be connected to.

h.   Type the Wi-Fi password.

i.   Touch **Join**. What happens?

Lab 10.4.1.4 - Install Linux in a Virtual Machine and Explore the GUI

Objectives

Part 1: Preparing a Computer for Virtualization

Part 2: Installing a Linux OS on the Virtual Machine

Part 3: Exploring the GUI

Background / Scenario

Computing power and resources have increased tremendously over the last 10 years. A benefit of multi-core processors and large amounts of RAM is the ability to install multiple operating systems or use virtualization on a computer. With more than one operating systems installed, the user can switch between operating systems by restarting the computer and choosing the operating system to boot.

With virtualization, one or more virtual computers can operate inside one physical computer. Virtual computers that run within physical computers are called virtual machines. Virtual machines are often called guests, and physical computers are often called hosts. Anyone with a modern computer and operating system can run virtual machines.

In this lab, you will install a Linux OS in a virtual machine using a desktop virtualization application, such as VirtualBox. After completing the installation, you will explore the GUI interface. You will also explore the command line interface using this virutal machine in a later lab in this course.

Required Resources

- Computer with a minimum of 2 GB of RAM and 10 GB of free disk space.
- High-speed Internet access to download Oracle VirtualBox and Linux OS image, such as Ubuntu Desktop 14.04.

Part 1: Preparing a Computer for Virtualization

In Part 1, you will download and install desktop virtualization software and a Linux OS image. Your instructor may provide you with a Linux OS image.

Step 1: Download and install VirtualBox.

VMware Player and Oracle VirtualBox are two virtualization programs that you can download and install to support the OS image file. In this lab, you will use the VirtualBox application. To download and install VirtualBox:

a. Navigate to http://www.oracle.com/technetwork/server-storage/virtualbox/downloads/index.html.

b. Choose and download the appropriate installation file based on your operating system. If you are running Windows OS, click the **Windows Installer** to download the file.

c. After the VirtualBox installation file is downloaded, run the installer and accept the default installation settings.

Step 2: Download a Linux image.

a. Navigate to the Ubuntu website at http://www.ubuntu.com/download/desktop to download and save a Ubuntu desktop image.

b. Select the 64-bit or 32-bit version of the OS. Click **Download** to start downloading the image. Scroll down the web page and click **Not now, take me to the download** if necessary to bypass the donation prompt. Then select **Save File** and click **OK** to save the file.

Note: The 64-bit version is recommended.

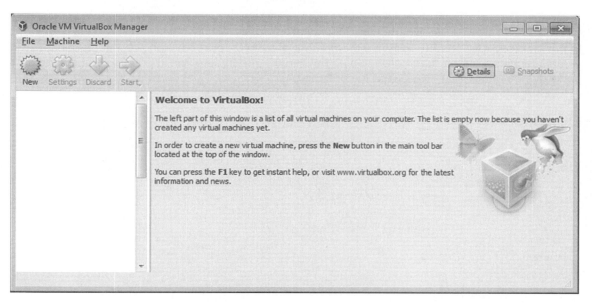

Part 2: Installing a Linux OS on the Virtual Machine

Step 1: Create a new virtual machine.

a. Click **Start** and search for **Virtualbox**. Click **Oracle VM VirtualBox** to open the manager. When the manager opens, click **New** to start the Ubuntu installation.

b. In the **Name and operating system** screen, type **Ubuntu** in the **Name** field. For the **Type** field, select **Linux**. In the **Version** field, select **Ubuntu (64-bit)** if that is the version downloaded from the Ubuntu website. Otherwise, select the corresponding downloaded version. Click **Next** to continue.

c. In the **Memory size** screen, increase the amount of RAM if desired as long as the amount of RAM for the virtual machine is in the green area. Going beyond the green area would adversely affect the performance of the host. Click **Next** to continue.

d. In the **Hard disk** screen, click **Create** to create a virtual hard disk now.

e. In the **Hard disk file type** screen, use the default file type settings of VDI (VirtualBox Disk Image). Click **Next** to continue.

f.   In the **Storage on physical hard disk** screen, use the default storage settings of dynamically allocated. Click **Next** to continue.

g.   In the **File location and size** screen, you can adjust the hard drive and change the name and location of the virtual hard drive. Click **Create** to use the default settings.

h. When the hard drive creation is done, the new virtual machine is listed in the **Oracle VM VirtualBox Manager** window. Select **Ubuntu** and click **Start** (➡) in the top menu.

Step 2: Install Ubuntu on the virtual machine.

a. When the virtual machine starts the first time without an installed OS, you are prompted to provide a location where an image of the OS can be found.

If you downloaded the operating system, click the file manager icon (🗁) to browse the OS image location in the file system. Select the file with .iso extension and click **Open** to start the installation.

If the operating system is on an optical disk, select the location of the optical driver that contains the optical disk.

Click **Start** to continue. Only complete the next step if you were not prompted for an operating system.

b. If you were able to locate the.iso and press **Start** in the previous step, skip this step. If you were not prompted an OS image, return to the **Oracle VM VirtualBox Manager** window. Right-click **Ubuntu** and select **Settings**. In the **Ubuntu – Settings** window, click **Storage** in the left panel. Click **Empty** in the middle panel. In the right panel, click the CD symbol ( ) and select the file location of the OS. Click **OK** to continue.

In the **Oracle VM VirtualBox Manager** window. Select **Ubuntu** and click **Start** ( ) in the top menu.

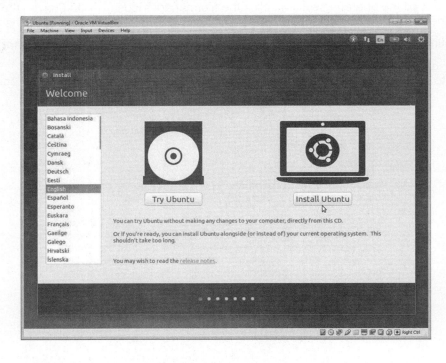

c. In the **Welcome** screen, you are prompted to try or install Ubuntu. In this lab, you will install the Ubuntu OS in this virtual machine. Click **Install Ubuntu**.

d. In the **Preparing to install Ubuntu** screen, verify that the computer meets the installation requirements represented by the green check marks. Select **Download updates while installing** and **Install this third-party software** if desired. Click **Continue**.

Note: If you are not connected to the Internet, you can continue to install and enable the network later.

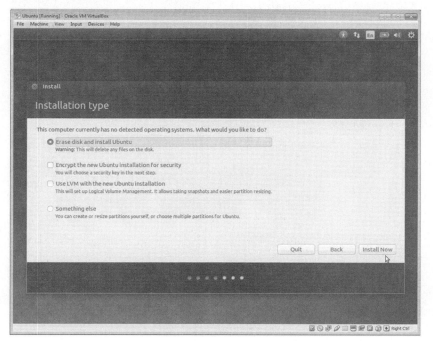

e. Because this Ubuntu installation is in a virtual machine, it is safe to erase the disk and install Ubuntu without affecting the host computer. Select **Erase disk and install Ubuntu**. Otherwise, installing Ubuntu on a physical computer would erase all data in the disk and replace the existing operating system with Ubuntu. Click **Install Now** to start the installation.

f.   Click **Continue** to erase the disk and install Ubuntu.

g.   In the **Where are you?** screen, verify that the location listed is correct. Otherwise, type your location in the field and select the desired location in the provided list. Then click **Continue**.

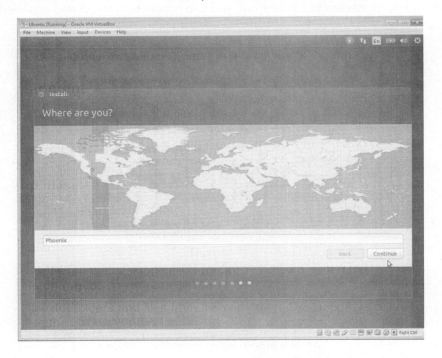

h.   In the **Keyboard layout** screen, verify that the correct keyboard layout is selected. If desired, type some text in the **Type here to test your keyboard** field to verify the keyboard layout. Click **Continue**.

i.   In the **Who are you?** screen, provide your name and choose a password. Use **ITEUser** for **Your Name** and **ITEpass!** for the password. You can use the username generated or enter a different username. If desired, you can change the other settings. Click **Continue**.

j.   The Ubuntu OS is now installing in the virtual machine. This will take several minutes. When the Installation Complete window displays, click **Restart Now** to use the new installation. If there is an installation disk in the optical drive, remove the media and close the tray and press **Enter** to continue.

Part 3: Exploring the GUI

In this part, you will install the VirtualBox guest additions and explore the Ubuntu GUI.

Step 1: Install guest additions.

a.   Log into your Ubuntu virtual machine using the user credentials created in the previous part.

b. Your Ubuntu Desktop window may be smaller than expected. This is especially true on high-resolution displays. Click **Device > Insert Guest Additions CD image…** to install the Guest Additions. This allows more functions, such as changing the screen resolution in the virtual machine.

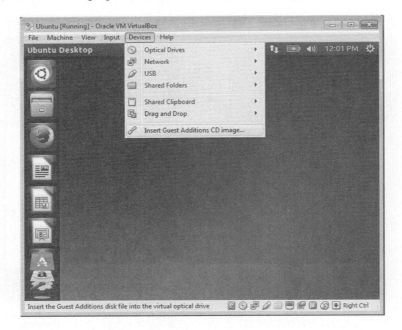

c. Click **Run** to install the additions. When prompted for a password, use the same password that you used to log in. Click **Authenticate** to continue.

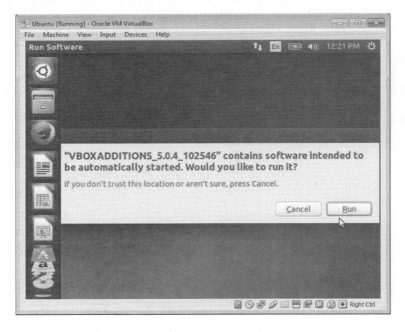

d. If the computer was not connected to the Internet during the installation, click **Devices > Network Settings** in the Oracle VirtualBox menu. Enable network adapters and configure the proper setting for network connections as necessary. Click **OK**.

e. When the installation of the additions is done, restart the virtual machine again. Click **Settings** ( ) in the upper-right corner and click **Shut down**. Click **Restart** to restart Ubuntu.

Step 2: Open a web browser.

a. Log into Ubuntu again. After you are logged in again, you can resize the virtual machine window.

b. Click **Dash** (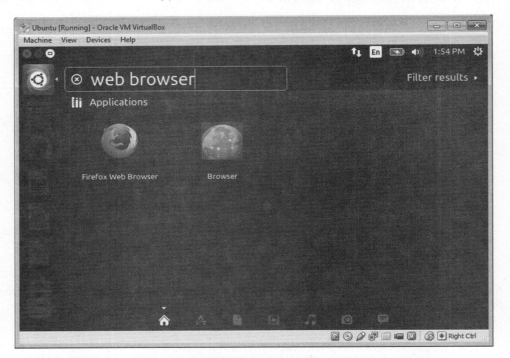) to search your computer and online resources. Type **web browser** and click your desired web browser under the Applications heading and navigate to different web sites.

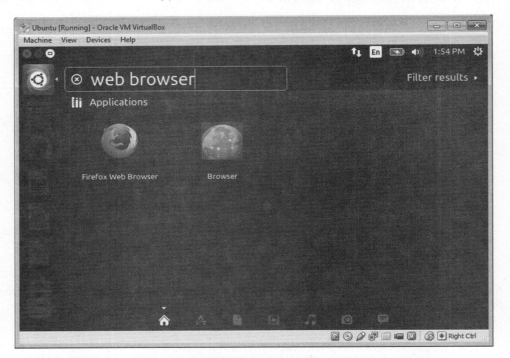

c. To access the command-line interface, click **Dash** and type **terminal** to display a list of terminal emulators listed under the Applications header.

How many are available to you and what are their names?

_____

_____

_____

Reflection

What are the advantages and disadvantages of using a virtual machine?

_____

_____

Lab 10.4.3.3 - Working with Linux Command Line

Introduction

In this lab, you will use the Linux command line to manage files and folders and perform some basic administrative tasks.

Recommended Equipment

- A computer with a Linux OS, either installed physically or in a virtual machine

Step 1:   Access the command line.

a.   Log on to a computer as a user with administrative privileges. The account **ITEUser** is used as the example user account throughout this lab.

b.   To access the command line, click **Dash**, and type **terminal** in the search field and press **Enter**. The default terminal emulator opens.

```
ITEUser@iteuser-VirtualBox: ~
ITEUser@iteuser-VirtualBox:~$
```

Step 2:   Display the man pages from the command line.

You can display command line help using the **man** command. A man page, short for manual page, is an online documentation of the Linux commands. A man page provides detailed information about a command and all the available options.

a.   To learn more about the man page, type **man man** at the command prompt and press **Enter**.

```
ITEUser@iteuser-VirtualBox: ~
MAN(1)                        Manual pager utils                        MAN(1)

NAME
       man - an interface to the on-line reference manuals

SYNOPSIS
       man [-C file] [-d] [-D] [--warnings[=warnings]] [-R encoding] [-L
       locale] [-m system[,...]] [-M path] [-S list] [-e extension] [-i|-I]
       [--regex|--wildcard] [--names-only] [-a] [-u] [--no-subpages] [-P
       pager] [-r prompt] [-7] [-E encoding] [--no-hyphenation] [--no-justifi-
       cation] [-p string] [-t] [-T[device]] [-H[browser]] [-X[dpi]] [-Z]
       [[section] page ...] ...
       man -k [apropos options] regexp ...
       man -K [-w|-W] [-S list] [-i|-I] [--regex] [section] term ...
Manual page man(1) line 1 (press h for help or q to quit)
```

Name a few sections that included in a man page.

_____

_____

b.   Type **q** to exit the man page.

c.   Type **man cp** at the prompt to display the information about the **cp** command.

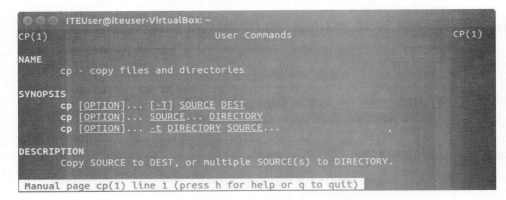

What command would you use to find out more information about the **pwd** command? What is the function of the **pwd** command?

_____

_____

Step 3:   Create and change directories.

In this step, you will use the change directory (**cd**), make directory (**mkdir**), and list directory (**ls**) commands.

Note: A directory is another word for folder. The terms directory and folder are used interchangeably throughout this lab.

a.   Type **pwd** at the prompt. What is the current directory?

_____

b.   Navigate to the /home/ITEUser directory if it is not your current directory. Type **cd /home/ITEUser**.

c.   Type **ls** at the command prompt to list the files and folders that are in the current folder.

d.   In the current directory, use the **mkdir** command to create three new folders: **ITEfolder1**, **ITEfolder2**, and **ITEfolder3**. Type **mkdir ITEfolder1** and press **Enter**. Create **ITEfolder2** and **ITEfolder3**.

e.   Type **ls** to verify the folders have been created.

f.   Type **cd ITEfolder3** at the command prompt and press **Enter**. Which folder are you in now?

_____

Another way to determine your location in the directory tree is to looking at the prompt. In this example, the prompt, **ITEUser@iteuser-VirtualBox:~/ITEfolder3$**, provides the name of the current user, the computer name, the current working directory, and the privilege level.

~/ITEfolder3: is the current working directory. The symbol **~** represents the current user's home directory. In this example, it is /home/ITEUser.

$: indicates regular user privilege. If **#** is displayed at the prompt, this indicates elevated privilege (root).

g.   Within the **ITEfolder3** folder, create a folder named **ITEfolder4**. Type **mkdir ITEfolder4**. Use the **ls** command to verify the folder creation.

h.   Type **cd ..** to change the current directory. Each **..** is a shortcut to move up one level in the directory tree.

After issuing the **cd ..** command, what is your directory now?

_____

What would be the current directory if you issue this command at **ITEUser@iteuser-VirtualBox:~$**?

_____

Step 4:   Create text files.

a.   Navigate to the **/home/ITEUser1/ITEfolder1 (~\ITEfolder1)** directory. Type **cd ITEfolder1** at the prompt.

b.   Type **echo This is doc1.txt > doc1.txt** at the command prompt. The **echo** command is used to display a message at the command prompt. The **>** is used to redirect the message from the screen to a file. For example, in the first line, the message **This is doc1.txt** is redirected into a new file named **doc1.txt**. Use the **echo** command and **>** redirect to create these files: **doc2.txt**, **file1.txt**, and **file2.txt**.

```
ITEUser@iteuser-VirtualBox: ~/ITEfolder1
ITEUser@iteuser-VirtualBox:~/ITEfolder1$ echo This is doc1.txt > doc1.txt
ITEUser@iteuser-VirtualBox:~/ITEfolder1$ echo This is doc2.txt > doc2.txt
ITEUser@iteuser-VirtualBox:~/ITEfolder1$ echo This is file1.txt > file1.txt
ITEUser@iteuser-VirtualBox:~/ITEfolder1$ echo This is file2.txt > file2.txt
ITEUser@iteuser-VirtualBox:~/ITEfolder1$
```

c.   Use the **ls** command to verify the files are in the **ITEfolder1** folder. To determine the file permission and other information, type the **ls –l** command at the prompt.

```
ITEUser@iteuser-VirtualBox: ~/ITEfolder1
ITEUser@iteuser-VirtualBox:~/ITEfolder1$ ls -l
total 16
-rw-rw-r-- 1 ITEUser ITEUser 17 Sep 21 08:58 doc1.txt
-rw-rw-r-- 1 ITEUser ITEUser 17 Sep 21 08:59 doc2.txt
-rw-rw-r-- 1 ITEUser ITEUser 18 Sep 21 08:59 file1.txt
-rw-rw-r-- 1 ITEUser ITEUser 18 Sep 21 08:59 file2.txt
ITEUser@iteuser-VirtualBox:~/ITEfolder1$
```

The following figure breaks down the information provided by the **ls –l** command. The user **ITEUser** is owner of file. The user can read and write to the file. The user **ITEUser** belongs to the group name **ITEUser**. Anyone in the group **ITEUser** has the same permission. The group can read and write to the file. If the user is not the owner or in the group **ITEUser**, the user can only read the file as indicated by the permission for other.

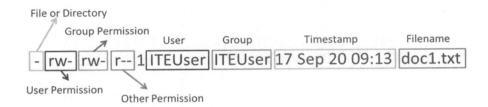

d. Type the **man ls** command at the prompt. What option would you use to list all the files in the directory, including the hidden files starting with .?

_____

e. Use the **cat** command to view the content of the text files. To view the content of doc2.txt, type **cat doc2.txt**.

Step 5: Copy, delete, and move files.

a. At the command prompt, type **mv doc2.txt ~/ITEfolder2** to move the file **doc2.txt** to the **/home/ITEUser/ITEfolder2** directory.

b. Type **ls** at the prompt to verify that **doc2.txt** is no longer in the current directory.

c. Type **cd ../ITEfolder2** to change the directory to **ITEfolder2**. Type **ls** at the prompt to verify **doc2.txt** has been moved.

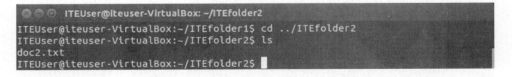

d. Type **cp doc2.txt doc2_copy.txt** to create a copy of **doc2.txt**. Type **ls** at the prompt to verify a copy of the file has been created. Use the **cat** command to look at the content of **doc2_copy.txt**. The content in the copy should be the same as the original file.

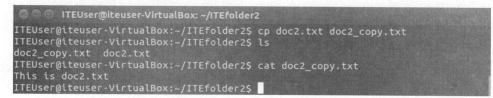

e. Now use the **mv** command to move **doc2_copy.txt** to **ITEfolder1**. Type **mv doc2_copy.txt ../ITEfolder1**. Use the **ls** command to verify that **doc2_copy.txt** is no longer in the directory.

f. A copy of **doc2.txt** can be created and renamed with the **cp** command. Type **cp doc2.txt ../ITEfoler1/doc2_new.txt** at the prompt.

g. Type **ls ..\ITEfolder1** to view the content in **ITEfolder1** without leaving the current directory.

h. Change the current directory to **ITEfolder1**. Type **cd ../ITEfolder1** at the prompt.

i. Move **file1.txt** and **file2.txt** into **ITEfolder3**. To move all the files that contain the word **file** into **ITEfolder3** with one command, use a **wildcard** (*) character to represent one or more characters. Type **mv file*.txt ..\ITEfolder3**.

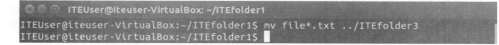

j. Now delete **doc2_copy.txt** from the **ITEfolder1** directory. Type **rm doc2_copy.txt**. Use the **ls** command to verify the file deletion.

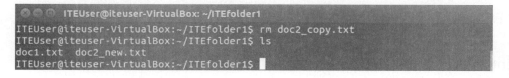

Step 6:   Delete directories.

In this step, you will delete a directory using the **rm** command. The **rm** command can be used to delete files and directories.

a. Navigate to the **/home/ITEUser/ITEfolder3** directory. Use the **ls** command to list the content of the directory.

b. Use the **rm ITEfolder4** to delete the empty directory, and the message **rm: cannot remove 'ITEfodler4/': Is a directory**.

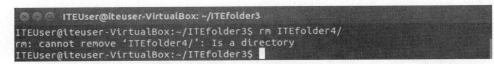

c. Use the man pages to determine what options are necessary so the **rm** command can delete directory. Type **man rm** at the prompt.

What option is needed to delete a directory?

_____

d. Use the **rm –d ITEfolder4** command to delete the empty directory and use the **ls** command to verify the removal of the directory.

e. Navigate to **/home/ITEUser**.

f. Now remove the folder **ITEfolder3** using the **rm –d ITEfolder3** command to delete the non-empty directory. The message indicates that the directory is not empty and cannot be deleted.

g. Use man pages to find out more information about the **rm** command.

What option is necessary to delete a non-empty folder using the **rm** command?

_____

h. To remove a non-empty directory, type the **rm –r ITEfolder3** command to delete the non-empty folder. Use the **ls** command to verify that the directory was deleted.

Step 7: Print lines matching a pattern.

The **cat** command is used to view the content of a text file. To search the content of a text file, you can use the **grep** command. The **grep** command can also be used to match a pattern with screen outputs.

In this step, you will create a few additional text files in the **/home/ITEUser/ITEfolder1** directory. The content and the filename are of your choosing. Three text files are used as examples in this step.

a. Navigate to **/home/ITEUser/ITEfolder1**.

b. Use the **echo** command and redirect **>** to create a few text files ~/**ITEfolder1** and verify that the files were created in **~/ITEfolder1**.

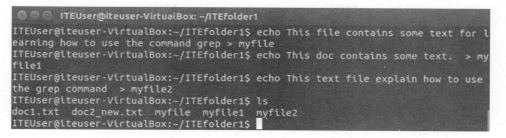

c. To determine which files contains the word **file** within the content of all the files, type **grep file *** to search for the word. The **wildcard** (*) allows any filename to be included in the search. The files **myfile** and **myfile2** have the word **file** in the content.

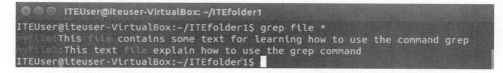

What command would you use to search for the word **doc** in the content of the files? Which files contains the word **doc** in this example?

d. Type **grep doc *.txt** to search for the files with **.txt** in the filename and has the word **doc** in the content.

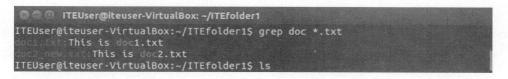

e. Type **grep "some text" *** at the prompt to determine which files contain the phrase **some text**. The files, **myfile** and **myfile1** have the phase **some text** in the content.

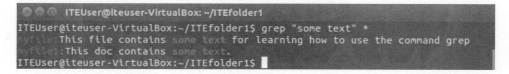

What command would you use to search for the word **the** in the file with the .txt extension? Which files met the requirements?

f.   The search pattern is case sensitive in the **grep** command. The option **–i** or **--ignore-case** is used to ignore the case distinction. To search for all the patterns of **th**, type the **grep –i th *** command at the prompt.

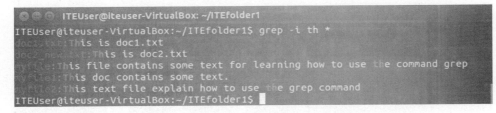

What command would you use to search for the pattern **th** or **Th** in the file with the .txt extension? Which files met the requirements?

_____

g.   To search for a certain pattern for a screen output, the vertical bar (|), commonly referred to as the pipe. The pipe (|) is used to direct the output from the first command into the input for the second command. Using the output of **ls** command as an example, type **ls | grep file** at the prompt to list all the filenames with the word **file**.

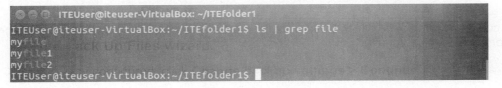

Step 8:   Display the IP address.

The **ifconfig** command allows you to configure a network interface. In this step, you will use the **ifconfig** to display the IP address associated with a network interface.

At the command prompt, type **ifconfig**. In this example, the **eth0** interface has been assigned an IP address of 192.168.1.7 with a subnet mask of 255.255.255.0.

```
ITEUser@iteuser-VirtualBox: ~
ITEUser@iteuser-VirtualBox:~$ ifconfig
eth0      Link encap:Ethernet  HWaddr 08:00:27:35:5c:6b
          inet addr:192.168.1.7  Bcast:192.168.1.255  Mask:255.255.255.0
          inet6 addr: fe80::a00:27ff:fe35:5c6b/64 Scope:Link
          UP BROADCAST RUNNING MULTICAST  MTU:1500  Metric:1
          RX packets:43107 errors:0 dropped:0 overruns:0 frame:0
          TX packets:819 errors:0 dropped:0 overruns:0 carrier:0
          collisions:0 txqueuelen:1000
          RX bytes:3392720 (3.3 MB)  TX bytes:126835 (126.8 KB)

lo        Link encap:Local Loopback
          inet addr:127.0.0.1  Mask:255.0.0.0
          inet6 addr: ::1/128 Scope:Host
          UP LOOPBACK RUNNING  MTU:65536  Metric:1
          RX packets:162 errors:0 dropped:0 overruns:0 frame:0
          TX packets:162 errors:0 dropped:0 overruns:0 carrier:0
          collisions:0 txqueuelen:0
          RX bytes:14250 (14.2 KB)  TX bytes:14250 (14.2 KB)

ITEUser@iteuser-VirtualBox:~$
```

Step 9:   Change your login password.

Changing your login password is a good practice in compute security and to unauthorized access to your information and your account.

In this step, you will change your login password. You will need your current password and choose a new password to access your account.

a. Type **passwd** at the prompt to start the process of changing your password. Enter the current password and provide your new password twice. When the message **passwd: password updated successfully** is displayed, your password has been changed.

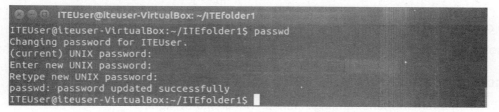

b. Log out of the computer and use the new password to log on to the computer again.

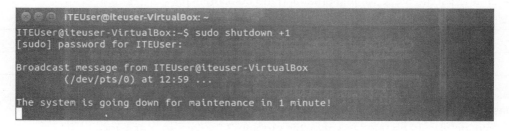

Step 10: Use the shutdown command.

The **shutdown** command is used to bring the computer down gracefully. It requires elevated privileges and a time parameter. Because the user ITEUser is the first user account on the computer, the **sudo** command and the password allows this user the elevated privileges. The time parameter can be now, number of minutes from now, or at a specific time, such as 13:00.

Type **sudo shutdown +1** to bring the computer down gracefully in 1 minute. When prompted, enter your password.

Reflection

What are the advantages of using the Linux command line?

_____

_____

Lab 10.5.2.2 - Troubleshooting Mobile Devices

Introduction

In this lab, you will analyze scenarios involving common problems for mobile devices and identify the solutions. You have been provided with a list of solutions for common problems. Each solution may be used more than once.

After the solutions have been identified, you will research and list the steps for implementing them.

Recommended Equipment

- Android tablet or smartphone running Android version 5.0 or higher
- iOS tablet or smartphone running iOS version 7.0 or higher

Troubleshooting Mobile Devices

Solutions for Common Problems		
Perform a hard shutdown	Pull the battery	Complete a factory restore/reset
Force the app to close	Replace the SIM card	Reconfigure network settings
Insert or replace the memory card	Delete unnecessary files or uninstall apps	Clean the phone

Select one solution from the box above for each common problem listed below. Each solution may be used more than once.

a. You have been using a social networking app on your phone without any problems. Suddenly the application freezes up while trying to upload a photo.

Which solution should be used to solve this problem? Explain your answer.

_____

Research and list the steps for implementing the solution.

_____

_____

_____

_____

b. The passcode, or passcode pattern, has been forgotten.

Which solution should be used to solve this problem? Explain your answer.

_____

Research and list the steps for implementing the solution.

_____

_____

_____

_____

c. A phone has been powered on, but it proceeds to loop through the startup process repeatedly.

Which solution should be used to solve this problem? Explain your answer.

_____

_____

Research and list the steps for implementing the solution.

_____

_____

_____

_____

d. You have had your Android smartphone for five months and have not experienced any problems. Suddenly, a "No SIM Card" message begins appearing regularly. You check your SIM card and there are no problems with the contacts on the SIM card and the SIM card is locked into place.

Which solution should be used to solve this problem? Explain your answer.

_____

_____

Research and list the steps for implementing the solution.

_____

_____

_____

_____

e. Friends and family have recently begun complaining about how hard it is to hear you during calls. You have already tried a hard reset for your phone, but that has not solved the problem.

Which solution should be used to solve the problem?

_____

Research and list the steps for implementing the solution.

_____

_____

_____

_____

f.   The phone is entirely unresponsive.

Which solution should be used to solve the problem?

_____

Research and list the steps for implementing the solution.

_____

_____

_____

_____

g.   The mobile device cannot send or receive email.

Which solution should be used to solve the problem?

_____

Research and list the steps for implementing the solution.

_____

_____

_____

_____

h.   The phone cannot install additional apps or save photos.

Which solution should be used to solve the problem?

_____

Research and list the steps for implementing the solution.

_____

_____

_____

_____

Chapter 11: Printers

Lab 11.2.1.6 - Install a Printer in Windows 7 and Vista

Introduction

In this lab, you will install a printer. You will find, download, and update the driver and the software for the printer.

Recommended Equipment

- A computer running Windows 7 or Vista
- Internet connection
- Printer

Step 1:   Connect a USB printer.

If you are installing a USB printer, plug the printer into the computer using a USB cable. Plug the printer power cord into an AC outlet, if necessary. Unlock the printer if it is locked. Refer to the instruction manual if you do not know how to unlock the printer. Printer heads are often locked to prevent damage during shipment.

Step 2:   Install the printer driver.

a. Windows detects the new hardware and attempts to load the appropriate driver.

b. If Windows is unable to load the appropriate driver, skip to **Step 3** to download and install the most recent printer driver.

c. Click the **Installing device driver software** bubble to determine the installation status.

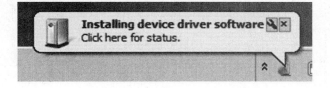

d. Click **Close** in the **Driver Software Installation** screen after viewing the messages.

Driver Software Installation		☒
Your device is ready to use		
USB Printing Support	✓ Ready to use	
Samsung CLP-310 Series (Mono)	✓ Ready to use	
		Close

Step 3:   Download a current version of the printer driver.

This step should be completed even if Windows installed a driver in **Step 2**. In order to ensure that your computer has the most current driver, find the manufacturer and the model number of the printer.

a. Visit the manufacturer's web site and navigate to the product downloads or support page. Download the most recent driver and software for the model of printer device that you have installed. The software and driver must be compatible with your operating system. Make sure to download the driver with a matching architecture for your computer (x64 or x32), if necessary.

b. Download the driver, often found in archive format, and extract to a temporary folder on your desktop, if necessary.

c. The installation wizard may start automatically after the file extraction.

d. Follow the installation wizard instructions until the software and driver installation is complete. Reboot the computer, if necessary.

Step 4:   Print a test page.

a. To verify printer functionality, click **Control Panel > Devices and Printers**.

b. Right-click the printer and select **Printer Properties**.

c. Click **Print Test Page**.

Reflection

Why would you download and install software and drivers when Windows already installs them for you?

_____

_____

_____

Lab 11.2.1.6 - Install a Printer in Windows 8

Introduction

In this lab, you will install a printer. You will find, download, and update the driver and the software for the printer.

Recommended Equipment

- A computer running Windows 8
- Internet connection
- Printer

Step 1: Connect a USB printer.

If you are installing a USB printer, plug the printer into the computer using a USB cable. Plug the printer power cord into an AC outlet if necessary. Unlock the printer if it is locked. Refer to the instruction manual if you do not know how to unlock the printer. Printer heads are often locked to prevent damage during shipment.

Step 2: Install the printer driver.

a. Windows detects the new hardware and attempts to load the appropriate driver.

b. Click **Close** when the installation is completed.

Step 3: Download an up-to-date printer driver.

In order to ensure that your computer has the most current driver, find the manufacturer and the model number of the printer.

Visit the manufacturer's web site and navigate to the product downloads or support page. Download the most recent driver and software for the model of printer device that you have installed. The software and driver must be compatible with your operating system. Make sure that you download the driver with a matching architecture for your computer (x64 or x32), if necessary.

a. Download the driver. The driver is often found in archive format.

b. Extract the driver to a temporary folder on your desktop, if necessary.

c. The installation wizard may start automatically after file extraction. If not, double-click the .exe file.

d. Follow the installation wizard instructions until the software and driver have been installed.

e. Reboot your computer if necessary.

Step 4:   Print a test page.

a. To verify printer functionality, click **Control Panel > Devices and Printers**.

b. Right-click the printer and select **Printer Properties**.

c. Click **Print Test Page** to print a test page.

Reflection

Why would you download and install software and drivers when Windows already installs them for you?

_____

_____

_____

Lab 11.3.2.5 - Share a Printer in Windows 7 and Vista

Introduction

In this lab, you will share a printer, configure the printer on a networked computer, and print a test page from the remote computer.

Recommended Equipment

- Two computers directly connected or connected through a switch
- Windows 7 or Vista installed on both computers
- A printer installed on one of the computers

Part 1: Windows 7

Step 1:   Share the printer.

a. Log on to the computer that has the printer connected. To access the folder options, click **Control Panel > Folder Options**. In the **View** tab, deselect **Use Sharing Wizard (Recommended)**. Click **OK** to continue.

b.   Click **Control Panel > Network and Sharing Center > Change advanced sharing settings** on the left side panel.

c.   In the **Change sharing options for different network profiles** screen, scroll down to **Password protected sharing** for the current profile. Select **Turn off password protected sharing** and click **Save changes**.

d.   Click **Control Panel > Devices and Printers**.

e.   Right-click the **printer > Printer properties**.

f.   In the **Sharing** tab, select **Share this printer**. Name the new share **All-in-One Printer** and click **OK**.

Step 2:   Add a shared printer.

a.   Log on to the computer that does not have the printer connected.

b.   Click **Control Panel > Devices and Printers**.

c.   In the **Devices and Printers** window, click **Add a printer**.

d.   Click **Add a network, wireless or Bluetooth printer**.

e.   The **Searching for available Printers** screen appears. When all printers are discovered, select *Printer name* on *ComputerName* in the **Select a printer** screen and click **Next**.

f.   To find a printer by name or TCP/IP address, select **The printer that I want isn't listed**.

g. Click **Select a shared printer by name** and type **\\computername\printer**, where *computername* is the name of the computer with the connected printer and *printer* is the name of the printer. Click **Next**.

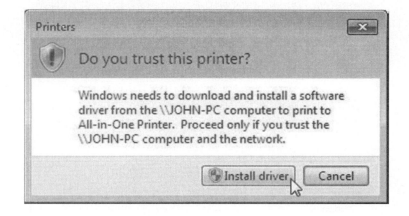

h. If prompted to install drivers, click **Install driver**.

i.   When the **You've successfully added a printer** screen appears, click **Next** and **Finish** to close the **Add Printer** window.

Step 3:   Print a test page.

a.   In the **Devices and Printers** window, right-click the **printer > Printer properties**.

b.   In the **General** tab, click **Print Test Page** to verify that the printer is working properly.

Part 2:   Windows Vista

Step 1:   Share the printer.

a.   Log on to the computer that has the printer connected. To access the folder options, click **Control Panel > Folder Options**. In the **View** tab, deselect **Use Sharing Wizard (Recommended)** and click **OK** to continue.

b.   Click **Control Panel > Network and Sharing Center > Password protected sharing**. Select **Turn off password protected sharing** and click **Apply**.

c. Click **Control Panel > Printers**. Right-click the printer **> Properties**.

d. In the **Sharing** tab, click **Change sharing options**.

e. Select **Share this printer**. Name the new share **Example** and click **OK**.

Step 2: Add a shared printer.

a. Log on to the computer that has no printer connected, and click **Control Panel > Printers**. Click **Add a printer**.

b. In the **Add Printer** screen, click **Add a network, wireless or Bluetooth printer**.

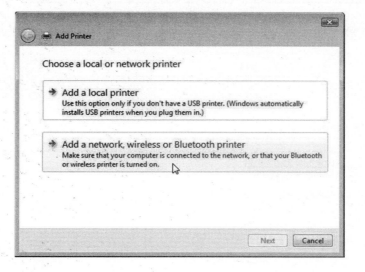

c. When all printers are discovered, the **Select a printer** screen opens. If the desired printer is displayed in the search list, select *Printer* on *Computername* and click **Next**.

Or to find a printer by name or TCP/IP address, select **The printer that I want isn't listed**.

Select the radio button **Select a shared printer by name** and type **\\computername\printer**, where *computername* is the name of the computer with the connected printer and *printer* is the name of the printer. Click **Next**.

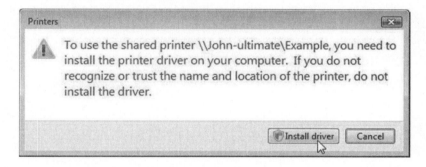

d.   If prompted to install drivers, click **Install driver**.

e.   Accept all default settings, click **Next,** and then click **Finish**.

Step 3:   Print a test page.

a.   Click **Control Panel >** double-click **Printers**.

b.   Right-click the **printer > Properties** and click **Print Test Page**.

Lab 11.3.2.5 - Share a Printer in Windows 8

Introduction

In this lab, you will share a printer, configure the printer on a networked computer, and print a test page from the remote computer.

Recommended Equipment

- Two computers directly connected or connected through a switch
- Windows 8 installed on both computers
- A printer installed on one of the computers

Step 1:   Share the printer.

a. Log on to the computer that has the printer connected. Click **Control Panel > Folder Options**. In the **View** tab, deselect **Use Sharing Wizard (Recommended)**. Click **OK** to continue.

b. Click **Control Panel > Network and Sharing Center > Change advanced sharing settings** on the left side panel.

c.   In the **Change sharing options for different network profiles** screen, expand the **All Networks** profile. Turn off password protected sharing for the All Networks profile. Select **Turn off password protected sharing** and click **Save changes**.

d.   Click **Control Panel > Devices and Printers**.

e.   Right-click the **printer > Printer properties**.

f.   In the **Sharing** tab, select **Share this printer**. Name the new share **All-in-One Printer**, and click **OK**.

Step 2:   Add a shared printer.

a. Log on to the computer with no printer connected.

b. Click **Control Panel > Devices and Printers**.

c. In the **Devices and Printers** window, click **Add a printer**.

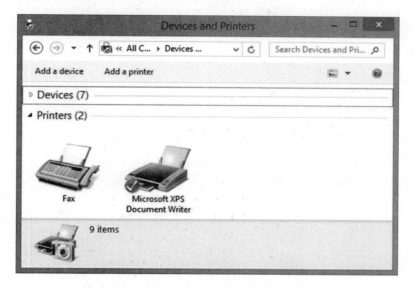

d. When all printers are discovered, select *Printer* on *ComputerName* in the **Select a printer** screen. Click **Next** to continue.

If the desired printer is not listed, click **The printer that I want isn't listed**. In the **Find a printer by other options** screen, click **Select a shared printer by name** and type **\\computername\printer**, where *computername* is the name of the computer with the connected printer and *printer* is the name of the printer. Click **Next**.

e.   If prompted to install drivers, allow the driver installation.

f.   When the **You've successfully added a printer** screen appears, click **Next** and **Finish** to close the **Add Printer** window.

Step 3:   Print a test page.

a.   In the **Devices and Printers** window, right-click and select **printer > Printer properties**.

b. In the **General** tab, click **Print Test Page** to verify that the printer is working properly.

Chapter 12: Security

Lab 12.2.1.8 - Configure Windows Local Security Policy

Introduction

In this lab, you will configure Windows Local Security Policy. Windows Local Security Policy is used to configure a variety of security requirements for stand-alone computers that are not part of an Active Directory domain. You will modify password requirements, enable auditing, configure some user rights, and set some security options. You will then use Event Manager to view logged information.

Recommended Equipment

*   A computer with Windows installed.

Note: Accessing the Local Security Policy tool is slightly different, depending on the version of Windows. But after it is open, the configurations are the same for the remaining steps in this lab.

Step 1: Review the security requirements.

A customer needs to have six stand-alone Windows computers at a branch office configured according to the security policy for the organization. These computers are not part of an Active Directory domain. The policies must be manually configured on each computer.

The security policy is as follows:

*   Passwords must be at least 8 characters.
*   Passwords must be changed every 90 days.
*   A user may change their password once a day.
*   A user must use a unique password for at least 8 changes of the password.
*   A password must consist of three of the following four elements:
    o   At least one lowercase alpha character.
    o   At least one uppercase alpha character.
    o   At least one numerical character.
    o   At least one symbol character.
*   Users are locked out of the computer after 5 attempts to enter the correct password. A user must wait 5 minutes for the lookout counter to reset.
*   Each security setting for Audit Policy should be enabled.
*   After 30 minutes of inactivity, the user will be automatically logged out. (Windows 8.1 and 8.0 only)
*   Users must login before removing a laptop from the docking station.
*   At login, users should be presented with the following title and text:
    o   Title: **Caution:**
    o   Text: **Your activity is monitored. This computer is for business use only.**
*   Users will receive a reminder to change the password 7 days before it expires.

The Windows Local Security Policy tool provides many more settings that are beyond the scope of this course.

Step 2: Open the Windows Local Security Policy tool.

a. To access Local Security Policy in Windows 7 and Vista, use the following path:

Start > Administrative Tools > Local Security Policy

b. To access Local Security Policy in Windows 8 and 8.1, use the following path:

Search > secpol.msc and then click **secpol**.

c. The **Local Security Policy** window opens. This lab will focus on the **Account Policies** and **Local Policies**, as highlighted in the figure below. The rest of the **Security Settings** are beyond the scope of this course.

Note: Screenshots from Windows 8.1 are used throughout this lab.

Step 3: Configure the Password Policy security settings.

The first six requirements of the company's security policy are configured in the **Account Policies** section of the **Local Security Policy** tool.

a. Click the arrow next to **Account Policies** to expand it, and then click **Password Policy**. Six policies are displayed in the right panel with their associated default security settings.

b. The first policy, **Enforce password history**, is used to set the number of unique passwords the user must enter before being allowed to reuse a password. According to the organization's security policy in Step 1, the security setting for this policy should be **8**. Double-click **Enforce password history** to open the **Enforce password history Properties** window. Set the value to **8**.

c. Using the security policy requirements in Step 1, fill in the values you should set in **Local Security Policy** for the remaining **Password Policy** security settings.

Policy	Security Setting
Enforce password history	8
Maximum password age	
Minimum password age	
Minimum password length	
Password must meet complexity requirements	
Store passwords using reversible encryption	Disabled

Note: The **Store passwords using reversible encryption** security setting should always be disabled. Storing passwords using reversible encryption is essentially the same as storing plaintext versions of the passwords. For this reason, this policy should never be enabled unless application requirements outweigh the need to protect password information.

d. Double-click on each of the policies and set the values according to your entries in the table above. When done, your configuration should look like the following:

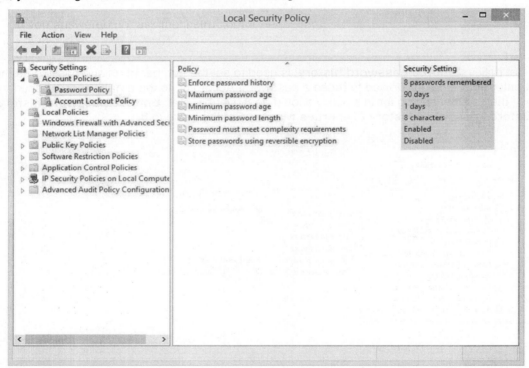

Step 4: Configure the Account Lockout Policy security settings.

a. According the security policy in Step 1, how many times is a user allowed to attempt to login before the account is locked?

_____

b.   How long should the user have to wait before attempting to log back in?

_____

c.   Use the **Account Lockout Policy** security settings in **Local Security Policy** to configure the policy requirements. When done, your configuration should look like the following.

Hint: You will need to configure the **Account lockout threshold** first.

Step 5: Configure the Audit Policy security settings.

a.   In **Local Security Policy**, expand the **Local Policies** menu, and then click **Audit Policy**.

b.   Double-click **Audit account logon events** to open the **Properties** window. Click the **Explain** tab to learn about this security setting.

c.   Click the **Security Setting** tab, and then click the check boxes for **Success** and **Failure**. Click **OK** to close the **Properties** window and apply the security settings.

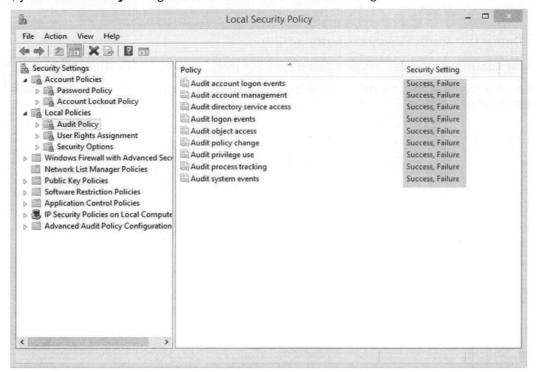

d.   Continue modifying the rest of the **Audit Policy** security settings. Click the **Explain** tab for each and read what it does. Click the **Success** and **Failure** check boxes in each **Properties** window. After you are done, your **Audit Policy** configuration should look like the following:

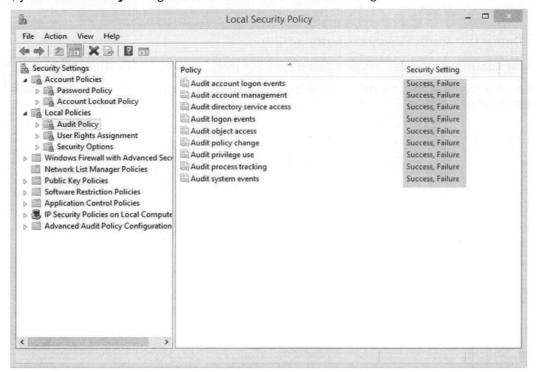

Step 6: Configure additional Local Policies security settings.

a. In **Local Security Policy**, click **User Rights Assignment** under **Local Policies** to view the security settings.

b. Although none of the security settings need to be modified to meet the security policy requirements, spend some time viewing the default settings. Are there any you would recommend changing? Why?

_____

_____

_____

c. In **Local Security Policy**, click **Security Options** under **Local Policies** to view the security settings.

d. Using the remaining security policy requirements in Step 1, list the policy and security setting values you need to change in **Security Options** in the table below. The first one is done for you.

Policy	Security Setting
Interactive logon: Machine inactivity limit (Windows 8.1 and 8.0 only)	1800 seconds

Step 7: Test the password policy security settings.

a. Test your password policy security settings by attempting to change the password. Try a new password that does not meet the length or complexity requirements.

In Windows 7 and Vista, use the following path:

Control Panel > User Accounts > Change your password.

In Windows 8.1, use the following path:

Control Panel > User Accounts > Make changes to my account in PC settings > Sign-in options, and then click **Change** under **Password**.

In Windows 8.0, use the following path:

Control Panel > User Accounts > Make changes to my account in PC settings, and then click **Change your password**.

b. You should be presented with a message that your new password does not meet password policy requirements, such as this message in Windows 8.1:

Step 8: Export and import security policy settings.

The customer has another five stand-alone computers that must meet the same security policy requirements. Instead of manually configuring the settings for each computer, export the settings on this computer.

a. From the menu bar in **Local Security Policy**, click **Action > Export policy...**.

b. Choose a name for the **.inf** file and save it to a location of your choice.

Copy the security policy **.inf** file to a flash drive. Take the flash drive to another computer. Insert the flash drive, open **Local Security Policy**, and click **Action > Import Policy...**. Locate the **.inf** on the flash drive and open it to apply the security policy to the new computer.

Lab 12.3.1.3 - Configure Data Backup and Recovery in Windows 7 and Vista

Introduction

In this lab, you will back up data. You will also perform a recovery of the data.

Recommended Equipment

- A computer with Windows 7 or Vista installed.

Part 1: Data Backup and Recovery in Windows 7

Step 1: Create backup files.

a.   Log on to the computer as an administrator.

b.   Create a text file on the desktop called **Backup File One**. Open the file and type the text "**The text in this file will not be changed.**"

c.   Create another text file on the desktop called **Backup File Two**. Open the file and type the text "**The text in this file will be changed.**"

   Note: Remove all extra folders and files from the computers Desktop. This will help to reduce the length of time to complete the backup for this lab.

Step 2: Open the Backup and Restore tool.

a.   To open Backup and Restore in Windows 7, use the following path:

   Control Panel > Backup and Restore

   In Vista, use the following path:

   Control Panel > Backup and Restore Center

b.   If backup has never been configured, your window will look like the following:

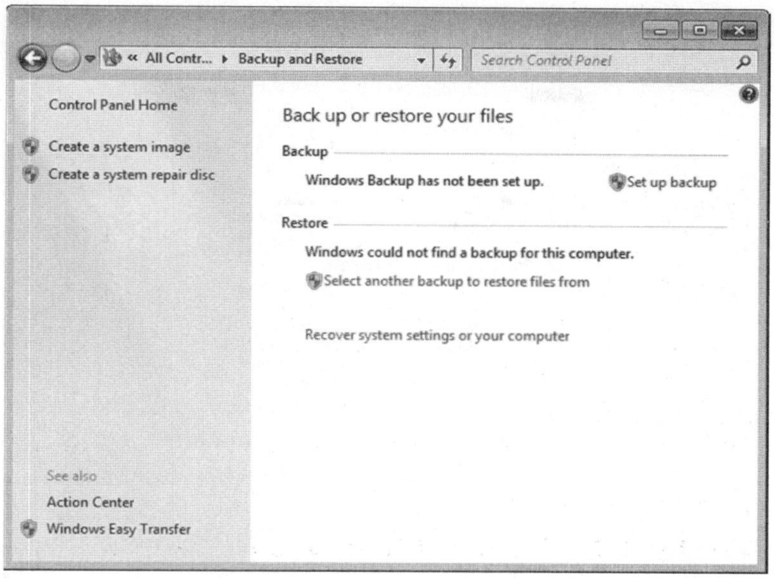

c. If a backup is scheduled to run, click **Turn off schedule**, as shown below.

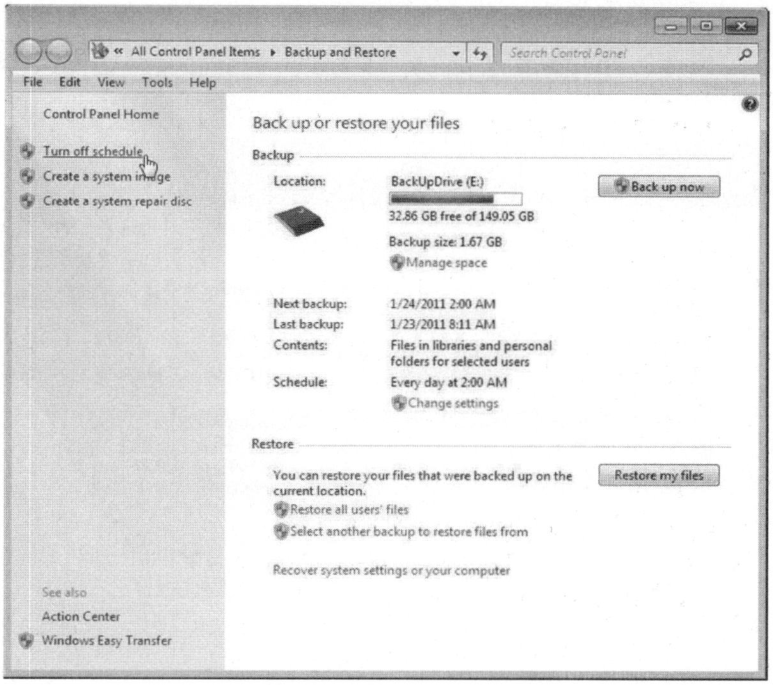

Step 3: Complete the Set Up Backup wizard.

a. If a backup method is already configured, click **Change settings**, as shown below, to start the **Set Up Backup** wizard. If a backup has never been configured, click **Set up backup** to start the wizard.

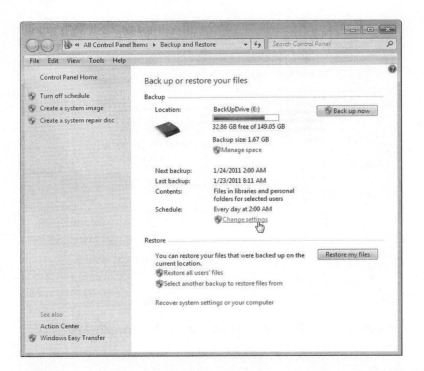

b.   Select the location where the backup will be stored. In this example, an external hard drive is used. Click **Next**.

c.   Select **Let me choose** on the **What do you want to back up?** screen. Click **Next**.

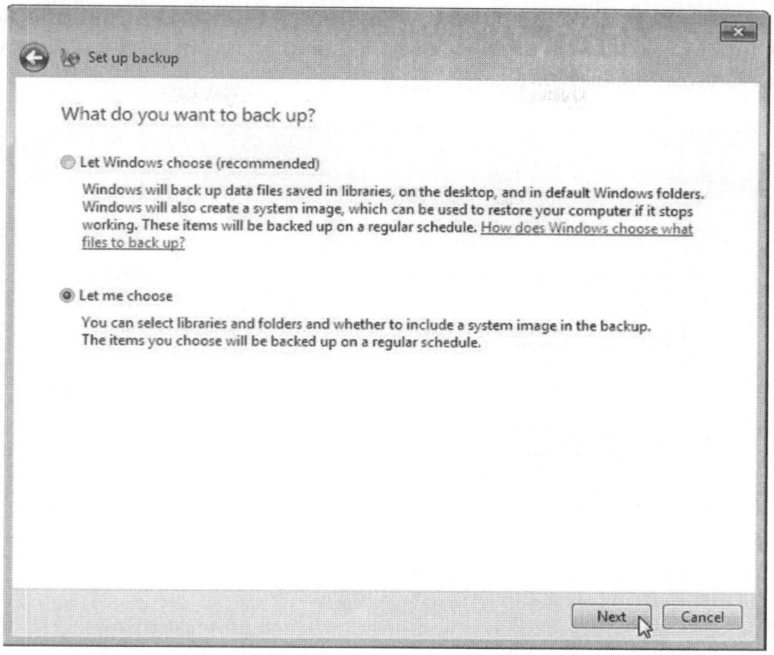

d. Expand the current user account so you can view the different libraries that you can back up. Click **What files are excluded by default from the backup?** and list the excluded files.

_____

_____

_____

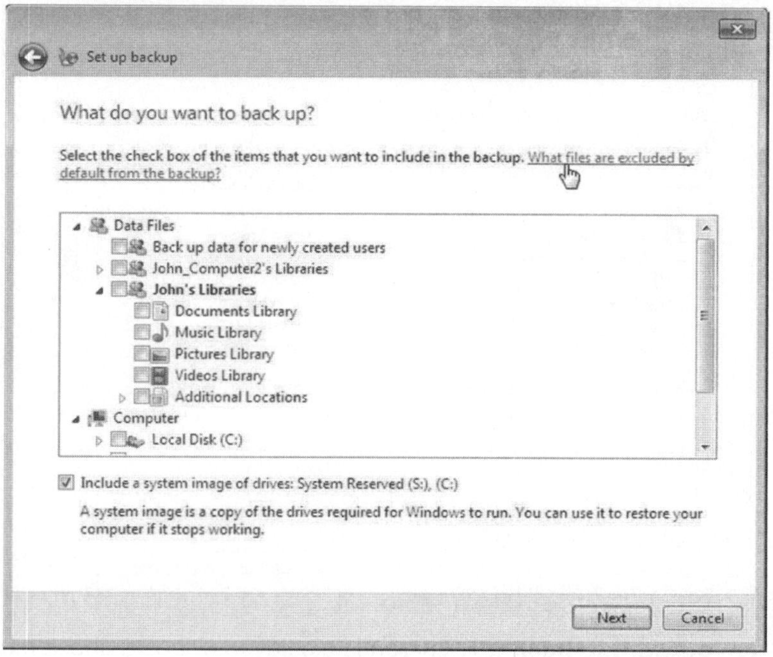

e. Close the **Windows Help and Support** window. Expand **Additional Locations** and make sure only **Desktop** is selected. Make sure no other location is selected. Remove the check mark from **Include a system image of drives:**. Click **Next**.

f. The **Review your backup settings** screen is displayed. Click **Change schedule**.

g. The **How often do you want to back up?** screen is displayed. Place a check mark in the checkbox **Run backup on a schedule (recommended)**. Set the following conditions and then click **OK.**

How often: **Daily**

What day: **blank**

What time: **2:00 AM**

Which files will be backed up?

---

h.   The **Review your backup settings** screen is displayed. Click **Save settings and exit**.

Note: If a backup schedule has never been created, then the button label is **Save settings and run backup**. Clicking the button will immediately start the backup process. If this is the case, move to Step 4b.

Step 4: Run the backup.

a. To test the backup configuration, click **Back up now**. To view the progress of the backup, click **View Details**. The **Windows Backup is currently in progress** screen is displayed.

b. When the **Windows Backup has completed successfully** message appears, click **Close**.

c. Review the information beneath the **Backup** section of the **Backup and Restore** window. When will the next backup take place?

What is the state of the schedule, on or off? _____

Step 5: Delete and restore files.

a. Navigate to the desktop and delete **Backup File One** and **Backup File Two**. Empty the Recycle Bin. In the **Backup and Restore** window, click **Select another backup to restore files from**.

b. The **Select the backup that you want to restore files from** screen is displayed. Select the location where the files are stored. Click **Next**.

c.   The **Browse or search your backup for files and folders to restore** screen is displayed. Click **Browse for files**.

d.   The **Browse the backup for files** window opens. Click the current user's backup. In the example, this user is **John.** Therefore, the folder is labeled **John's backup**. Double-click **Desktop** and locate files **Backup File One** and **Backup File Two**. Select both files by clicking **Backup File One** and then holding down the Ctrl key while clicking **Backup File Two**. Click **Add files**.

e.   The two files are listed in the **Browse or search your backup for files and folders to restore** screen. Click **Next**.

f. The **Where do you want to save the restored files?** screen is displayed. Select **In the original location**, and then click **Restore**.

g. The **Your files have been restored** screen is displayed. Click **Finish**.

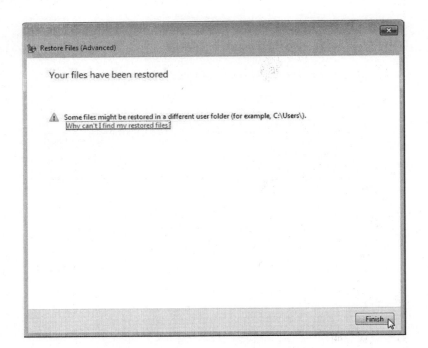

h.   Navigate to the **Desktop**. Are the two files restored to the desktop? _____

Step 6: Modify, back up, delete, and restore a file.

a.   Open file **Backup File Two**. Add the following text "More text added." to the file. Save the file.

b.   Click the **Backup and Restore** window so it is active. Click **Back up now**.

c.   Navigate to the **Desktop**. Delete **Backup File Two**. Empty the Recycle Bin. Click on the **Backup and Restore** window so it is activated. Click **Select another backup to restore files from**.

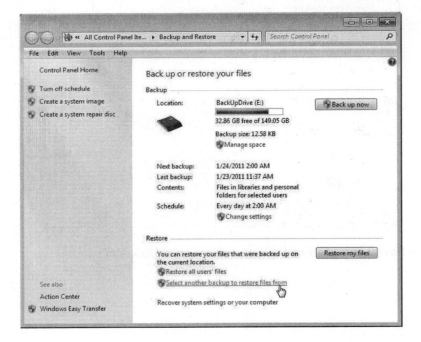

d. Select the location where the files are stored and then repeat **Step 5**:

Next > Browse for files > User's backup > Desktop

e. Restore **Backup File Two**. Navigate to the **Desktop**. Open file **Backup File Two**. What text is in the file?

Part 2: Backup and Data Recovery in Windows Vista

Step 1: Create backup files.

a. Log on to the computer as an administrator.

b. Create a text file on the desktop called **Backup File One**. Open the file and type the text "**The text in this file will not be changed.**"

c. Create another text file on the desktop called **Backup File Two**. Open the file and type the text "**The text in this file will be changed.**"

Note: Remove all extra folders and files from the computer's desktop. This will help to reduce the length of time to complete the backup for this lab.

Step 2: Open the Backup Status and Configuration tool.

a. To open the **Backup Status and Configuration** tool in Windows Vista, use the following path:

Start > All Programs > Accessories > System Tools > Backup Status and Configuration

b. If backup has never been configured, your window will look like the following:

c. If a backup is scheduled to run, click **Turn off**, as shown below.

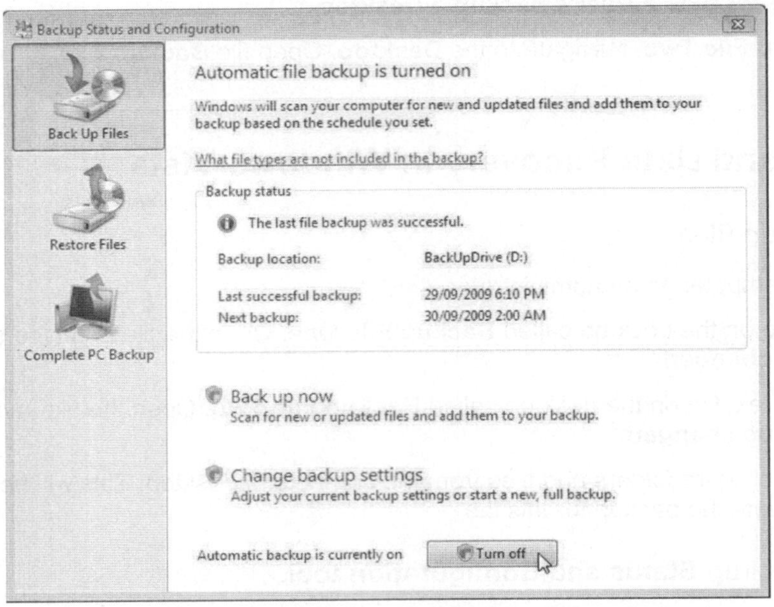

Step 3: Complete the Back Up Files wizard.

a. If a backup is already configured, click **Change backup settings > Continue**. If a backup configuration does not exist, click **Setup automatic file backup > Continue**.

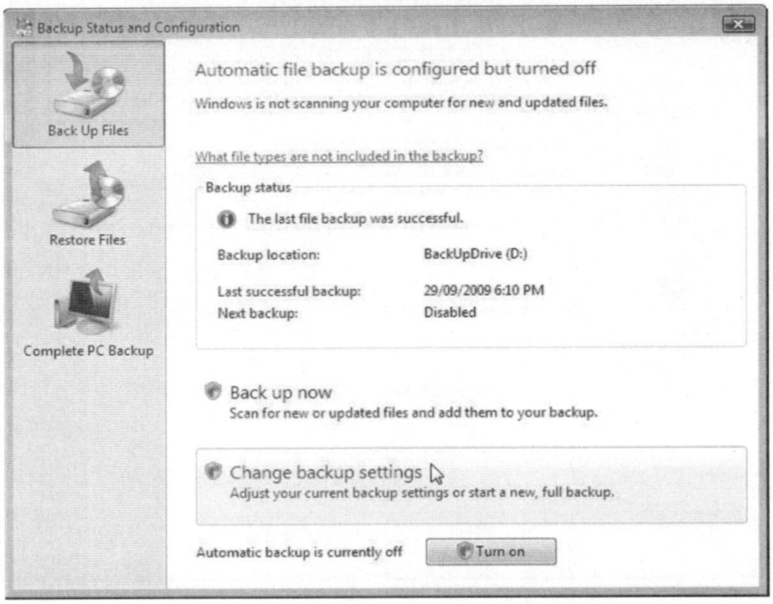

b. The **Where do you want to save your backup?** screen is displayed. Select the location where the backup will be stored. In this example, an external hard drive is used. Click **Next**.

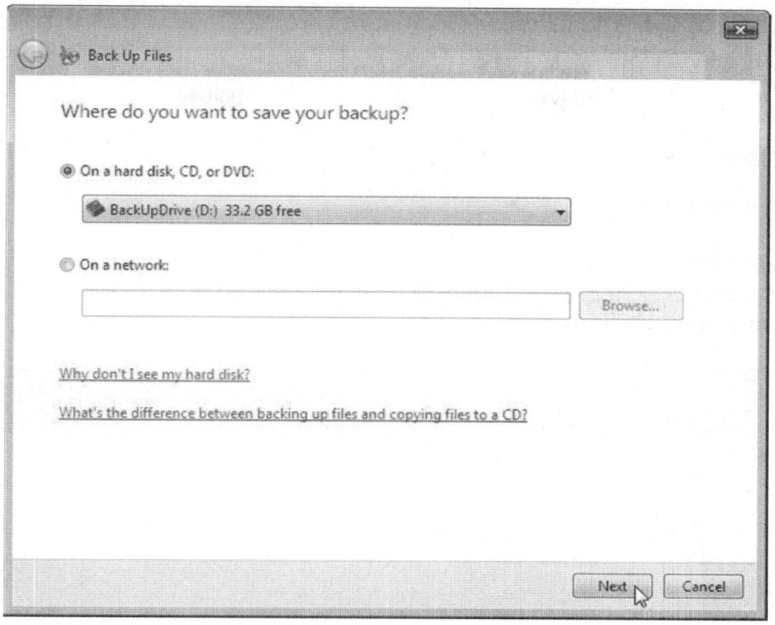

c. The **Which file types do you want to back up?** screen is displayed. Answer the following questions:

What file type can be backed up?

_____

What file types will not be backed up?

_____

Only files on what type of disk can be backed up?

_____

d. Select the file type **Documents**. Click **Next**.

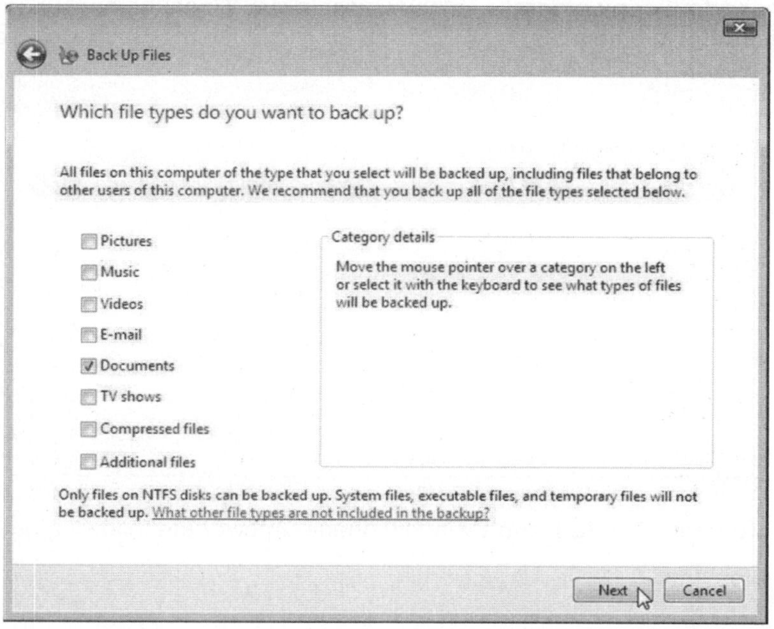

e. The **How often do you want to create a backup?** screen is displayed. Set the following conditions:

How often: **Daily**

What day: **blank**

What time: **2:00 AM**

Which files will be backed up?

_____

f. Place a check mark in the checkbox. Create a new, full backup now in addition to saving settings. Click **Save settings and start backup**.

g. The **Creating a shadow copy** progress screen is displayed. When the backup is done, **The backup has finished successfully** screen is displayed. Click **Close** to finish the **Back Up Files** wizard.

h. The **Backup Status and Configuration** window opens. Answer the following questions:

When will the next backup take place?

_____

What is the state of automatic backup? On or Off?   _____

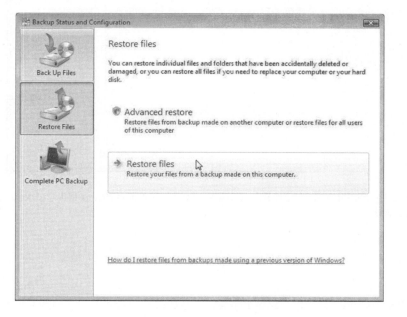

Step 4: Delete and restore files.

a. Navigate to the **Desktop**. Delete **Backup File One** and **Backup File Two**. Empty the Recycle Bin.

b. In the **Backup Status and Configuration**, click **Restore Files** in the left panel. Click **Restore Files** in the main window, as shown below.

c. The **Restore Files** wizard starts and the **What do you want to restore?** screen is displayed. Select **Files from the latest backup**. Click **Next**.

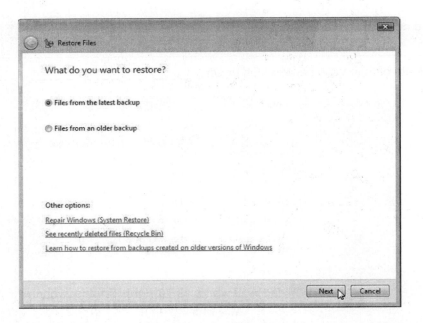

d.   The **Select the files and folders to restore** screen is displayed. Click **Add files...**, and then navigate to the desktop to locate files **Backup File One** and **Backup File Two**.

e.   Select both files by clicking **Backup File One** and then holding down the Ctrl key while clicking **Backup File Two**. Click **Add**.

f.   The two files should show up in the **Select the files and folders to restore** screen. Click **Next**.

g.   The **Where do you want to save the restored files?** screen is displayed. Select **In the original location**. Click **Start restore**.

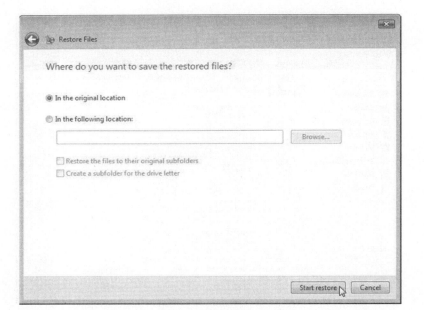

h. When the **Successfully restored files** screen is displayed, click **Finish**.

i. To verify that the files are restored, navigate to the desktop. Are the two files restored to the desktop?

_____

Step 5: Modify, back up, delete, and restore a file.

a. Open file **Backup File Two**. Add the following text "**More text added.**" to the file. Save the file.

b. Click **Backup Status and Configuration**, and then click **Back Up Files**.

c. Click **Back up now > Continue**. The progress bar opens. When the backup is complete, click **Close**.

d. Navigate to the **Desktop**. Delete **Backup File Two**. Empty the Recycle Bin.

e. Click **Backup Status and Configuration**. Click **Restore Files** from the left panel. Click **Restore files** in the main window.

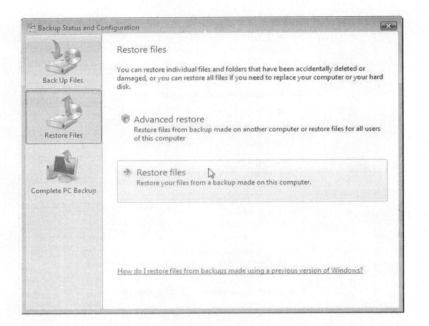

f.   Restore **Backup File Two**. Navigate to the **Desktop**. Open file **Backup File Two**. What text is in the file?

_____

Lab 12.3.1.3 - Configure Data Backup and Recovery in Windows 8

Introduction

Microsoft introduced a new way to protect your data files in Windows 8 called File History. File History supersedes the Backup and Restore features of Windows 7 and functions similarly to Apple's Time Machine application, where it periodically (hourly by default) scans the file system and copies any changed files to another partition or external drive. Over time, a complete history of file changes can be viewed and restored, using the new Restore personal files utility. In this lab, you will turn on the File History utility and allow it to back up your data files. You will then use the Restore personal files utility to restore some of your data files.

Recommended Equipment

- A computer with Windows 8 installed.
- Computer should have a second partition available to store backup.

Step 1: Open the File History tool.

a. Log on to the computer as an administrator.

b. To open File History, click **Search > Control Panel > File History**.

c. The **File History** window opens. File History is turned off by default. To turn it on, click **Turn on**.

Where will File History save files?

d. File History will save your data files when you turn it on. It displays a timestamp of the save in the **File History is on** box. You can click **Run now**, at any time, to have File History save your files immediately.

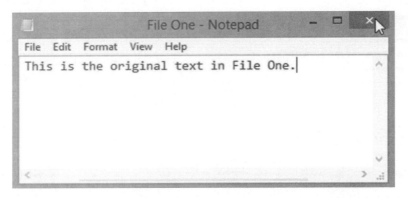

Step 2: Create two text files on the desktop.

a. Create a text file on the desktop called **File One**. Right-click the **Desktop**, and select **New > Text Document**. Name the document **File One**.

b. Double-click on **Files One** and type **This is the original text in file one** in the **File One - Notepad** window, then close and save the text file.

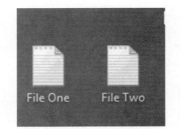

c. Create a second file on the desktop called **File Two**. Open the file and type the text **The text in this file will be changed.**, then close and save the text file.

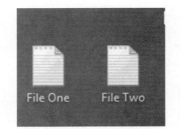

Step 3: Run File History a second time.

In the File History window, click **Run now**. This will create a backup of the files you just created on the desktop.

Step 4: Use the Restore personal files utility to view File History.

a.   In the **File History** window, click **Restore personal files**.

b.   The **Home – File History** window opens. This window displays the date and time of the last backup, along with file folder and library icons to navigate the backup locations. There is also file history navigation controls at the bottom of the window. Double-click on the **Desktop folder**.

c.   The **Desktop – File History** window opens displaying the two text files that you saved to the desktop. Notice at the top of the window, to the right of the date and time of the backup, there displays **2 of 2**. These numbers are telling you that this is the second backup of two backups. Click the **left arrow icon** on the bottom of the window.

d. Notice the timestamp changes to an earlier date and time, and the numbers to the right of the timestamp change to **1 of 2**. You are now looking at the first backup, made immediately after you turned on File History. **File One** and **File Two** are no longer showing.

Why are the two text files missing from the desktop folder of the first backup?

_____

e. Close the **Desktop – File History** window.

Step 5: Make changes to the text files on the desktop and create another backup history.

a. Right-click **File One** and select **Delete**.

b. Open and edit **File Two**. Add the following text: **This was added in step 5 of the lab. Exit** Notepad and **save** your changes.

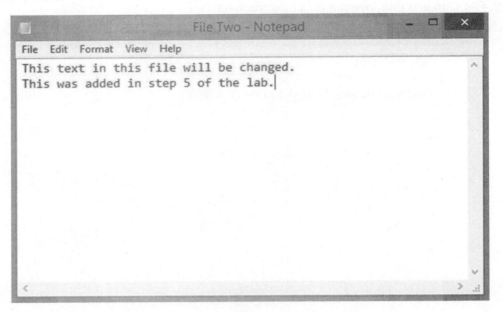

c. In the **File History** window, click **Run now** to create another save to the File History.

Step 6: Open the Restore personal files utility to review the File History.

a. In the **File History** window, click **Restore personal files**.

b. Double-click the **Desktop folder**.

What files are shown in the desktop folder for the most recent backup?

_____

c. Click the **Previous version** icon at the bottom of the screen to view the way the desktop looked before the last save.

Step 7: Restore user files.

a. Select **File One** from the **2 of 3 File History** window and then click the green **Restore** icon at the bottom-center of the window.

b.   The **Desktop** window opens. Notice that **File One** is back on the Desktop. Close the **Desktop** window.

c.   In the **Desktop – File History** window, select **File Two** and then click the green **Restore** icon.

d.   The **Replace or Skip Files** window opens; click **Replace the file in the destination**.

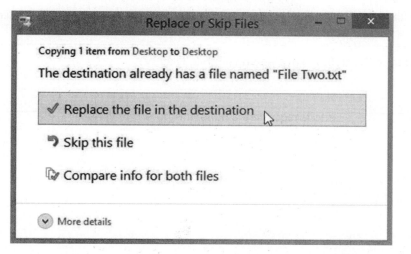

e.   The **Desktop** window opens with **File Two** highlighted. Close all open windows.

f.   You should be able to locate both **File One** and **File Two** on your desktop. Double-click **File Two**.

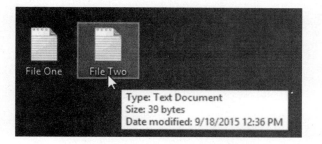

g.   **Notepad** opens, displaying the contents of **File Two**. Notice that the second line that you added to File Two is now missing.

How would you use File History to restore the second line back into File Two?

_____

_____

h.   Close all open windows.

Step 8: Delete text files and turn off File History.

a.   Highlight the **File One** and **File Two** text files on your desktop, right-click, and then select **Delete**.

b.   Click **Control Panel > File History**, and then click **Turn off**.

Reflection

1. Once File History has been activated, how often does it automatically save your data files?

   _____

2. How would you change the default save settings in File History?

   _____

   _____

Lab 12.3.1.5 - Configure the Firewall in Windows 7 and Vista

Introduction

In this lab, you will explore the Windows Firewall and configure some advanced settings.

Recommended Equipment

- Two computers directly connected or connected on a network.
- Windows installed on both computers.
- Computers are in the same workgroup and share the same subnet mask.

Part 1: Configure the Firewall in Windows 7

Step 1: Create and share a folder.

a. On computer 1, right-click on the desktop and select **New > Folder**. Name the folder **Cisco**.

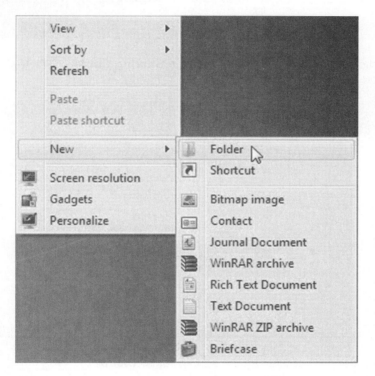

b. Right-click the Cisco folder, and then select **Share with > Advanced Sharing**. The **Advanced Sharing** window opens. Share the folder. Use the default name **Cisco**.

c. On computer 2, click **Control Panel > Network and Sharing Center**. Click the icon with the network name to which you are connected.

d. Double-click **computer 1**. Can you see the shared folder **Cisco**? _____

Note: If you answered no, ask the instructor for help.

e. Close **Network**.

Note: Use computer 1 for the rest of the lab unless otherwise stated.

Step 2: Open Windows Firewall.

a. To open the **Windows Firewall**, use the following path:

Control Panel > System and Security > Windows Firewall

b.   The normal state for the Windows Firewall is **On**.

c.   What are the benefits of Windows Firewall?

_____

_____

_____

Step 3: Investigate the Windows Firewall Allowed Programs feature.

a.   Click **Allow a program or feature through Windows Firewall**.

b.   The **Allowed Programs** window opens. Programs and services that Windows Firewall is not blocking will be listed with a check mark. You can add applications to this list. This may be necessary if your customer has an application that requires outside communications, but for some reason the Windows Firewall cannot perform the configuration automatically. You must be logged on to this computer as an administrator to complete this procedure.

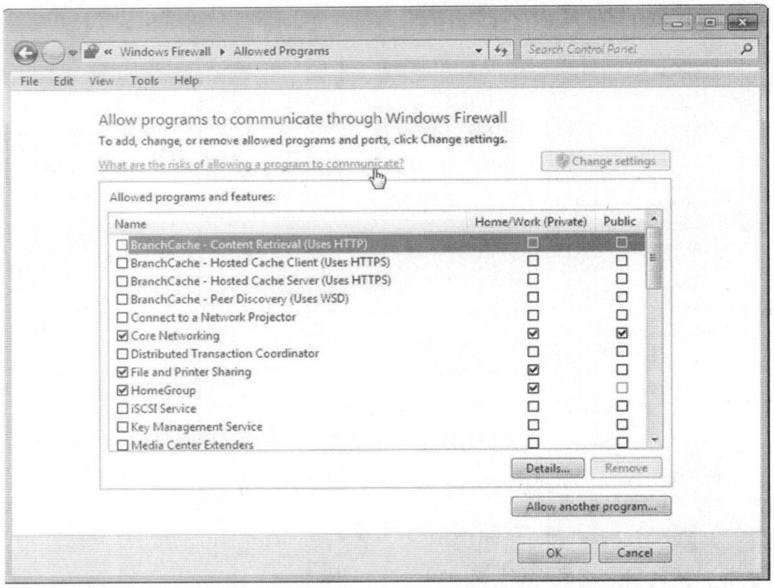

c. Click **What are the risks of allowing a program to communicate?**. The **Windows Help and Support** window opens. Creating too many exceptions in your Programs and Services file can have negative consequences.

Describe a negative consequence of having too many exceptions.

_____

_____

_____

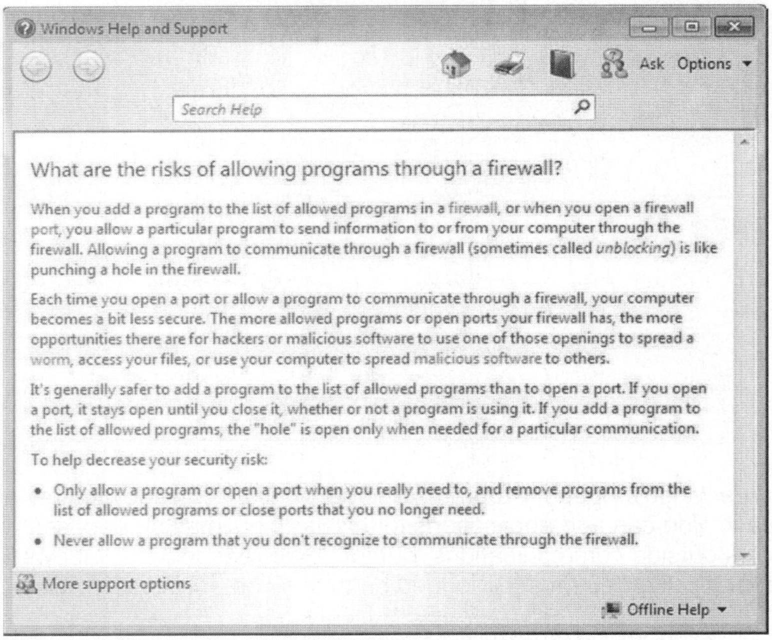

d.   Close the **Windows Help and Support** window.

Step 4: Configure the Windows Firewall Allowed Programs feature.

a.   On computer 1, click the **Allowed Programs** window so it is active. Click **Change settings**, if necessary. To turn off an exception, remove the check mark from **File and Printer Sharing**, and then click **OK**.

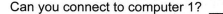

b.   On computer 2, attempt to open a connection to computer 1, using the following path:

Control Panel > Network and Sharing Center > Network icon.

Can you connect to computer 1? _____

c. On computer 1, add a check mark to **File and Printer Sharing**. Click **OK**.

d. On computer 2, refresh the **Network** screen and attempt to connect to computer 1. Can you connect to computer 1? _____

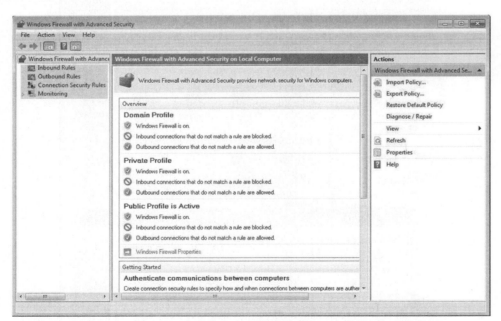

e. Log off computer 2. Use computer 1 for the rest of the lab.

Step 5: Configure Advanced Security features in Windows Firewall.

a. To configure advanced security, use the following path:

Control Panel > Administrative Tools > Windows Firewall with Advanced Security

b. In the panel on the left, you can select items to configure **Inbound Rules**, **Outbound Rules**, or **Connection Security Rules**. You can also click **Monitoring** to view the status of configured rules. Click **Inbound Rules**.

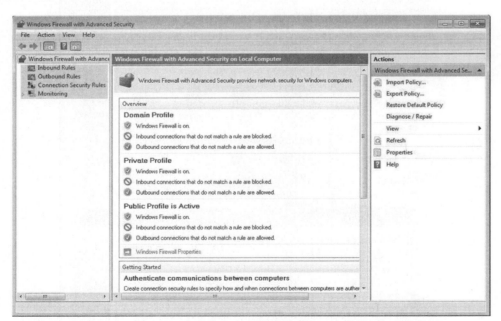

c. In the middle panel, scroll down until you find the inbound rule **named Files and Printer Sharing (Echo Request – ICMPv4-In)**. Right-click on the rule and select **Properties > Advanced** tab **> Customize**.

d. The **Advanced** tab displays the profile(s) used by the computer and the **Customize Interface Types** window displays the different connections configured for your computer. Click **OK**.

e.   Click the **Programs and Services** tab. Click **Settings....** The **Customize Service Settings** window opens. In the space below, list the short name of four services that are available. When done, click **Cancel**.

f.   There are many applications that users do not normally see that also need to get through the Windows Firewall to access your computer. These are the network level programs that direct traffic on the network and the Internet. Click **Protocols and Ports** tab.

File and Printer Sharing (Echo Request - ICMPv4-In) Properties

General	Programs and Services	Computers
Protocols and Ports	Scope	Advanced	Users

Protocols and ports

Protocol type: ICMPv4

Protocol number: 1

Local port: All Ports

Remote port: All Ports

Internet Control Message Protocol   Customize...
(ICMP) settings:

Learn more about protocol and ports

OK   Cancel   Apply

g. For the ICMP settings, click the **Customize** button. The **Customize ICMP Settings** window opens. In the example here, allowing incoming echo requests is what allows network users to ping your computer to determine if it is present on the network. In the space below, list four of the specific ICMP types.

_____

_____

h.   Close all windows.

Part 2: Configure the Firewall in Windows Vista

Step 1: Create and share a folder.

a.   On computer 1, right-click on the desktop, select **New > Folder**. Name the folder **Cisco**.

b.   Right-click the **Cisco** folder, and then select **Share > Continue**. The **Advanced Sharing** window opens. Share the folder. Use the default name **Cisco**.

c. On computer 2, click **Control Panel > Network and Sharing Center > Network** icon (icon with the network name to which you are connected).

d. Double-click **computer 1**. Can you see the shared folder **Cisco**? _____

   Note: If you answered no, ask the instructor for help.

e. Close **Network**.

   Note: Use computer 1 for the rest of the lab unless otherwise stated.

Step 2: Open Windows Firewall.

a. To open the Windows Firewall, use the following path:

   Control Panel > Security Center

b. The normal state for the Windows Firewall is **On**. Click **Windows Firewall** in the left panel.

c. The **Windows Firewall** window opens. Click **Change settings > Continue**.

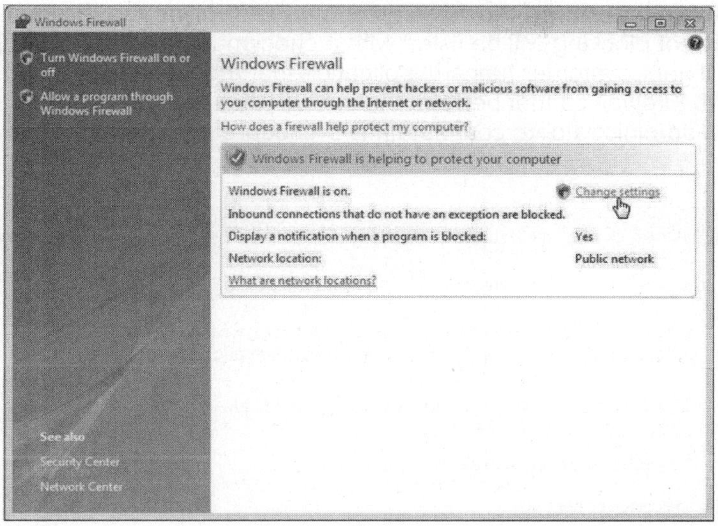

d. The **Windows Firewall Settings** window opens.

Why is turning off the Windows Firewall not advised?

_____

_____

_____

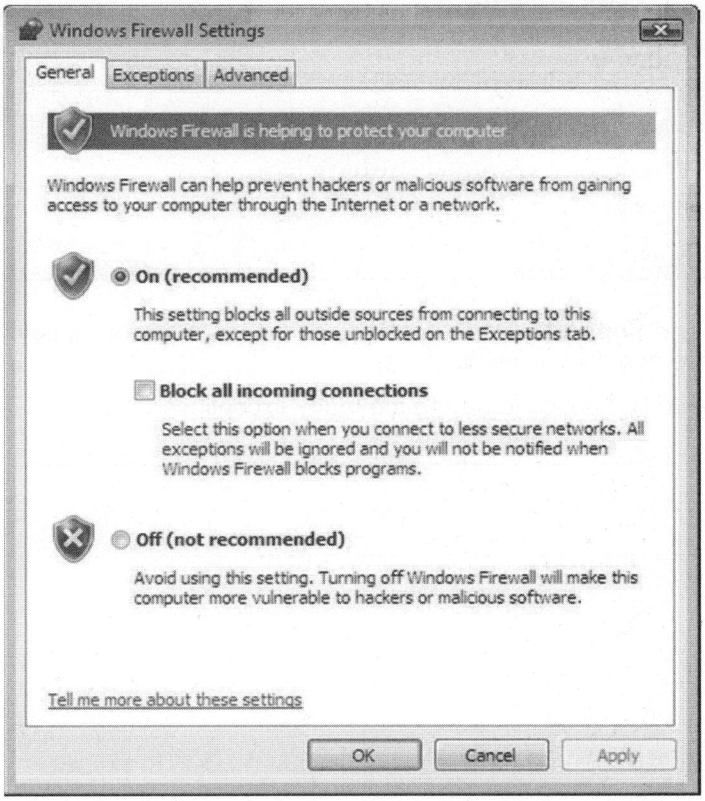

Step 3: Investigate the Windows Firewall Exceptions tab.

a.   In the **Windows Firewall Settings** window, select the **Exceptions** tab. Programs and services that Windows Firewall is not blocking will be listed with a checkmark. You can add applications to this list. This may be necessary if your customer has an application that requires outside communications but for some reason the Windows Firewall cannot perform the configuration automatically. You must be logged on to this computer as an administrator to complete this procedure. Click **What are the risks of unblocking a program?**.

b.   The **Window Help and Support** window opens. Creating too many exceptions in your Programs and Services file can have negative consequences.

Describe a negative consequence to having too many exceptions.

_____

_____

_____

c. Close the **Windows Help and Support** window.

Step 4: Configure exceptions to the Windows Firewall.

a. On computer 1, click the **Windows Firewall Settings** window so it is active. Click **Change settings**, if necessary. To turn off an exception, remove the check mark from **File and Printer Sharing**. Click **OK**.

b. From **computer 2**, attempt to open the network connect to **computer 1**, using the following path:

Control Panel > Network and Sharing Center > Network icon.

Can you connect to computer 1? _____

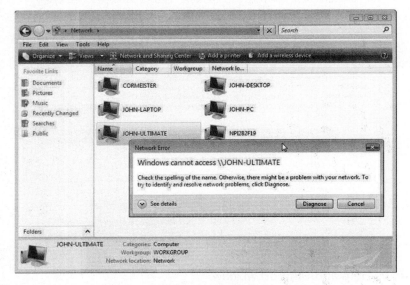

c. On **computer 1**, add back the exception for **File and Printer Sharing**. Click **OK**.

d. On **computer 2**, refresh **Network** screen and attempt connect to **computer 1**. Can you connect to computer 1? _____

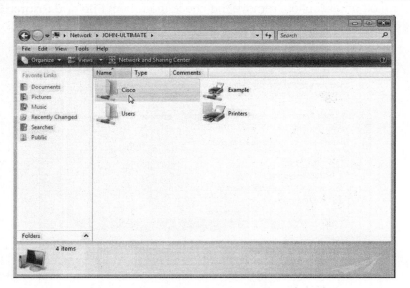

e. Log off **computer 2**. Use **computer 1** for the rest of the lab.

Step 5: Configure Advanced Security features in Windows Firewall.

a. To configure advanced security, use the following path:

Control Panel > Administrative Tools > Windows Firewall with Advanced Security

b.   In the panel on the left, you can select items to configure **Inbound Rules**, **Outbound Rules**, or **Connection Security Rules**. You can also click **Monitoring** to view the status of configured rules. Click **Inbound Rules**.

c.   In the middle panel, scroll down until you find the inbound rule named **Files and Printer Sharing (Echo Request – ICMPv4-In)**. Right-click on the rule and select **Properties > Advanced** tab > **Customize**.

d.   The **Advanced** tab displays the profile(s) used by the computer and the **Customize Interface Types** window displays the different connections configured for your computer. Click **OK**.

File and Printer Sharing (Echo Request - ICMPv4-In) Properties   ⌧

| General | Programs and Services |
| Users and Computers | Protocols and Ports | Scope | Advanced |

Profiles

Customize Interface Types   ⌧

This rule applies to connections on the following interface types.

⦿ All interface types

○ These interface types:

☐ Local area network
☐ Remote access
☐ Wireless

Learn more about interface types

OK   Cancel

Allow edge traversal

Learn more about these settings

OK   Cancel   Apply

e. Click the **Programs and Services** tab. Click **Settings....** The **Customize Service Settings** window opens. In the space below, list the short name of four services that are available. When done, click **Cancel**.

f.   There are many applications that users do not normally see that also need to get through the Windows Firewall to access your computer. These are the network level programs that direct traffic on the network and the Internet. Click **Protocols and Ports** tab.

g. For the ICMP settings, click the **Customize** button. The **Customize ICMP Settings** window opens. In the example here, allowing incoming echo requests is what allows network users to ping your computer to determine if it is present on the network.

List four of the specific ICMP types.

_____

_____

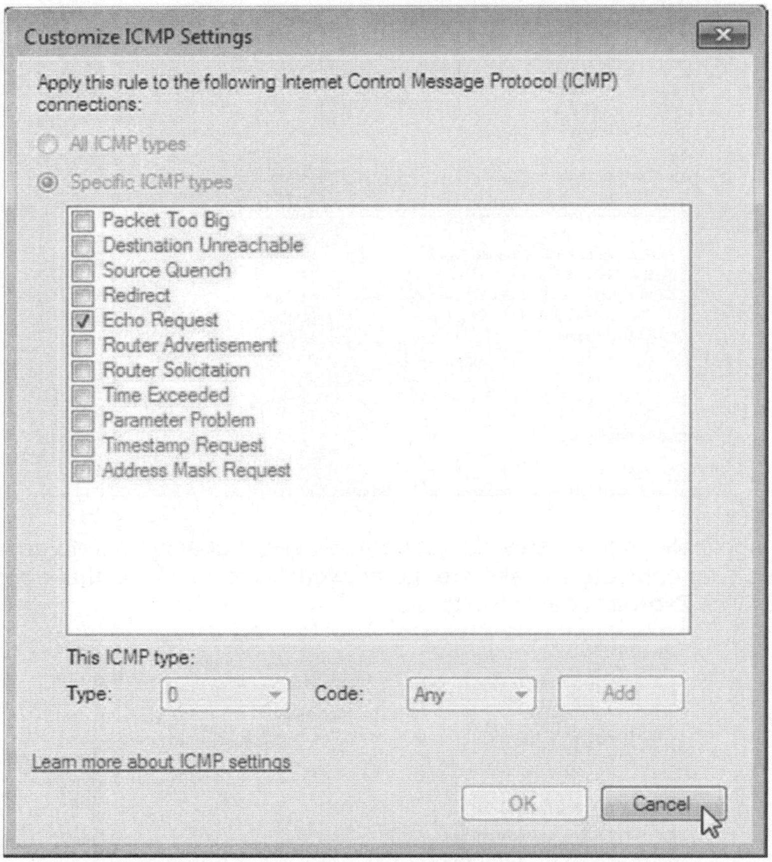

h. Close all windows.

Lab 12.3.1.5 - Configure the Firewall in Windows 8

Introduction

In this lab, you will explore the Windows Firewall and configure some advanced settings.

Recommended Equipment

- Two computers directly connected or connected over the network.
- Windows 8 installed on both computers.
- Computers must be in the same workgroup and share the same subnet mask.

Step 1: Create and share a folder on PC-1.

a. Log on to **PC-1** as a member of the administrator group. Ask your instructor for the user name and password.

b. On **PC-1**, right-click the desktop, select **New > Folder**. Name the folder **Cisco**.

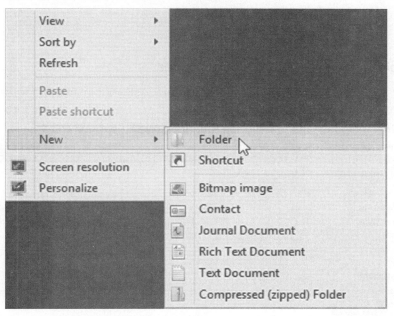

c. Right-click the Cisco folder, and then select **Properties > Sharing > Advanced Sharing**. The **Advanced Sharing** window opens. Click **Share this folder** and use the default name **Cisco**. Click **OK**. Close the **Cisco Properties** window.

Step 2: Use File Explorer to view PC-1's shared folder.

a.   Log on to **PC-2** as a member of the administrator group. Ask your instructor for the user name and password.

b.   Open **File Explorer** window. In the left pane, under **Network**, expand **PC-1**.

Under PC-1, are you able to see the shared folder **Cisco**? _____

Note: If you answered no, ask the instructor for help.

c.   Close **File Explorer**.

Step 3: Open Windows Firewall on PC-1.

Note: Use **PC-1** for the rest of the lab unless otherwise stated.

a.   To open the **Windows Firewall** window, click **Control Panel > Windows Firewall**.

b.   The normal state for the Windows Firewall is **On**.

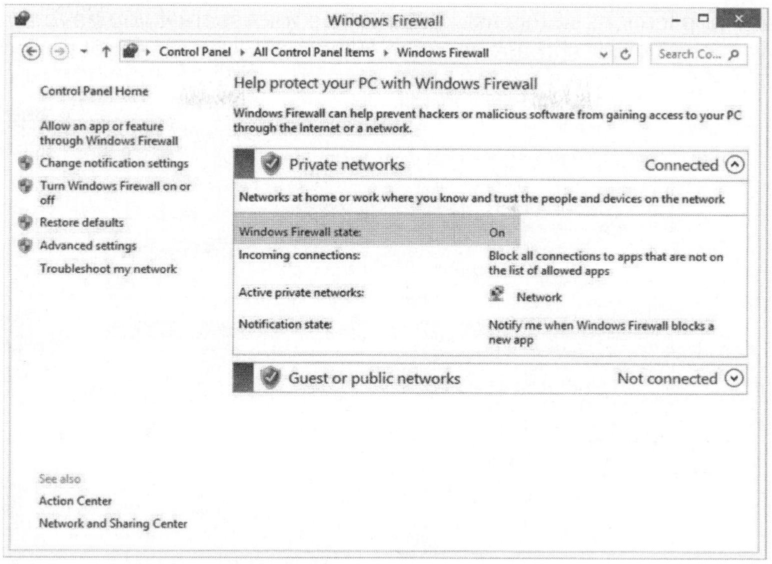

c.   What are the benefits of Windows Firewall?

_____

_____

_____

Step 4: Investigate the Windows Firewall Allowed Programs feature.

a.   Click **Allow an app or feature through Windows Firewall**.

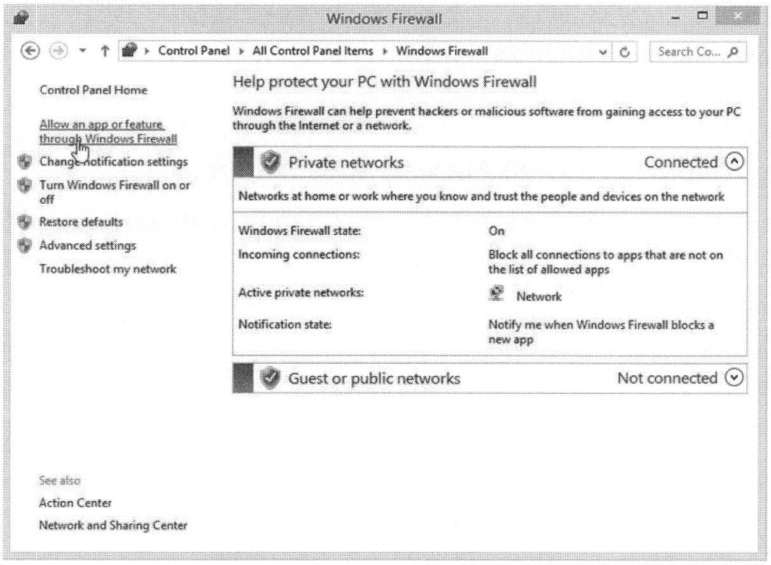

b.   The **Allowed apps** window opens. Programs and services that Windows Firewall is not blocking will be listed with a check mark. Click **What are the risks of allowing an app to communicate?**.

Note: You can add applications to this list. This may be necessary if you have an application that requires outside communications but for some reason the Windows Firewall cannot perform the configuration automatically.

Creating too many exceptions in your Programs and Services file can have negative consequences. Describe a negative consequence of having too many exceptions.

_____

_____

_____

c.   Close the **Windows Help and Support** window.

Step 5: Configure the Windows Firewall Allowed apps feature.

a.   Click the **Allowed apps** window so it is active. Click **Change settings**. Remove the check mark from **File and Printer Sharing**. Click **OK**.

b. On **PC-2**, using **File Explorer**, attempt to open the network connect to **PC-1**.

Can you connect to PC-1 and view the Cisco shared folder? _____

Did you receive an error message on PC-2? If so, what was the error message?

_____

c. Close all open windows on **PC-2**.

d. On **PC-1**, add a check mark to **File and Printer Sharing**. Click **OK**.

Note: You should be able to add the check mark without needing to click **Change settings**.

e. On **PC-2**, re-open File Explorer and attempt to connect to **PC-1**.

Can you connect to computer 1? Why?

_____

f. Close all open windows on **PC-2** and log off.

g. Close all windows on **PC-1**.

Step 6: Configure Advanced Security features in Windows Firewall.

Note: Use **PC-1** for the rest of this lab.

a. Click **Control Panel > Administrative Tools > Windows Firewall with Advanced Security**.

b. The **Windows Firewall with Advanced Security** window opens. In the panel on the left, you can select items to configure **Inbound Rules**, **Outbound Rules**, or **Connection Security Rules**. You can also click **Monitoring** to view the status of configured rules. Click **Inbound Rules**.

c. In the middle panel, scroll down until you find the inbound rule named **Files and Printer Sharing (Echo Request – ICMPv4-In)**. Right-click the rule and select **Properties**, then select the **Advanced** tab.

d. The **Advanced** tab displays the profile(s) used by the computer. Click **Customize** in the **Interface Types** area of the window.

e.   The **Customize Interface Types** window opens. It displays the different connections configured for your computer. Leave **All interface types** selected, then click **OK**.

f.   Click the **Programs and Services** tab. In the **Services** section, click **Settings....**

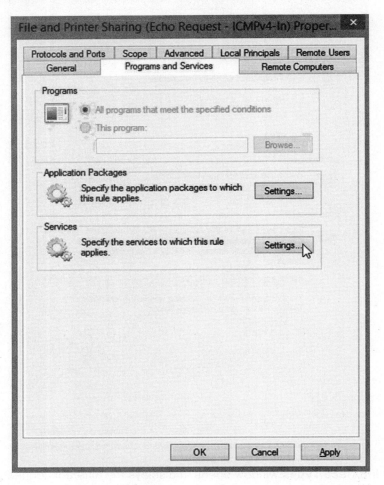

g.   The **Customize Service Settings** window opens.

h. List the short name of four services that are available.

_____

i. Click **Cancel** to close the **Customize Service Settings window**.

j. Click the **Protocols and Ports** tab.

Note: There are many applications that users do not normally see that also need to get through the Windows Firewall to access your computer. These are the network level programs that direct traffic on the network and the Internet.

k. For the ICMP settings, click the **Customize** button.

l. The **Customize ICMP Settings** window opens. Allowing incoming echo requests is what allows network users to ping your computer to determine if it is present on the network.

List four of the specific ICMP types.

_____

_____

m. Close all open windows on **PC-1**.

n. Right-click the **Cisco** folder on the desktop, then select **Delete**.

Reflection

What are some possible reasons you may need to make firewall changes?

_____

_____

_____

_____

_____

Lab 12.3.1.9 - Configure Users and Groups in Windows

Introduction

In this lab, you will create users and groups and delete users using the Local Users and Groups Manager. You will also assign group and user permission to the folders.

Recommended Equipment

- A computer with Windows installed.

Part 1: Creating New Users

New users can be created individually or you can create a list of new users and groups with the Local Users and Groups Manager.

Step 1: Access Local Users and Groups Manager.

In this step, log on the computer using an account with administrative privileges provided by the instructor. In this lab, the initial user ITEUser is used and Studentxx and Staffxx accounts will be created in this lab.

a. Click **Control Panel > Administrative Tools > Computer Management**. Click **Local Users and Groups**.

b. In the Local Users and Groups Manager, select the **Users** folder. What are the names of the accounts listed?

_____

c. Select the **Groups** folder. Name five groups from the list.

d. Click the **Users** folder. Right-click your account and select **Properties**. Click the **Member Of** tab. Which group does your account belong to?

e. Click **OK** to close the Properties window.

Step 2: Create new users.

In this step, you will create a few more local users using the **Local Users and Groups Manager**.

a. In the **Local Users and Groups** window with the **Users** folder selected, click **More Actions** under **Users** and select **New User** in the right column.

b. In the **New User** window, enter **Student01** as a new user name and **cisco12345** as the password. If desired, provide a full name and description for the user. Click **Create**.

What is Student01 required to do when logging in the first time?

c.   Create users **Student02**, **Staff01**, and **Staff02** or a list of user names provided by the instructor. Use **cisco12345** as the password for these users. Unselect **User must change password at next logon** for each user. Click **Close** when finished creating all the users.

d.   Double-click **Student01**. Unselect the **User must change password at next logon**.

What group does User01 belong to? _____

e.   Click **OK**.

f.   Click the **Groups** folder. Double-click the **Users** group.

From the description, can the members of the Users group make system-wide changes? What can the Users group do on the computer?

_____

_____

Who are the group members?

_____

_____

g.   Click **OK** to continue.

Step 3: Verify user and group permissions.

The permission for the Users group allows the members to run most applications on the local computer. The group member inherited the permission when they joined the group during the creation of the account. These members cannot make any system-wide changes. In this step, you will try to create another new user as a member of the Users group and use Internet Explorer to navigate to www.cisco.com.

a.   Log off the computer.

b.   Log on as any member of the Users group.

c.   Navigate to the **Local Users and Groups Manager**. Click **Users**.

d.   Create a new user account using the name **Test** and password **cisco12345**. Were you successful in creating the new account? Explain.

_____

_____

e.   Navigate to **www.cisco.com** using Internet Explorer. Were you able to navigate to **www.cisco.com**? Explain.

_____

_____

Part 2: Creating New Groups

In this part, you will create new groups named **ITEStudent** and **ITEStaff** and add members to the group. You will also create folders and assign permissions.

Step 1: Create new groups.

a.   Log off the computer. Log on to the computer using an account with administrative privileges. In this example, the account **ITEUser** has administrative privileges.

b.   Navigate to the **Local Users and Groups Manager**.

c. Right-click the **Groups** folder and select **New Group**.

d. Enter **ITEStaff** as the group name. Click **Add** to add users to this group.

e. In the **Select Users** window, enter **Staff01** under the heading **Enter the object names to select**. Click **Check Names** to verify the object was entered correctly. Click **OK** to add **Staff01** to the group **ITEStaff**. Repeat this procedure to add **Staff02** to the group **ITEStaff**.

f.   Click **Create** to complete the group creation process.

g.   Repeat the same procedure to add users **Student01** and **Student02** to the group **ITEStudent**. Click **Create**. Click **Close** when finished with new group creation.

h.   Click **Users** and double-click each of the four users and verify they are members of the correct groups by clicking the **Member Of** tab. Click **Cancel** to close each user after verification.

Step 2: Assign group permissions to folders.

a.   Create folders named **Staff** and **Students** in the C:\ drive.

b.   Select and then right-click the **Students** folder and select **Properties**.

c.   Select the **Security** tab. Click **Edit** to change the permission for this folder.

d.   Click **Add** to add group permission to this folder.

e. In the **Select Users or Groups** window, enter **ITEStaff** under the heading **Enter the object names to select**. Click **Check Names** for verification. Click **OK** to continue.

With the group **ITEStaff** highlighted, what can the members do in this folder?

_____

f.   Repeat the same procedure to add permissions for the group **ITEStudent**. In addition, the members of this group should have full control for this folder.

Which additional checkbox would you select?

_____

g.   Click **OK** to continue. Click **OK** to close the **Properties** window.

h.   Select the **Staff** folder. Right-click the folder and select **Properties**.

i.   Click the **Security** tab to add group permission as follows:

   o   Allow the group **ITEStaff** Full control.

   o   Deny Full control for the group **ITEStudent**.

j.   Click **OK**.

k.   Click **Yes** when prompted to deny permission to a group.

l.   Click **OK** to close the **Properties** window.

Part 3: Modifying User and Group Permissions

In this part, you will verify the results of the group permission on the folders **Staff** and **Student**. You will also modify user and group permissions.

Step 1: Verify and modify folder permissions.

a.   Log off the computer. Log on the computer as **Student01**.

b. Navigate to the folder **C:\Students**. Create a folder named **Student01** and create a text document in the folder. Were you successful? Explain.

_____

_____

c. Navigate to the folder **C:\Staff**. Create a folder named **Student01** and place a text file in the folder. Were you successful? Explain.

_____

_____

d. Now log off the computer and log on as **Student02**.

e. Navigate to **C:**. Can you place a text file in the **Staff** folder? Can you modify the text file in folder **Student01**? Explain.

_____

_____

f. Create a new folder named **Student02** in the folder **C:\Students** and create a text document in the folder.

g. To prevent the user **Student01** and other **ITEStudent** group members from modifying this folder and its content, right-click the folder **Student02** and select **Properties**.

h. In the **Security** tab, click **Edit**.

i. Add the user **Student02** with Full control permission to this folder. Select **Full Control** under the **Allow** column.

j. Select the group **ITEStudent**. Select the **Modify** checkbox under the **Deny** column to prevent other **ITEStudent** group members from modifying this folder and its content. Click **OK**. Click **Yes** in the **Windows Security** window when prompted. Click **OK** to close the **Properties** window.

k. Log off the computer and log on as **Student01**.

l. Navigate to the folder **C:\Students**. Are you able to access the content in the **Student01** and **Student02** folders? Explain.

_____

_____

m. Log off the computer and log on as **Staff01**.

n. Navigate to the folder **C:**. Were you able to access the content in the folders **Staff**, **Student\Student01**, and **Student\Student02**? Explain.

_____

_____

Step 2: Disable a user account.

At this time, the user account **Staff02** is not used. In this step, you will disable this account.

a. Log off the computer and log on as **ITEUser** or an account with administrative privileges.

b. Navigate to the **Local Users and Groups Manager**.

c. Select the **Users** folder. Double-click **Staff02**.

    d.   Check **Account is disabled**.

    e.   Click **OK** to continue.

    f.   Log off the computer. Can you log on as **Staff02**? Explain.

_____

_____

Step 3: Clean up.

In this step, you will delete the users, groups, files, and folders created in this lab.

    a.   Log on using an account with administrative privileges.

    b.   Navigate to **C:** and delete the folders **Staff** and **Student**.

    c.   Navigate to the **Local Users and Groups Manager**.

    d.   Select **Users**.

e. Right-click **Staff01** and select **Delete**. Click **Yes** to confirm the user deletion. Repeat this for **Staff02**, **Student01, and Student02**.

f. Select **Groups**.

g. Right-click **ITEStaff** and select **Delete**. Click **Yes** to confirm the group deletion. Repeat this for **ITEStudent**.

Reflection

1. How would you give administrative privileges on the local computer to all the members of ITEStaff?

2. How would you deny access to a file for everyone, except the owner?

Lab 12.4.2.2 - Document Customer Information in a Work Order

Introduction

As a help desk technician, it is your job to gather data from the customer to begin the troubleshooting process. As a Level 1 technician, you do not have administrative rights to the customer's computer. Issues that require administrative rights must be escalated to a Level 2 technician. Use the Customer Information sheet on page 2 or one provided by your instructor to document the customer's problem in the work order below. Assign a case number of your choice and set the Priority as a P2 (Significant Issue). Describe the problem and recommend a solution.

Technician Sheet

Company Name:

Contact:

Company Address:

Company Phone:

Work Order

Generating a New Ticket

Category: _____   **Status:** _____   **Escalated:** _____

Business Impacting   ○ Yes   ○ No

Summary: _____

Case ID#: _____   **Priority:** _____

User Platform: _____

Problem Description:

_____

_____

_____

Problem Solution:

_____

_____

_____

_____

Customer Information

Use the contact information and problem description below to report the following information to a level-one technician:

Contact Information

Company Name: .....Organization of Associated Chartered Federations, Inc.

Contact: ....Braxton Jones

Note: Braxton contributes significantly to the organization's daily operations.

Company Address:...123 E. Main Street

Company Phone: 480-555-1234

Category:..................Security

Problem Description

I am not able to login. I was able to login yesterday and all days previously. I tried to login with a different computer but was unsuccessful there also. I received an email last week about changing my password, but I have not changed my password yet.

Additional Information

- Windows 7

Chapter 13: The IT Professional

Lab 13.1.1.3 - Technician Resources

In this lab, you will use the Internet to find resources for a specific computer component. Search online for resources that can help you troubleshoot the component. In the table below, list at least one website for each of the following types of resources: FAQs, manuals, troubleshooting/help site, and blogs. Give a brief description of the content on the site. Be prepared to discuss the usefulness of the resources you found.

Component to research: _____

Type of Resource	Website Address

Chapter 14: Advanced Troubleshooting

Lab 14.1.1.2 - Troubleshooting Hardware Problems

Introduction

In this lab, you will diagnose the cause of various hardware problems and solve them.

Recommended Equipment

- A computer with an operating system installed

Scenario

You must solve hardware problems for a customer. You might also need to troubleshoot hardware connected to the computer. Make sure you document all the problems and the solutions.

There are several possible errors. Follow through the lab, solving one problem at a time until you can successfully start the computers and all devices are fully functional. You may need to ask the instructor for hardware when needed.

Step 1: Start and log in to the computer.

a. Start the computer. Did the computer boot successfully?

_____

_____

b. If the computer started, log on with an account with administrative privileges. Test all internal and external hardware devices. Did all devices operate properly?

_____

_____

c. If the computer successfully started and all devices are fully functional, you have successfully solved all hardware problems. Hand the lab to your instructor.

Step 2: Troubleshoot the hardware problem.

If you could not successfully start the computer and all devices are not fully functional, continue troubleshooting the problem.

Answer the following questions after each problem is solved.

a. What problem did you find?

_____

_____

_____

_____

b. What steps did you take to determine the problem?

_____

_____

_____

_____

_____

_____

c. What is causing the problem?

_____

_____

_____

_____

_____

_____

d. List the steps taken to fix the problem.

_____

_____

_____

_____

_____

_____

Lab 14.1.1.3 - Remote Technician - Repair Boot Problem

Introduction

In this lab, you will gather data from the customer, and then instruct the customer to fix a computer that does not boot. Document the customer's problem in the work order below.

Student Technician Sheet

Company Name: JH Travel, Inc.

Contact: Dan Handy

Company Address: 204 N. Main Street

Company Phone: 1-866-555-0998

Work Order

Generating a New Ticket

Category:		**Closure Code:**	N/A	**Status:**	Open
Type:	N/A	**Escalated:**	Yes	**Pending:**	N/A
Item:	N/A			**Pending Until Date:**	N/A

Business Impacting?   X **Yes**   O **No**

Summary:

Case ID#:	47	**Connection Type:**	N/A
Priority:	2	**Environment:**	N/A
User Platform:			

Problem Description:

_____

_____

_____

_____

Problem Solution:

_____

_____

_____

_____

_____

Student Customer Sheet

Use the contact information and problem description below to report the following information to a level-two technician.

Contact Information

Company Name: JH Travel, Inc.

Contact: Dan Handy

Company Address: 204 N. Main Street

Company Phone: 1-866-555-0998

Problem Description

Ok, so I work with cars all the time and I know how they work, but I do not know how my computer works. This morning was pretty slow because I guess more and more people are using those Internet travel sites. So, after my morning coffee, I decided to figure out what makes my computer work. I opened up the case and just started looking at the different things inside. When I put everything back together, everything seemed to fit and I didn't see any leftover parts. Now it does not work at all. It beeps at me all the time.

Note: After you have given the level-two tech the problem description, use the Additional Information to answer any follow-up questions the technician may ask.

Additional Information

- Windows 7.
- Computer has no new hardware.
- Computer has not been moved recently.
- Except for the beeping, I did not hear any other strange sounds from the computer.
- I do not smell any electronics burning or smoke.
- Computer looks the same as it did yesterday.

Lab 14.2.1.2 - Troubleshoot Operating System Problems

Introduction

In this lab, you will diagnose the cause of various operating system problems and solve them.

Recommended Equipment

- A computer with Windows installed
- Windows installation media

Scenario

You must solve operating system problems for a customer. Make sure you document and solve the problems, and then document the solutions.

There are several possible errors. Follow through the lab, solving one problem at a time until you can successfully start the computer, the desktop contains the appropriate open programs, and the display is set to the native resolution or the resolution given to you by your instructor.

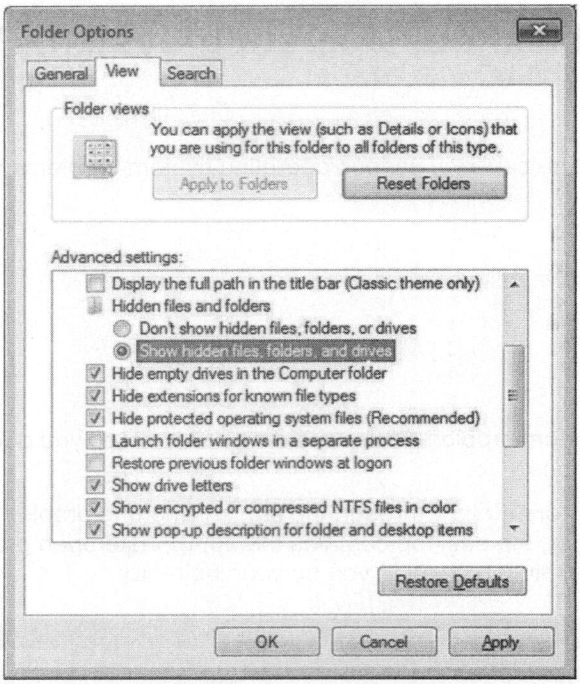
Folder Options
General
View
Search
Folder views
You can apply the view (such as Details or Icons) that you are using for this folder to all folders of this type.
Apply to Folders
Reset Folders
Advanced settings:
Display the full path in the title bar (Classic theme only)
Hidden files and folders
Don't show hidden files, folders, or drives
Show hidden files, folders, and drives
Hide empty drives in the Computer folder
Hide extensions for known file types
Hide protected operating system files (Recommended)
Launch folder windows in a separate process
Restore previous folder windows at logon
Show drive letters
Show encrypted or compressed NTFS files in color
Show pop-up description for folder and desktop items
Restore Defaults
OK
Cancel
Apply

Folder Options
General
View
Search
Folder views
You can apply the view (such as Details or Icons) that you are using for this folder to all folders of this type.
Apply to Folders
Reset Folders
Advanced settings:
Show hidden files, folders, and drives
Hide empty drives in the Computer folder
Hide extensions for known file types
Hide protected operating system files (Recommended)
Warning
You have chosen to display protected operating system files (files labeled System and Hidden) in Windows Explorer.
These files are required to start and run Windows. Deleting or editing them can make your computer inoperable.
Are you sure you want to display these files?
Yes
No

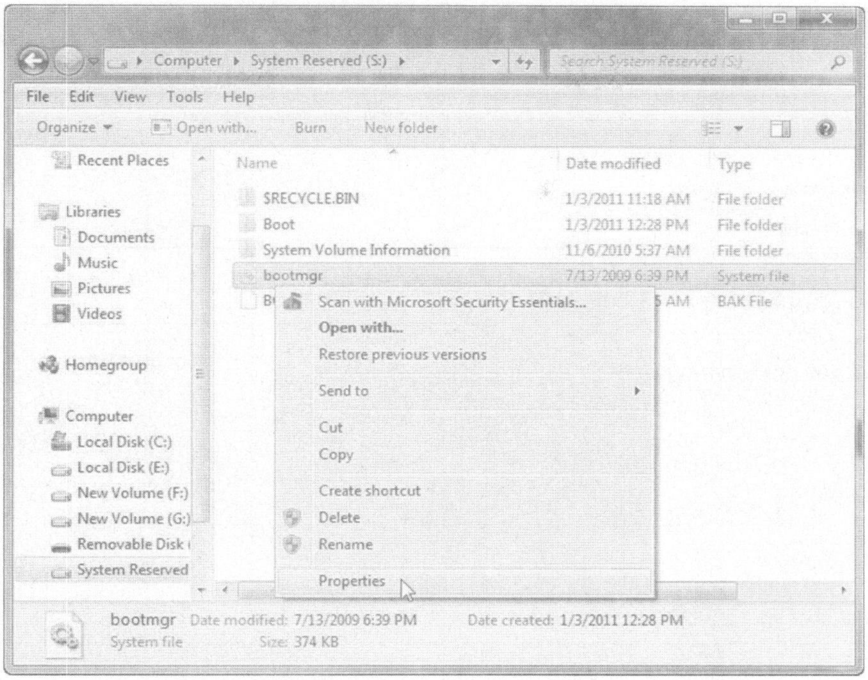

Computer ▸ System Reserved (S:) ▸
Search System Reserved (S:)
File Edit View Tools Help
Organize ▾ Open with... Burn New folder
Recent Places
Libraries
Documents
Music
Pictures
Videos
Homegroup
Computer
Local Disk (C:)
Local Disk (E:)
New Volume (F:)
New Volume (G:)
Removable Disk
System Reserved
Name
Date modified
Type
$RECYCLE.BIN 1/3/2011 11:18 AM File folder
Boot 1/3/2011 12:28 PM File folder
System Volume Information 11/6/2010 5:37 AM File folder
bootmgr 7/13/2009 6:39 PM System file
BAK File
Scan with Microsoft Security Essentials...
Open with...
Restore previous versions
Send to
Cut
Copy
Create shortcut
Delete
Rename
Properties
bootmgr Date modified: 7/13/2009 6:39 PM Date created: 1/3/2011 12:28 PM
System file Size: 374 KB

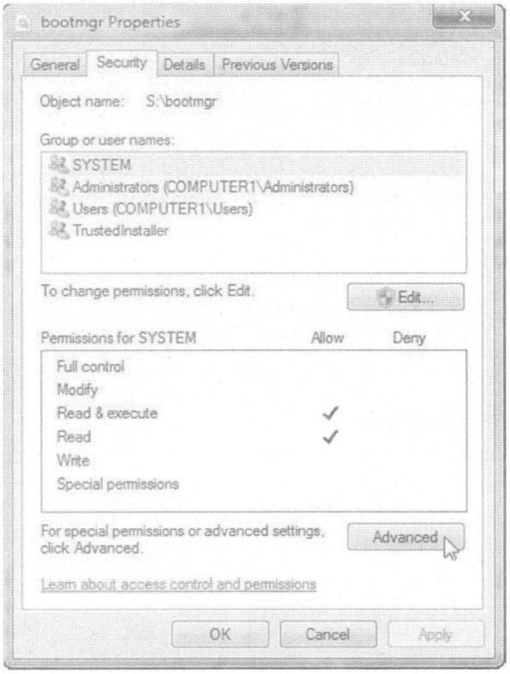

bootmgr Properties
General Security Details Previous Versions
Object name: S:\bootmgr
Group or user names:
SYSTEM
Administrators (COMPUTER1\Administrators)
Users (COMPUTER1\Users)
TrustedInstaller
To change permissions, click Edit.
Edit...
Permissions for SYSTEM Allow Deny
Full control
Modify
Read & execute ✓
Read ✓
Write
Special permissions
For special permissions or advanced settings, click Advanced.
Advanced
Learn about access control and permissions
OK Cancel Apply

Advanced Security Settings for bootmgr

Permissions | Auditing | Owner | Effective Permissions

You can take or assign ownership of this object if you have the required permissions or privileges.

Object name: S:\bootmgr

Current owner:

TrustedInstaller

Change owner to:

Name
Vicki (COMPUTER1\Vicki)

Edit...

Learn about object ownership

OK | Cancel | Apply

Advanced Security Settings for bootmgr

Owner

You can take or assign o...

Object name: S:\boc

Current owner:

TrustedInstaller

Change owner to:

Name
Administrators (COMPUTER1\Administrators)
Vicki (COMPUTER1\Vicki)

Other users or groups...

Learn about object ownership

OK | Cancel | Apply

Windows Security

If you have just taken ownership of this object, you will need to close and reopen this object's properties before you can view or change permissions.

OK

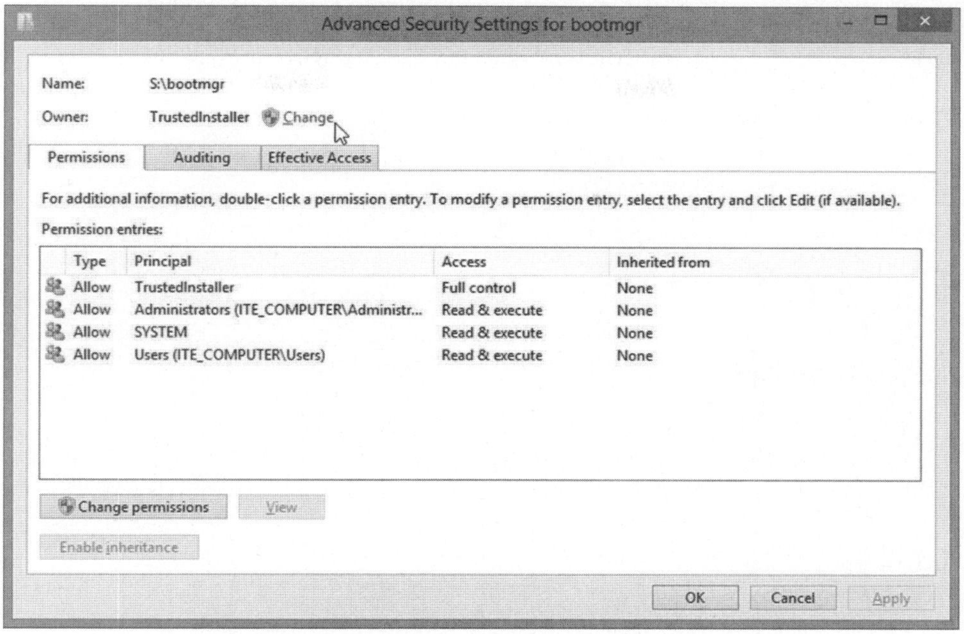
Advanced Security Settings for bootmgr
Name: S:\bootmgr
Owner: TrustedInstaller Change
Permissions
Auditing
Effective Access
For additional information, double-click a permission entry. To modify a permission entry, select the entry and click Edit (if available).
Permission entries:
Type Principal Access Inherited from
Allow TrustedInstaller Full control None
Allow Administrators (ITE_COMPUTER\Administr... Read & execute None
Allow SYSTEM Read & execute None
Allow Users (ITE_COMPUTER\Users) Read & execute None
Change permissions
View
Enable inheritance
OK
Cancel
Apply

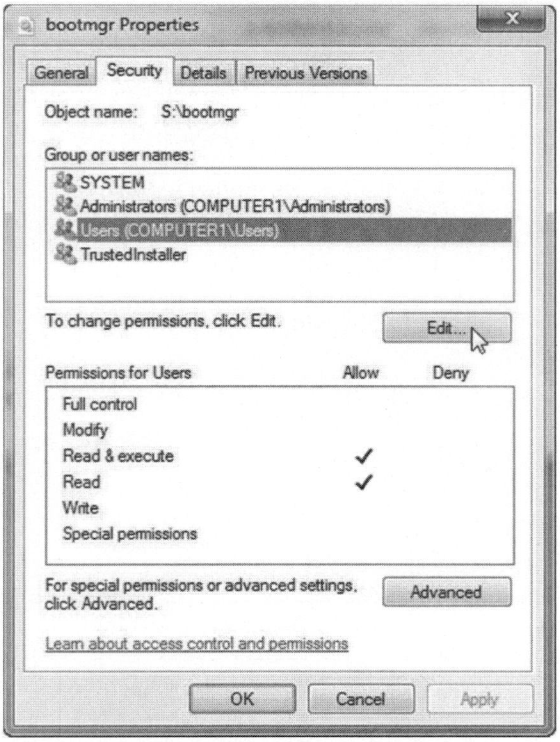
bootmgr Properties
General
Security
Details
Previous Versions
Object name: S:\bootmgr
Group or user names:
SYSTEM
Administrators (COMPUTER1\Administrators)
Users (COMPUTER1\Users)
TrustedInstaller
To change permissions, click Edit.
Edit...
Permissions for Users Allow Deny
Full control
Modify
Read & execute
Read
Write
Special permissions
For special permissions or advanced settings, click Advanced.
Advanced
Learn about access control and permissions
OK
Cancel
Apply

Permissions for bootmgr

Security

Object name: S:\bootmgr

Group or user names:

- SYSTEM
- Administrators (COMPUTER1\Administrators)
- Users (COMPUTER1\Users)
- TrustedInstaller

Add...   Remove

Permissions for Users	Allow	Deny
Full control	✓	☐
Modify	✓	☐
Read & execute	✓	☐
Read	✓	☐
Write	✓	☐

Learn about access control and permissions

OK   Cancel   Apply

Delete File

Are you sure you want to move this system file to the Recycle Bin?

If you remove this file, Windows or another program may no longer work correctly.

bootmgr
Date created: 1/3/2011 12:28 PM
Size: 374 KB

Yes   No

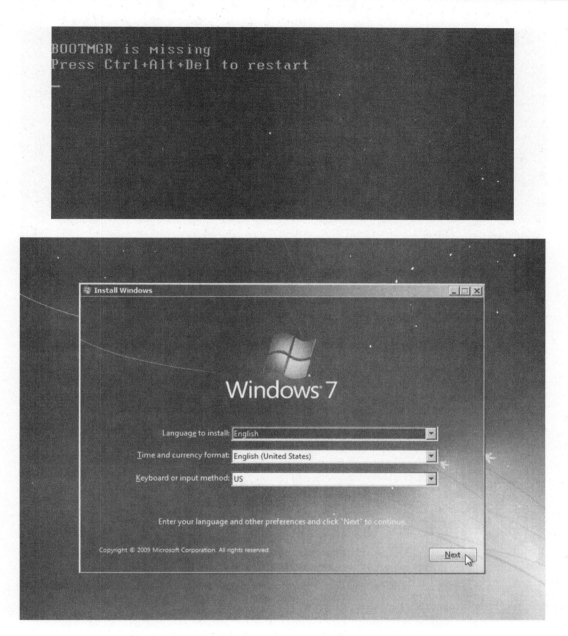

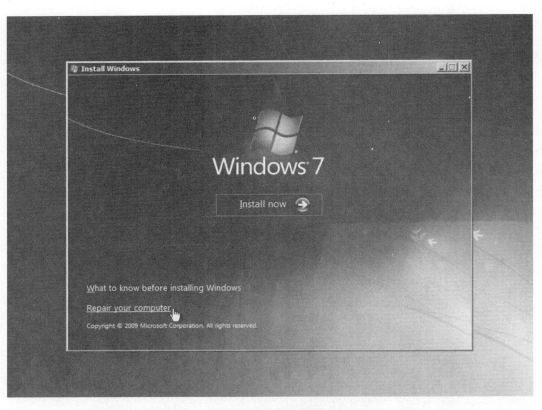

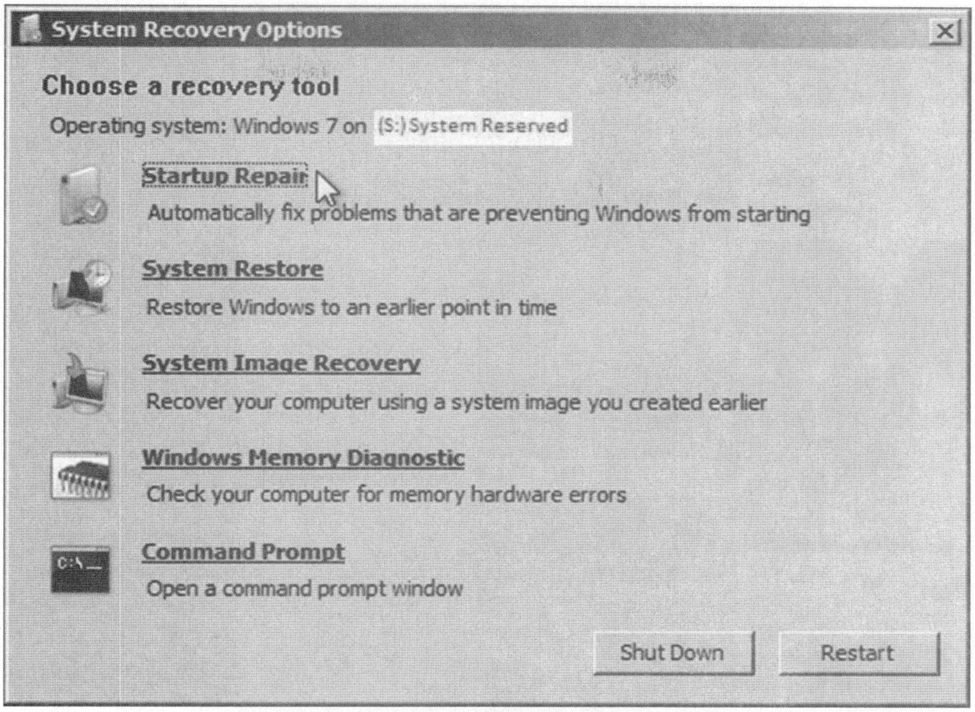
System Recovery Options
Choose a recovery tool
Operating system: Windows 7 on (S:) System Reserved
Startup Repair
Automatically fix problems that are preventing Windows from starting
System Restore
Restore Windows to an earlier point in time
System Image Recovery
Recover your computer using a system image you created earlier
Windows Memory Diagnostic
Check your computer for memory hardware errors
Command Prompt
Open a command prompt window
Shut Down
Restart

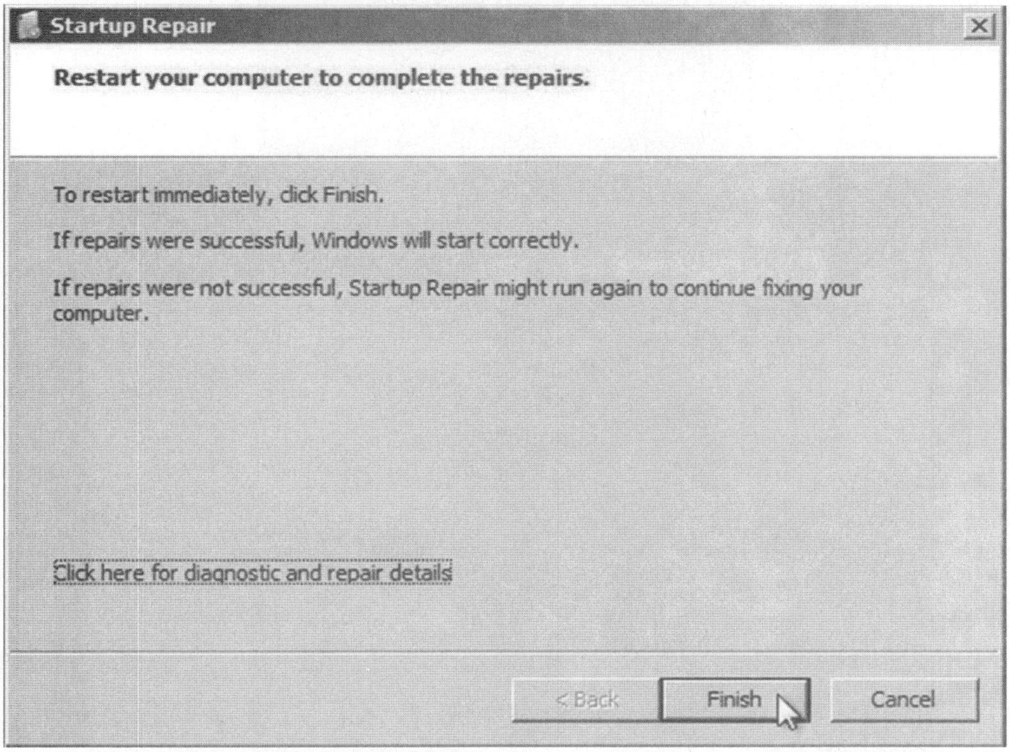
Startup Repair
Restart your computer to complete the repairs.
To restart immediately, click Finish.
If repairs were successful, Windows will start correctly.
If repairs were not successful, Startup Repair might run again to continue fixing your computer.
Click here for diagnostic and repair details
< Back
Finish
Cancel

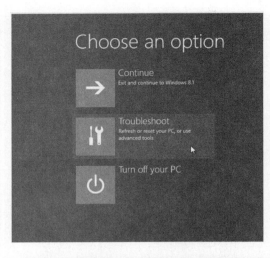

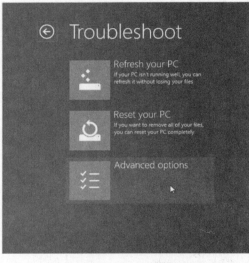

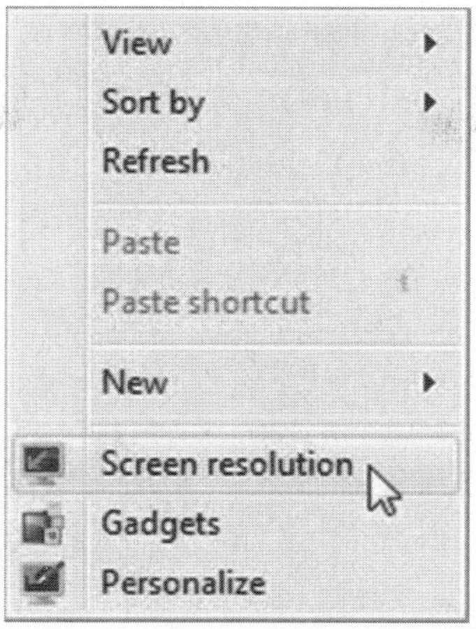

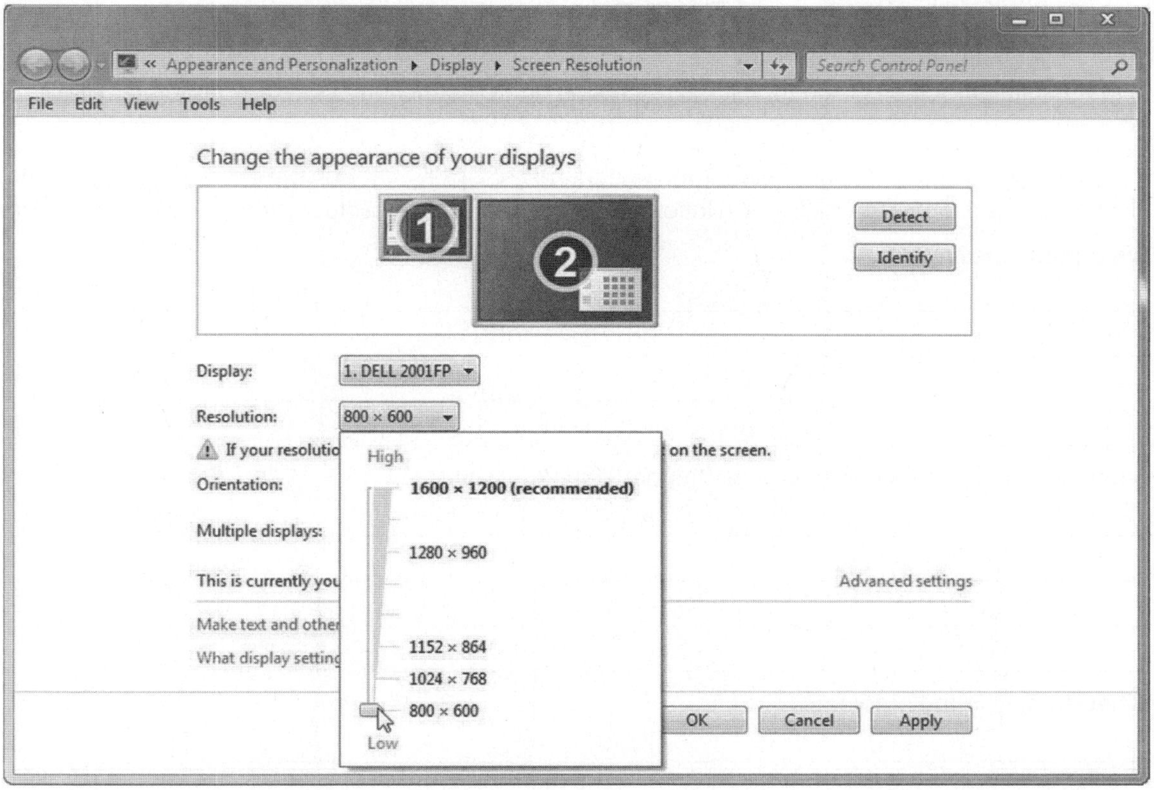

Step 1:   Start the computer.

a.   Start the computer.

Does the computer boot properly?

_____

b.   If the computer started Windows, log on to the computer using a **Standard User** account provided by your instructor.

Were you able to log in?

_____

If you are unable to log in, log in as an administrator and change the credentials of the standard user.

Step 2:   Troubleshoot the operating system problems.

a. If the computer did not start Windows, troubleshoot the operating system until the computer successfully boots. Because all hardware is correctly connected, you do not need to troubleshoot hardware in this lab.

b. If the operating system is missing the required files to boot the computer, you can replace these files by booting the computer with the Windows installation media, or the F8 key. Use the Startup Repair option to replace any missing files.

c. Is the mouse working properly?

_____

If the mouse is not working properly, modify the mouse settings so that it works correctly.

d. Is the keyboard working properly?

_____

If the keyboard is not working properly, modify the keyboard settings so that it works correctly.

e. Is the resolution of the screen the native resolution or the resolution chosen by your instructor?

_____

If the screen resolution is not native or the resolution chosen by your instructor, configure Windows to display the desktop at the native resolution of the monitor or the resolution chosen by your instructor.

f. What problems did you find?

_____

_____

_____

_____

g. What steps did you take to determine the problems?

_____

_____

_____

_____

h. What is causing the problems?

_____

_____

_____

_____

i. List the steps taken to fix the problems.

_____

_____

_____

_____

Lab 14.2.1.3 - Remote Technician - Fix an Operating System Problem

Introduction

In this lab, you will gather data from the customer, and then instruct the customer to fix a computer that does not connect to the network. Document the customer's problem in the work order below.

Student Technician Sheet

Company Name:	Main Street Stoneworks
Contact:	Karin Jones
Company Address:	4252 W. Main Street
Company Phone:	1-888-774-4444

Work Order

Generating a New Ticket

Category:		**Closure Code:**	N/A	**Status:**	Open
Type:	N/A	**Escalated:**	Yes	**Pending:**	N/A
Item:	N/A			**Pending Until Date:**	N/A

Business Impacting?   X **Yes**   O **No**

Summary:

Case ID#:	78	**Connection Type:**	Ethernet
Priority:	2	**Environment:**	N/A

User Platform:

Problem Description:

_____

_____

_____

_____

Problem Solution:

_____

_____

_____

_____

_____

Student Customer Sheet

Use the contact information and problem description below to report the following information to a level-two technician:

Contact Information

Company Name: Main Street Stoneworks

Contact: Karin Jones

Company Address: 4252 W. Main St.

Company Phone: 1-888-774-4444

Problem Description

When I came into the office today, I could not get my email. The Internet does not work either. I tried to restart my computer, but that did not help. None of the files that I need are available to me either. It is like someone pulled the plug, but the plug is still there. I need to get some files from my folder that I was working on yesterday. It is very important for me to get my files so that I can send them to my client. I do not know how to get the files or send them because my computer cannot find them. What do I do?

Note: After you have given the level-two tech the problem description, use the Additional Information to answer any follow-up questions the technician may ask.

Additional Information

- Windows 7.
- Computer has not had any new hardware installed recently.
- There is no wireless network available at work.
- Computer detected new hardware at boot-up.
- Computer could not install new hardware.

Lab 14.3.1.2 - Troubleshooting Network Problems

Introduction

In this lab, you will diagnose the causes and solve the network problems.

Recommended Equipment

- Two computers running Windows
- A wireless router
- Two Ethernet cables
- Internet access

Scenario

You must solve network problems for a customer. You may need to troubleshoot both the router and two computers. Make sure you document and solve the problems, and then document the solutions.

There are several possible errors. Solve one problem at a time until you can successfully establish a connection between the two computers.

To better identify which steps should be done on which computer, the lab will refer to them as computer01, computer02, or both.

Step 1: Log on to the computers.

a. List the computer name used for computer01 and computer02. Use these names whenever the lab refers to computer01 and computer02.

Computer01 name:

_____

Computer02 name:

_____

b. Log on to **computer01** with an account that has administrative privileges.

c. Click **Start > Computer > Network**.

If computer02 is available, double-click **computer02**. Did the connection open?

_____

Step 2:   Troubleshoot network problems.

Use a command prompt to display IP address information, open the network control panel and review the adapter configuration, and log on to the router and review all of the configuration options to troubleshoot the router or computers for problems. Answer the following questions after each problem is solved.

a. What problem did you find?

_____

_____

_____

_____

b. What steps did you take to determine the problem?

_____

_____

_____

_____

c. What is causing the problem?

_____

_____

_____

_____

d. List the steps taken to fix the problem.

_____

_____

_____

_____

e. If you can see computer02, what is the name of shared folder?

_____

Open the text file in the shared folder. What does the hidden message say?

_____

f. If you opened and recorded the message from the shared folder, you have successfully solved all networking problems. Hand in the lab to your instructor.

Lab 14.3.1.3 - Remote Technician - Fix a Network Problem

Introduction

In this lab, you will gather data from the customer, and then instruct the customer to fix a computer that does not connect to the network. Document the customer's problem in the work order below.

Student Technician Sheet

Company Name:	JH Paint Supply
Contact:	Jill Henderson
Company Address:	114 W. Main Street
Company Phone:	1-888-555-2143

Work Order

Generating a New Ticket

Category:		**Closure Code:**	N/A	**Status:**	Open
Type:	N/A	**Escalated:**	Yes	**Pending:**	N/A
Item:	N/A			**Pending Until Date:**	N/A

Business Impacting?   X **Yes**   O **No**

Summary:

Case ID#:	50	**Connection Type:**	Wireless
Priority:	2	**Environment:**	N/A
User Platform:			

Problem Description:

_____

_____

_____

_____

Problem Solution:

_____

_____

_____

_____

_____

Student Customer Sheet

Use the contact information and problem description below to report the following information to a level-two technician:

Contact Information

Company Name: JH Paint Supply

Contact: Jill Henderson

Company Address: 114 W. Main Street

Company Phone: 1-888-555-2143

Problem Description

Well, the problem does not always seem to be there. Typically, not all computers on the network are used all of the time, so everything seems to be fine. On some busy days, every computer is being used, and there is always one computer that cannot connect. I cannot figure out what the problem is because it is not usually on the same computer. When a computer cannot make connectivity, I check to make sure all cables and connections are fine.

Note: After you have given the level-two tech the problem description, use the Additional Information to answer any follow-up questions the technician may ask.

Additional Information

- Windows 7.
- Computer has no new hardware.
- Computer has not been moved recently.
- An extra computer was added to the network recently.
- Computer looks the same as it did yesterday.

Lab 14.4.1.2 - Troubleshoot Security Problems

Introduction

In this lab, you will diagnose the cause of various access security problems and solve them.

Recommended Equipment

- One computer running Windows

Scenario

Company XYZ has hired Devon to manage the training department. Shawna was also hired as a temporary employee to replace Brooks, who is no longer working for the company. You must solve access security problems for the training department. You might need to access the computers as each user and the administrator. Make sure to document the problems and the solutions.

There are several possible errors. Solve one problem at a time until there are no more access problems. Use the following tables when solving problems. The user account information is listed in Table 1. Use only the groups shown in Table 2. They are set up with the proper permissions. The instructor will provide the administrator's account information.

Table 1: Accounts

User Name	Password	Group for User
Brooks	Cisco2001	Guests
Devon	Cisco2010	Academy Student
Shawna	Cisco2100	Guests
Administrator user name:	Administrator password:	Administrators

Table 2: Groups

Groups	Group Permissions
Academy Student	Read & Execute, List Folder Contents, Read, Write
Guests	Read & Execute, List Folder Contents, Read
Administrators	Full Control

Note: There is a file, with a message, in the C:\ITE\Class01 folder.

Troubleshooting

You will try to log on as different users Brooks, Shawna, and Devon and determine the possible issue. You will fix possible security issues using an account with administrative privileges.

Step 1:   Determine security issues with Brooks' account.

Log on to the computer as Brooks and save text to the file **C:\ITE\Class01\Curriculum.txt**.

Using the information from the tables in the Scenario section, should Brooks be able to log on to the computer and change the file? Explain.

_____

_____

Can Brooks log on to the computer? Can Brooks access the file?

_____

_____

If you determine there is a security breach, how would you fix and validate the solution?

_____

_____

_____

_____

Step 2:   Determine security issues with Devon's account.

Log on to the computer as Devon and save text to the file **C:\ITE\Class01\Curriculum.txt**.

Using the information from the tables in the Scenario section, should Devon be able to log on to the computer and change the file? Explain.

_____

_____

Can Devon log on to the computer? Is the account disabled? Do you have the correct password? Explain the problem.

_____

_____

How would you fix the issue and validate the solution?

_____

_____

_____

_____

Navigate to **C:\ITE\Class01**. Can Devon write to the file? Is there a permission issue? Explain.

_____

_____

_____

_____

How would you fix the issue and validate the solution?

_____

_____

_____

_____

Step 3:   Determine security issues with Shawna's account.

Log on to the computer as **Shawna** and save text to the file **C:\ITE\Class01\Curriculum.txt**.

Using the information from the tables in the Scenario section, should Shawna be able to log on to the computer and change the file? Explain.

_____

_____

Can Shawna write to the file? Explain.

_____

_____

How would you fix and validate the solution?

_____

_____

_____

_____

Lab 14.4.1.3 - Remote Technician - Fix a Security Problem

Introduction

You will gather data from the customer to begin the troubleshooting process. You will document the customer's problem and possible solution in the work order.

Student Technician Sheet

Company Name: Smith Lumber Supply

Contact: James Smith

Company Address: 1234 S. Main Street

Company Phone: 801-555-1212

| Work Order |

Generating a New Ticket

Category: _____	Closure Code: N/A	Status: Open
Type: N/A	Escalated: Yes	Pending: N/A
Item: N/A		Pending Until Date: N/A
	Business Impacting? X **Yes** O **No**	

Summary: _____

Case ID#: 102	Connection Type: _____
Priority: 2	Environment: N/A

User Platform: _____

Problem Description:

_____

_____

_____

_____

Problem Solution:

_____

_____

_____

_____

_____

Student Customer Sheet

Use the contact information and problem description below to report the following information to a level-two technician:

Contact Information

Company Name: Smith Lumber Supply

Contact: James Smith

Company Address: 1234 S. Main Street

Company Phone: 801-555-1212

Category: Security

Problem Description

You are unable to use your laptop's wireless connection while at work. The wireless connection works fine at home and the coffee shop downstairs, but for some reason, it will not connect to the wireless anywhere in the office. Since you are unable to access the wireless connection, you have been using the Ethernet cable connection instead. The cable connection is working fine.

Note: After you have given the problem description, use the Additional Information to answer any follow-up questions your lab partner may ask.

Additional Information

- Windows 7.
- Wireless client can see the wireless network.
- My wireless connection worked yesterday at work.
- I can connect using an Ethernet cable.
- My wireless account is in good standing.
- Wireless connection works for other employees.
- I have not made any changes to my wireless security settings.
- A new wireless router was installed on the network yesterday.